WORK ROLES AND RESPONSIBILITIES
IN GENITOURINARY MEDICINE CLINICS

The Policy Studies Institute (PSI) is Britain's leading independent research organisation undertaking studies of economic, industrial and social policy, and the workings of political institutions.

PSI is a registered charity, run on a non-profit basis, and is not associated with any political party, pressure group or commercial interest.

PSI attaches great importance to covering a wide range of subject areas with its multi-disciplinary approach. The Institute's 40+ researchers are organised in teams which currently cover the following programmes:

Family Finances – Employment – Information Policy – Social Justice and Social Order – Health Studies and Social Care – Education – Industrial Policy and Futures – Arts and the Cultural Industries – Environment and Quality of Life

This publication arises from the Health Studies programme and is one of over 30 publications made available by the Institute each year.

Information about the work of PSI, and a catalogue of available books can be obtained from:

Marketing Department, PSI
100 Park Village East, London NW1 3SR

Work Roles and Responsibilities in Genitourinary Medicine Clinics

Isobel Allen and Debra Hogg

Policy Studies Institute
London

The publishing imprint of the independent
POLICY STUDIES INSTITUTE
100 Park Village East, London NW1 3SR
Telephone: 071-387 2171 Fax: 071-388 0914

ISBN 0 85374 570 6

A CIP catalogue record of this book is available from the British Library.

PSI Research Report 720

1 2 3 4 5 6 7 8 9

PSI publications are available from
BEBC Distribution Ltd
P O Box 1496, Poole, Dorset, BH12 3YD

Books will normally be despatched within 24 hours. Cheques should be made payable to BEBC Distribution Ltd.

Credit card and telephone/fax orders may be placed on the following freephone numbers:

FREEPHONE: 0800 262260
FREEFAX: 0800 262266

Booktrade representation (UK & Eire):
Book Representation and Distribution Ltd (BRAD)
244a London Road, Hadleigh, Essex SS7 2DE

PSI subscriptions are available from PSI's subscription agent
Carfax Publishing Company Ltd
P O Box 25, Abingdon, Oxford OX14 3UE

Laserset by Policy Studies Institute
Printed in Great Britain by BPCC Wheatons Ltd, Exeter

Acknowledgements

This study was initiated and funded by the Department of Health. Many members of staff at the Department were involved at various stages of the research, but particular thanks are due to Tom Snee of the AIDS Unit, Dr Judith Hilton, Senior Medical Officer, and Dr Veronica Bishop, formerly of Research and Development Division. All three were members of the Advisory Group which gave valuable help, guidance and advice to the research team at all stages of the study.

Other members of the Advisory Group were Dr Tom McManus, Consultant in Genitourinary Medicine at King's College Hospital, London; Sue Trotter, Senior Health Adviser, Radcliffe Infirmary, Oxford; Andrea Game, Clinical Specialist Manager, Genitourinary Medicine Services, Derbyshire Royal Infirmary; Howard Wood, GUM Clinics Manager, Charing Cross and Westminster Hospitals; Ian Hicken, English National Board for Nursing, Midwifery and Health Visiting; Len Wilson and Dr Christopher Maggs of the Department of Health.

We wish to acknowledge the enormous help given to us by the staff in the twenty Genitourinary Medicine (GUM) Clinics in which we conducted this study. The clinics must remain anonymous, but it should be recorded that the research team were most grateful for the cooperation and interest shown by all the staff who were involved with us in this research. We are also indebted to staff in the clinics in which we carried out the extensive pilot work on this study and to the GUM consultants who gave us help in designing research instruments.

The study was designed and directed by Isobel Allen. Debra Hogg was responsible for the management of the project, and carried out much of the analysis of the data. The study owes a great deal to her organising skills. Deborah Charnock and Isobel Bowler were responsible for fieldwork in a number of clinics and played a valuable role in data analysis. Lynda Clarke was involved in fieldwork in one of the clinics. Karen MacKinnon was responsible for the computing and preparation of tables. Karin Erskine prepared the text for desk-top publishing.

Contents

Tables

1 Introduction

The purpose of the study on which this report is based was to identify the roles and responsibilities of staff working in Genitourinary Medicine (GUM) clinics, to identify areas of overlap and duplication, and to make recommendations in the light of the need for efficiency and cost-effectiveness, for changes in existing roles. Particular attention was paid to reviewing the provision of counselling services within GUM clinics.

The report was commissioned by the Department of Health to look specifically at the work roles and responsibilities of doctors, nurses, health advisers and administrative, clerical and reception staff in GUM clinics. The study was an in-depth investigation of twenty GUM clinics selected at random from each health region in England, having stratified the sampling as described below to ensure representation of both large and small clinics. The study can therefore claim to give a representative account of what was going on in GUM clinics in 1990-1991 at the time of the fieldwork.

It should be emphasised that the timing of the research coincided with marked changes in the organisation of the health service and its local management structures with the introduction of the purchaser/provider split. The study chronicles the structure and organisation of GUM clinics and the experience of their staff at a time of change. The impact or the potential impact of the changes was more noticeable in some clinics than in others, but there can be little doubt that change was at least on the horizon for all clinics.

However, although some of the practices identified in this research may have been affected or modified by these changes, it is likely that most of the findings of our investigation still have considerable relevance for the organisation and management of GUM clinics both now and in the future. It is important that the unique history and culture of GUM clinics and the evolution of work roles and responsibilities within them, as described in this report, are understood. Without this understanding, there may be problems in achieving the implementation of changes which are necessary for the development of GUM clinics to meet the needs of the public in the most effective and appropriate ways.

Background to the study: the Monks Report

The study sprang directly from the recommendations of the *Report of the Working Group to Examine Workloads in Genitourinary Medicine Clinics*, more commonly known as the *Monks Report*, (Department of Health, 1988). Since

1

the findings and recommendations of the Monks Report were so central to the genesis of the present study, it is important to describe them in some detail as background to the research.

The workloads in Genitourinary Medicine (GUM) clinics have been increasing for many years, as indicated by Department of Health statistics, but in recent years the spread of HIV infection has led to a substantial increase in the demand for both treatment and counselling at these clinics. In 1988, as a result of concern about the rising workload and pressure on GUM clinics, the Department of Health set up a working group chaired by a retired District General Manager, Mr A Monks, with a membership of a consultant in genitourinary medicine, a health adviser and a nurse manager. The terms of reference were:

> to examine current and forecast workloads in GUM clinics, taking account of AIDS and other STDs, and to recommend any action which may need to be taken on manpower (including nursing manpower), training, resources and accommodation.

The Monks team visited 20 GUM clinics, representing approximately 10 per cent of the clinics in England, over a period of three months in the late spring of 1988. At least one clinic in every region was visited. The Monks Report made detailed recommendations, some of which were directed at the Department of Health. The Department issued a response to the first three priority recommendations in February 1989 through Health Circular EL(89)P/36, which stated that ministers expected health authorities to give special attention to GUM services. It made additional resources available in 1989-90 as part of the AIDS-related expenditure package to assist this process.

Subsequently, the yearly Executive Letters issued by the Department of Health have requested health authorities to give an up-date of progress in implementing the recommendations of the Monks Report (EL(90)P/30; EL(91)52; EL(92)18; Department of Health, 1990; 1991; 1992). All regions have been asked to agree with district health authorities a 3-year programme of implementation.

Other Monks Report recommendations directed at the Department of Health related to manpower, staff roles, training for nurses and health advisers and pay structures, as well as recommending that regions should be required to review the distribution of their main GUM services and improve distribution where required (see recommendations 12-17, 20, 22, Department of Health, 1988). In addition, the report made recommendations on the need for comprehensive counselling services with support from clinical psychologists or psychiatrists, stressing that HIV antibody testing should be offered with appropriate pre- and post-test counselling and support (see recommendations 18, 28 and 29, Department of Health, 1988). The report also recommended that arrangements should be made for some evening clinic sessions, and, in general, recommended that districts should be made aware of the views of patients and their level of satisfaction with the quality of service (see recommendations 31-32, Department of Health, 1988).

The research described in the present report, *Work Roles and Responsibilities in Genitourinary Medicine Clinics*, was initiated by the Department of Health as a result of these recommendations of the Monks Report. The Monks working group found evidence of considerable variation in the work done by the members of staff in different clinics, evidence of overlap between the various members of staff and no clear lines of direction. Policy Studies Institute was asked to carry out the present research with particular reference to the need to examine the roles of doctors, nurses, health advisers and administrative and clerical staff, together with their interaction with the working of the whole GUM clinic. We were asked to pay special attention to counselling services provided in the GUM clinics. These were felt to need reviewing in the light of the actual and projected increase in work related to HIV infection and AIDS.

Apart from the Monks Report, there had been surprisingly little research which had examined either the workloads of GUM clinics or, more especially, the work roles and responsibilities of staff within GUM clinics. We were often told that genitourinary medicine had traditionally been regarded as a 'Cinderella' specialty, and this, combined with the impression of isolation and fear of stigma which was a prevailing characteristic of the GUM clinics in this study, appeared to have contributed to a paucity of research material on the organisation and structure of an important area of medical work.

Preliminary research for the present study found that medical staffing was said to vary considerably among GUM clinics, with different levels of staffing found in teaching and non-teaching hospitals. In general, the level of medical staffing was thought to be inadequate, particularly in the light of the changes in recent years in the types of cases and conditions seen in GUM clinics. The Monks Report drew attention to the effect this had on the doctor consultation times available to patients which were generally considered to be too short, and made a recommendation that guidelines for staff requirements should be established, based on patient attendances and time required per patient. It also recommended that staffing levels should be reviewed and adjusted accordingly (see section 4.2 and recommendations 13 and 14, Department of Health, 1988).

The report on 'The Role and Training of Nurses Working in Departments of Genitourinary Medicine in England and Wales' (Rogers and Adler, 1987) indicated that there was a great diversity of work and responsibilities among nursing staff in GUM clinics, and recommended improvements in their teaching, recruitment and role. The Monks Report also identified the diversity in the amount of responsibility given to nurses working in GUM clinics, which it found 'does not necessarily reflect the experience of the staff but rather local custom and practice'. The report recommended that the English National Board should be approached and asked to review the entrance criteria and curricula of existing courses (ENB 275 and ENB 932) in order to meet the needs of nurses and departments of GU medicine. The report also recommended that new patients, and old patients presenting with a new clinical problem, should be clinically examined by a doctor rather than a nurse (see section 4.3 and recommendations 15 and 19, Department of Health, 1988).

It was generally accepted that health advisers could be drawn from any number of backgrounds, with a wide range of skills, training and qualifications. Their duties were said to vary enormously from clinic to clinic and their pay also ranged widely. They were thought to suffer from a lack of recognition, lack of status and no career structure. The Monks Report recommended that every clinic should have at least one health adviser and that a certificated course of sufficient content and duration should be established for health advisers and endorsed by the Department of Health. It also recommended that common career structures and pay scales for health advisers should be laid down with job descriptions and properly evaluated staffing levels (see section 4.4 and recommendations 16 and 17, Department of Health, 1988).

The responsibilities of clerical and administrative staff in GUM clinics were also said to vary, and doubts were expressed about the quality of some reception staff, particularly in certain areas where recruitment and retention were said to be difficult and there was a heavy reliance on temporary and agency staff. The Monks working group were concerned about the adequacy of clerical and administrative support and recommended the revision of pay scales to attract and retain staff of a suitable calibre in order not only to avoid exploitation of existing staff but also to ensure that other health care professionals did not have to undertake clerical work. They were particularly concerned about the lack of secretarial and administrative support for health advisers (see sections 4.4 and 4.5 and recommendations 20 and 21, Department of Health, 1988).

The increase in HIV infection was said to have brought about changes not only in the numbers attending the clinics, but also in the type of work undertaken, including an increased need for counselling, both for those who had the infection and those who did not. Counselling was said to be undertaken mainly by health advisers, but, again, there was little evidence about the practice in GUM clinics as a whole. There was a fear that there might well be a duplication of effort, not all of which was based on good training and good practice. This diversity in counselling services has also been found in other areas of health care, as illustrated in *Counselling Services for Sterilisation, Vasectomy and Termination of Pregnancy* (Allen, 1985).

The Monks Report recommended that all GUM clinics should continue to provide comprehensive counselling for patients and clients, and that those who provided counselling should be able to deal with the full range of GUM problems. In addition, it recommended that HIV antibody testing should only be offered with informed consent and with pre- and post-test counselling and support (see section 7 and recommendations 18, 28 and 29, Department of Health, 1988), and that counselling should be available in dedicated soundproof accommodation, integral to the GU medicine department (see recommendation 11, Department of Health, 1988).

Although the projected increase in HIV infection was difficult to substantiate, and the Monks Report pointed out that most districts were unable to base their projections on 'anything stronger than a speculative hypothesis', it was generally agreed that the workload of GUM clinics would continue to increase. The Monks working group were firmly of the opinion that staffing in GUM clinics was falling behind current workload in all areas of work in most clinics (see para 4.1, Department of Health, 1988). However, there was clearly not enough evidence on which to base recommendations on the optimum use of staff resources, and the Monks Report recommended that 'the individual roles of the doctor, nurse, health adviser and other staff should be examined, together with their interaction with the working of the whole GUM clinic' (see recommendation 12, Department of Health, 1988).

In the light of the findings and recommendations of the Monks Report outlined above, the Department of Health considered that there was an urgent need to collect evidence on who does what in GUM clinics and to make recommendations for rationalisation of the service provision. It was against this background that PSI conducted the present study, the fieldwork for which took place in 1990 and 1991.

Purpose of the research

The Department of Health identified the following aims for the PSI study:
i)   to identify what all staff personnel do in GUM clinics;
ii) to identify areas of overlap or duplication of work;
iii) to make recommendations, in the light of the need for efficiency and cost-effectiveness, for changes in existing roles.

It should be emphasised that this study was primarily about staff roles and responsibilities within GUM clinics, and was designed to give a description of what was going on within the clinics at the time of the research. It was not designed to explore the external management of GUM clinics, and did not seek the formal views of staff outside the clinics, although, as described below, a small number of informal interviews took place with staff working in related areas outside the clinics. It should also be emphasised that the study was about work roles and responsibilities rather than about workload as such. Information about the workload of the clinics was collected and collated by analysing the statistics collected for the Department of Health on clinic sessions and patient visits (the KH 09 returns) and the records of diagnoses made in GUM clinics (the KC 60 returns). These are presented in Chapters 2 and 6 and in the Appendix and are discussed in Chapter 6. However, as we note in Chapters 2 and 6, there must be some doubt about the extent to which the official data, as collected at the time of the research, truly reflected the workload of GUM clinics, particularly as far as work in connection with HIV infection was concerned.

We were asked to pay special attention to counselling services provided within the clinics. These were of particular importance in contributing to the apparent increase in workload experienced by staff in the clinics, although, as we shall see, the reported increase was poorly represented in the official workload statistics. In addition, the Department of Health was concerned that the nature of counselling services within the clinics should be reviewed.

Finally, it should be stressed that the study did not set out to provide a sophisticated audit of work in GUM clinics. For the purpose of the study, staff kept a record of their activities within the clinic, which provided valuable information on their roles and responsibilities and the extent to which there was overlap between types of staff. However, clinical audit was in its infancy at the time of the fieldwork and, although we designed the staff activity records with the help of consultants who were designing instruments for use in the audit of GUM clinics, this study used these activity records as ancillary information rather than as audit material as such.

Preparation and piloting

An Advisory Group was set up to give assistance to the PSI team of researchers. The group included a consultant in GU medicine, a nurse manager and two health advisers working in GUM clinics, members of staff from the Department of Health with responsibility for GUM clinics, members of the AIDS Unit, and a a representative of the English National Board for Nursing, Midwifery and Health Visiting.

The research team spent time at the beginning of the research period consulting members of the Advisory Group on an individual basis, and carried out extensive pre-piloting and piloting of questionnaires and research instruments in the GUM clinics in which members of the group worked. Other GUM consultants provided invaluable help in the preliminary stages of the research. We derived great benefit from this opportunity to explore issues and methods with a wide variety of staff in a number of clinics. Given the acknowledged diversity of clinics, we considered it important to develop and test our research instruments in as many settings as possible before embarking on the main study.

Selection of clinics

The fieldwork for the study took place in 20 GUM clinics, with one clinic selected in eight regions and two clinics in six regions which had a higher than average incidence of HIV infection and AIDS cases. Regions from which two clinics were selected included the Northern, North-West Thames, South-East Thames, South Western, West Midlands and Mersey Regional Health Authorities. This weighting was agreed with the Department of Health on the grounds that these regions were thought more likely to have had experience of the problems that others had yet to encounter, and might therefore contribute more to the study.

The clinics for each region were arranged in rank order of size, measured by the number of cases seen in a specific quarter. The aim was to ensure that both large and small clinics were represented in the sample of 20 clinics; the mean number of cases seen was therefore calculated for each region, and the lists of clinics divided into those above and below the mean for each region. The eight regions in which one clinic was to be selected were divided at random into two groups, with the aim of selecting 'large' clinics from four of them and 'small' clinics from the other four. Both 'large' and 'small' clinics were selected from the other six regions. Each clinic was given a number, and random numbers were generated to select one clinic from each appropriate group. The final sample of clinics was then checked against the pattern for GUM clinics as a whole to ensure that it was representative, given the stratification by size which we had imposed. The final sample ranged from very large clinics in teaching hospitals, which ran daily clinics offering a wide range of services with large numbers of staff, to very small 'peripheral' clinics which ran one session a week with a few staff.

Interviews

The aim of the study was to interview all the staff working in the clinics, although it was recognised that this might not be feasible in the very large clinics. In the event, all staff were interviewed in 17 of the 20 clinics in which fieldwork took place. In two clinics where a high number of clinical assistants did one session each, a decision was made to restrict the number of interviews to half of these clinical assistants. In the final clinic, which was by far the largest, it was not thought necessary to interview all the staff. All medical staff, apart from the senior house officers (SHOs) and academic staff, and a random selection of nursing, health adviser, and reception, clerical and administrative staff were interviewed in this clinic.

Interviews were carried out with a total of 89 medical staff, 98 nursing staff, 22 health advisers, 52 administrative, clerical and reception staff, and 8 other professionals working in the GUM clinics (3 counsellors, 4 MLSOs, 1 microscopist), a total of 269 interviews in all. In addition, informal interviews took place with a number of senior administrators, consultants in other specialties, HIV coordinators and others working in the areas selected for this study. Details of the staff establishment of the 20 clinics are given in the Appendix.

Methods

The following research methods were used:

i) an activity record of the work of all staff in the GUM clinic was compiled. Staff were asked to record details of their activities on a check-list or 'activity form'. This required careful design, negotiation and handling. It provided evidence on all the activities ever carried out by each member of staff, and, for each activity carried out, information on the frequency with which the staff member performed this function. The activities covered are outlined in (iii) b) in the next section, since they were discussed in interviews with staff as well as being recorded by staff on the activity forms;

ii) personal interviews were carried out with all types of staff working in the clinic, using semi-structured questionnaires. These questionnaires included

7

a fairly high proportion of open-ended questions, giving the respondents plenty of opportunity to illustrate the reasons for their answers and to develop the points they wanted to make in their own way;

iii) detailed information was collected on the staffing, location, facilities, equipment and other aspects of the clinic. Statistics were collected on attendances and diagnoses at the clinic for 1989 and the first 6-9 months of 1990. Particular additional questions were asked on the incidence of HIV positive and AIDS patients;

iv) PSI research staff spent up to three working weeks in each clinic. Although 'observational' techniques as such were not used, the researchers kept a detailed account of what they observed, especially regarding the use of staff time. A standard check-list was devised. Staff/patient interaction was observed outside the consulting and examination rooms. A 'career history of patients' was constructed for each clinic.

Contents of interviews with staff

The interviews with staff covered certain broad areas, including:

i) personal characteristics (eg. sex, age, etc.)

ii) professional characteristics (eg. post held, training, qualifications, previous job history, pay, etc.)

iii) aspects of their current job:

a) responsibilities, job description, structure of working week, time spent on various duties, managerial lines of responsibility, liaison with other staff, changes over last twelve months etc.

b) specific areas of work:*
counselling, contact tracing, partner notification, health education, liaison with other agencies (statutory, voluntary, private), clerical and administrative, reception, statistical returns, patient care, clinical duties (including history taking, examining patients, special procedures, performing microscopy, ordering treatment);

* (as noted in the previous section, most of these topics were also covered in the activity forms completed by staff)

iv) their reasons for entering the specialty or for working in GU medicine;

v) the extent and nature of their job satisfaction, including aspects of their jobs found most/least satisfying, the main constraints they experienced, whether they felt they had too much/too little responsibility;

vi) what they would like to do in their jobs; how they would like to change their jobs/roles;

vii) how they saw the jobs/roles of other members of the GUM clinic staff; the nature and extent of any overlap between their job/role and that of others; what they felt about overlap/duplication; how they would like to change the jobs/roles of other clinic staff;

viii)recommendations for changes or improvements in:

a) the content and nature of their own job/role;

b) the content and nature of the jobs/roles of others;
c) the way in which the GUM clinic operated in general;
d) specific changes relating to treatment and counselling connected with HIV infection.

Questionnaires, other research instruments and interviewing

All interviews were carried out on a personal basis using a series of questionnaires which were fully structured in that all the questions were asked in a pre-determined order and the exact working of each question was specified. Each staff member within the given category was asked the same questions. There was fairly extensive duplication across the questionnaires used for different staff categories, with many questions being asked of all four types of staff. Certain questions relating specifically to practice were asked only of the type of staff to whom these questions were relevant. The questionnaire for administrative, clerical and reception staff was shorter than that for the other three categories of staff.

As noted above, a fairly high proportion of questions allowed for an open-ended response, and the interviewers recorded the answers verbatim. The interviews with medical, nursing and health advisers lasted on average about an hour and a half, although some were shorter and some were considerably longer. The interviews with administrative, clerical and reception staff usually lasted about an hour, although again there was some variation, often depending on the length of experience the respondent had in the clinic. Interviewers included the authors of this report, other staff from Policy Studies Institute and an experienced health researcher working on a freelance basis.

Questionnaires were developed after extensive pre-piloting and piloting in a number of GUM clinics which were not part of the final sample. This was also true of the other research instruments used, which included the self-completed staff activity records, forms recording information about staffing, location, facilities, equipment and other aspects of the clinic, and forms recording information on clinic attendances and diagnoses, as well as specific information on HIV positive and AIDS patients. We were particularly indebted to consultants who had been developing audit instruments for use in GUM clinics.

Analysis of data

The research was a study of staff roles and responsibilities in 20 clinics. It took a dual approach in that it looked at the 20 clinics as case-studies, but, at the same time, it collected data on the four main types of staff across the 20 clinics.

The data collected were diverse and were analysed in a number of ways, as outlined below, but essentially we had to make a decision on whether to concentrate on an analysis across the types of staff or whether to develop the case-study approach and analyse the material in terms of 'typologies' or groups of clinics.

One of the main aims of the researchers was to establish criteria by which the clinics could be grouped in some way, so that recommendations on staff roles and responsibilities could be made on the basis of such factors as size, location, workload, type of work or mix of staffing. The difficulties in establishing clear 'typologies' of clinics are described in Chapter 2, and they should be borne in mind throughout the reading of the report.

It was difficult to escape the conclusion that the clinics represented 20 typologies, and that each clinic had several unique features which inhibited comparison across clinics. This enormous diversity clearly influenced the way in which we analysed the material. Having struggled with attempting to impose a clinic typology approach on the analysis of the data, we reluctantly decided that the most informative way of presenting the material collected from the staff was to analyse it by discipline rather than by clinic or type of clinic.

Throughout the report we have attempted to use the material as a basis for illustrating the differences between clinics. But we have concluded that, in many ways, the general picture of the views and experience of the staff in all 20 clinics was easier to present and to understand than the much more intricate, and potentially incomprehensible, method of analysing each aspect of work roles and responsibilities in terms of clinic typology.

A study of this kind generates a considerable amount of data from a number of different sources. The nature of the data is also diverse. Some, such as the data on staffing, location, facilities, equipment and other aspects of the clinic, are hard, factual data which can be seen and measured scientifically.

The statistical data on attendances and diagnoses at the clinics for 1989-90 can also be considered to be 'hard' data, although, as we have noted and will explore in more detail in the report, they were not always as reliable as they might have been.

The activity records completed by staff describing what they did and how often they did it constitute a measurement of what was going on in the clinics. The reliability of such self-completed data may vary, particularly in determining the extent to which non-specific tasks are carried out. There is inevitably a certain crudity in the results, but the data are usually regarded as 'hard' data by scientific observers.

The data collected in interviews with staff can broadly be divided into two types – the 'hard' data describing characteristics such as sex, age, qualifications, job title, hours of work, their responsibilities, activities and so on, and the 'softer' data describing the experience of the respondents and the views they held about certain aspects of the clinic, their own work roles and responsibilities and those of others within the clinic. (The data collected in interviews with staff referring to their activities were checked against the data they supplied on their 'activity form'. A high degree of congruence was found.)

The questionnaires were coded using their predetermined codes, as well as coding frames developed from detailed textual analysis of the 'open-ended' questions. Verbatim quotes were also extracted from the questionnaires and selected for inclusion in the report in a rigorous manner in proportion to the numbers making such comments. Some readers may be unfamiliar with the use of quotes from interviews to illustrate the points made, although it is a conventional technique for dealing with the type of rich material generated in research of this kind. Members of staff often described common views and experience in such a lucid manner that it would have been a loss to the report not to have presented them.

Structure and presentation of the report

The report covers a lot of ground, some of which may be of more interest to some readers than to others. Chapter 2 gives a detailed factual description of the 20 GUM clinics in which the research took place, in terms of location, times and sessions, attendances and staffing. It groups the clinics into four main types of clinics. Details of the staff establishment of each clinic are given in the Appendix.

Chapters 3 to 6 look at the characteristics, the roles and the responsibilities of the four main types of staff working in GUM clinics – the medical, nursing, health advising and clerical, administrative and reception staff. Chapter 7 describes the location and physical characteristics of the clinics and examines the effects these had on the work roles and responsibilities of staff.

Chapter 8 describes the workload of the clinics in terms of the official statistics on diagnoses of conditions recorded in the period leading up to the research, details of which are given in graphs in the Appendix. It also examines the views of staff about workload in the clinics. In addition, it describes the two main types of official statistical returns required from the clinics and examines problems associated with the compilation and collation of the statistics.

Chapter 9 looks in detail at the effects on the clinics of work in connection with HIV infection and AIDS, and examines the question of contact tracing and partner notification. Chapter 10 is devoted to a description and assessment of counselling within the GUM clinics. Chapter 11 looks at the extension of the boundaries of the work of GUM clinics, including liaison with other professionals and the relationship with family planning clinics in particular. Chapter 12 examines the extent to which there was overlap and duplication of work between staff in the clinics, and assesses the views of staff on this important issue.

Chapter 13 is a discussion of the main findings of the research and Chapter 14 summarises the policy implications of the key findings and suggests action which might be taken.

Some tables are included in the text, but the report is written in such a way that the reader does not have to refer to tables except to check details. Reference is made to other literature only when it is felt to be essential. Our main aim has been to present the results of an empirical study addressed to a more general audience, including those working in clinics and related areas, rather than an exclusively academic one.

This research was designed to provide factual evidence describing the organisation, functions and activities of the GUM clinics studied. The report also provides a considerable amount of evidence describing the characteristics of the staff. But, in addition, it provides an insight into the views and experience of the staff. As we have observed, the research took place at a time of change, and this report documents the process by which these changes were making their effects felt not only on practice but also on the culture of the clinics.

The distinct culture of GUM clinics, despite their great diversity, often shines through the quotes from respondents in a way which would be impossible to capture through a presentation of the bare facts alone. It can be argued that many of the comments made by respondents reflect only their own experience and that they can be interpreted as 'perceptions'. It is to be hoped that readers recognise that perceptions affect behaviour and often dominate the culture of an organisation, and that custom and practice may be slow to respond to change unless the nature and strength of 'perceptions' are recognised and tackled in an appropriate manner.

2   The GUM clinics

This study was carried out in 20 genitourinary medicine (GUM) clinics, the selection of which was described in Chapter 1. Anonymity was guaranteed for all clinics in the survey. However, it was recognised that it would be necessary to make some reference to individual clinics for illustrative purposes, so each clinic was given a code number, based simply on geographical distribution. These code numbers are used in the tables and graphs in the Appendix and referred to in the text where appropriate.

Our aim was to create a 'typology' of different types of clinics, based on set criteria, which could have a more universal application. This proved difficult, mainly because of the marked individual differences in the organisation of the clinics, even if they appeared, on the surface, to be serving similar communities in similar locations with similar staffing and attendance levels. Many of these differences were related to the way in which the clinics had evolved over the years, and often appeared to be rooted in historical accident or strong consultant direction rather than in logical development.

A number of criteria could have been used as a basis for grouping the clinics, but, having tried and rejected several combinations, we decided upon a relatively simple set of four main criteria which had a firm factual basis:
(i)   the location of the clinic,
(ii) the clinic times and sessions,
(iii) patient attendances, including HIV-related work, and
(iv) the staffing of the clinic.

Using the four criteria, we grouped the 20 clinics into four main types of clinic, but even within these four groups, there was considerable variation among the constituent clinics, and there was inevitable cutting across the groups.

In this chapter, we first discuss the clinics in terms of the four main groupings, and then describe them in terms of the criteria we applied.

Types of clinic
Type 1
These were the 'large' city-based clinics. They were all located in hospitals, with buildings or areas dedicated to GUM clinic use and, as a rule, were not part of the out-patients department. All of them were full-time (ie open all day every weekday), with more than 20 clinic sessions per week and around 5,000 or more patient attendances per quarter. Each had more than one consultant and all of

13

them had medical training posts. Each had more than one full-time health adviser. Nursing staff were dedicated GUM nurses, generally with an extended role in the clinics. HIV/AIDS work was an important part of the work of these clinics, with 50 or more HIV positive patients ever registered with each clinic. This group included four clinics (code numbers 6, 8, 9, 14)

Type 2
These were medium to large clinics. They were all located in a city hospital in dedicated accommodation and were not usually part of the out-patients department. They were all full-time, or virtually full-time, with between 10 and 20 clinic sessions per week and more than 3,000 patient attendances per quarter. They each had one or two consultants but only one of the three had medical training posts. The number of health advisers varied from 1 whole time equivalent (WTE) to 3.5 WTE. The nursing staff were dedicated GUM nurses with quite an extended role in each of the clinics. The importance of HIV/AIDS work varied among the clinics, with the number of HIV positive patients ever registered with the clinic ranging from 10 to 50. This group included three clinics (code numbers 3, 13, 16)

Type 3
These were the medium to small clinics. They were all hospital- based and were more likely than not to be located in the out-patients department. Some had dedicated accommodation but some shared with other clinics, such as other out-patient clinics. They were all part-time, with between 4 and 10 clinic sessions per week and c.1,000 to 2,000 patient attendances per quarter. Most had only one part-time consultant and, as a rule, had no medical training posts. The health adviser establishment ranged from 0 to 1 WTE. Three of the clinics did not have a dedicated health adviser. In one clinic, there was a combined sister/health adviser post, one clinic employed HIV counsellors and in one clinic the medical and nursing staff were fulfilling the health advising duties. The nursing staff were often general out-patient nurses and, as such, tended not to have an extended role. HIV/AIDS work was a relatively small part of the clinic's work, and the number of HIV positive patients ever registered ranged from 5 to 26. This group included six clinics (code numbers 1, 2, 5, 7, 12, 18)

Type 4
These were the small peripheral clinics. They were usually located in the out-patient department of a district general hospital, although two were community-based. Some had dedicated accommodation; some shared with other out-patient clinics. They were all part-time, with 2 or 3 clinic sessions per week and fewer than 700 patient attendances per quarter. All of them had only one part-time consultant and all but one had clinical assistant sessions. The health advising establishment ranged from 0 to 1 WTE. Two clinics did not have a health adviser. In these clinics, the sister was carrying out the health advising

duties. The role of the nursing staff varied. Three of the clinics had dedicated GUM nurses with quite an extended role. But four were staffed by general out-patient nurses whose role was rather limited. HIV/AIDS work was a relatively small part of the clinics' work, with the number of HIV positive patients ever registered ranging from 0 to 12. This group included seven clinics (code numbers 4, 10, 11, 15, 17, 19, 20)

We now look in detail at how the clinics fitted into the four main criteria used for grouping them.

Location of clinics
There were four types of clinic location:
i) hospital-based clinics which were part of, and located in, the main out-patients department;
ii) hospital-based clinics which were part of the out-patients department but separate from other out-patient clinics;
iii) hospital-based clinics which were not part of the out-patients department;
iv) community-based clinics.

Eighteen of the 20 clinics were hospital-based: 5 in a teaching hospital and 13 in a district general hospital. The remaining 2 clinics were community-based.

Hospital-based clinics
Eleven of the hospital-based clinics were located in the out-patients department: eight in the main out-patients department, sharing accommodation with other out-patient clinics; the other three had accommodation separate from the other clinics and used only by the GUM clinic.

The other seven hospital-based clinics were not part of the out-patients department, but were located in separate buildings or areas used only by the GUM clinic.

Community-based clinics
One of the two community-based clinics had previously been hospital-based. The hospital had been closed down and the out-patient clinics, including the GUM clinic, had been relocated in the community. The accommodation was shared by the GUM clinic and other 'out-patient' clinics. The other community-based clinic had its own exclusive accommodation in a community health centre.

Clinic times and sessions
Full-time and part-time clinics
Six of the clinics were full-time clinics, ie open all day every weekday, while a seventh was open almost full-time (open all day every weekday, apart from one afternoon).

The other 13 clinics were part-time clinics:
• four were open on 5 days a week

15

- one on 4 days a week
- two on 3 days a week
- five clinics on 2 days a week
- one clinic on only 1 day a week

Clinic sessions

The clinics routinely collect information for the KH 09 statistical return on the number of clinic sessions held. However, there were clear problems of comparability of data between them, since different clinics defined 'clinic sessions' in different ways. For example, some clinics recorded male and female clinics running concurrently as one clinic session, while others recorded this as two clinic sessions. (These problems are discussed further in Chapter 8).

In order to establish comparability between the 20 clinics in this study, we defined a clinic session as a *doctor-run* clinic, and this definition for 'clinic sessions' is used in Table 2.1. Two clinics running concurrently (eg a male clinic and a female clinic, or a mixed sex clinic and an HIV clinic) were counted as two clinic sessions. This method was still not ideal, not only because clinic sessions were of different lengths but also because it did not take into account the number of doctors working in a clinic session at any one time. Nevertheless, we found it a more useful measure than the quarterly KH 09 data on 'clinic sessions' which were based on different interpretations in different clinics.

The clinics varied widely in the number of clinic sessions held each week, as can be seen in Table 2.1:

- two held between 31 and 40 clinic sessions
- two held between 21 and 30 clinic sessions
- three held between 11 and 20 clinic sessions
- five held between 5 and 10 clinic sessions
- eight held fewer than five clinic sessions

The maximum number of clinic sessions held per week was 38 and the minimum number two sessions per week.

Doctor sessions

The KH 09 data did not take into account the number of doctors working in the clinic at any one time. We defined 'doctor sessions' as the number of doctors working in each clinic session. The number of doctor sessions per week was, therefore, a count of the total number of sessions worked by all doctors in the clinic. We considered that this gave a better measure of the size and workload of the clinic than simply counting the clinic sessions, and we have used it as the main measure of workload in 'session' terms in Table 2.1, as shown in the first column.

Table 2.1 shows that four of the clinics held more than 40 doctor sessions per week. This included one very large clinic with over 100 doctor sessions per week. This high number was largely accounted for by the fact that the clinic ran

Table 2.1   Doctor sessions and clinic sessions

Clinic code	Doctor sessions (per week)	Clinic sessions (per week)	Patient attendances* (per quarter)
6	117	38	13,100
14	44	23	5,400
8	43	28	4,900
9	41	31	5,70
13	36	13	3,900
16	27	16	3,100
3	23	20	3,500
5	13	8	1,100
18	12	7	1,400
12	12	4	1,100
2	9	9	1,400
1	8	8	900
7	8	8	1,800
11	5	3	700
17	5	3	600
19	4	2	600
20	4	2	400
10	4	3	500
15	3	3	600
4	2	2	200

Clinic sessions - separate 'clinics' (eg male, female, warts, HIV etc.) run by a doctor

Doctor sessions - separate sessions run by a doctor within 'clinic sessions'

* Patient attendances in a quarter in 1990 taken from KH09 statistical data

separate STD and HIV clinics. (The term HIV clinic was used in this GUM clinic and we have followed its terminology.) Both the STD clinic and the HIV clinic were open all day every weekday. Between two and five doctors worked in the STD clinic at any one time and between one and four GUM doctors worked in the HIV clinic at any one time.

Three clinics held between 20 and 40 doctor sessions per week, while six held between six and 20 doctor sessions per week. Seven of the smaller clinics held five or fewer doctor sessions per week.

Patients

Patient attendances

We also found many inconsistencies in the recording of patient attendances on the KH 09 returns. Nevertheless, the number of patient attendances gave some measure of how busy the clinics were. (It should be noted that patient attendances are 'threshold crossings' and do not represent the actual number of patients.)

The data on patient attendances are given in Table 2.1, alongside the data on clinic and doctor sessions per week. We have used the KH09 data for one of the quarters of 1990, but to ensure anonymity we have not identified the quarter and have rounded the figures to the nearest hundred. The table is useful in giving an indication of the workload of the clinics in terms of numbers of people passing through in relation to the weekly sessions held.

Around 5,000 or more patients per quarter (three months) were recorded as attending the four largest clinics, including more than 13,000 patient attendances in the largest of these clinics. In three clinics there were between 3 and 4,000 and in six clinics there were between 900 and 2,000 patient attendances per quarter. In seven clinics there were fewer than 700 patient attendances in a quarter.

Number of HIV positive patients

There was a huge variation in the number of HIV positive patients who had ever been registered with the GUM clinics, ranging from more than 1,000 in the largest city clinic to none in two of the small peripheral clinics. However, the location of the clinic often seemed to have as much effect on the number of HIV positive patients as the overall size of the clinic did. Some of the smaller clinics, which were relatively close to a city, had had more HIV positive patients registered than some of the larger northern clinics.

The largest, city-based, clinic had registered more than 1,000 HIV positive patients, while another large city clinic had registered around 125. Three clinics, all based in southern cities, had registered around 50 HIV positive patients; two clinics, including one of the smaller clinics, had registered between 25 and 35; three clinics had registered between 10 and 20. Of the remaining ten clinics, eight had registered fewer than 10, and two had never registered a patient as HIV positive. The implications of this are discussed further in Chapter 9.

The staffing of the clinics

We collected details from each clinic of its staff establishment and the actual number of staff in post. Table A.1 in the Appendix gives details of the establishment of each clinic, with indications of posts which were unfilled at the time of the fieldwork. The following text should be read in conjunction with Table A.1.

Medical establishment

Consultants

Twelve of the 20 clinics were staffed by one consultant only. In only one instance did this single consultant work full-time in the selected clinic. In the other 11 cases, the consultant worked part-time in the clinic (ranging from 2 to 7 sessions per week), although all but one of these consultants were working full-time overall, including their work in other clinics.

Six clinics were staffed by two consultants. In one case, there were two part-time consultants (4 sessions and 6 sessions), and in one clinic, there were two full-time consultants. The other four clinics were each staffed by one full-time and one part-time consultant. All but one of the 'part-time' consultants were working full-time overall.

The remaining two clinics each had more than two consultants working in the clinic. One was staffed by four consultants who all worked part-time in the clinic and the other was staffed by six consultants, 2 full-time and four part-time in the clinic. All of the 'part-time' consultants worked full-time overall.

In total, therefore, there were 34 consultants working in the 20 clinics, 9 of whom worked full-time in the selected GUM clinics and 25 part-time. Of the 34 consultants, 32 worked full-time, including their work in other clinics. Only two held part-time appointments: one with 9 sessions, all in GU medicine, and one with 7 sessions, 4 of which were in GU medicine.

Other career grades
Two clinics employed an associate specialist, one on a full-time basis, the other on a part-time basis (6 sessions). One clinic employed a full-time staff grade physician.

Training grades
Six of the 20 clinics included doctors in training grades in their medical establishment: five had senior registrars, six had registrars and two had senior house officers (SHOs).

Of the five clinics with senior registrars, one had three full-time posts, one had one full-time post and three shared a full-time senior registrar post with another clinic. All the clinics with senior registrars also had at least one registrar post, but only two had SHO posts.

Of the six clinics with registrars, one had four full-time posts, four had one full-time post and one shared a full-time registrar post with another GUM clinic. In one of these clinics, the registrar post was the only training grade post.

Of the two clinics with SHOs, one had three full-time posts and the other had two full-time posts.

Clinical assistants
Clinical assistants worked in all but one of the 20 clinics. The number of clinical assistants employed ranged from one to nine, and the number of clinical assistant sessions ranged from one to 14. Seven clinics employed GP clinical assistants only, seven employed other (non-GP) clinical assistants only and five employed both GP and other clinical assistants.

Total medical establishment
The total medical establishment of the clinics varied considerably:

- one clinic was staffed by one part-time consultant only, with no additional medical staff
- twelve clinics were staffed by consultant(s) and clinical assistant(s) only
- one clinic was staffed by consultants, clinical assistants and a staff physician
- four were staffed by consultant(s), clinical assistant(s) and training grade doctors
- two were staffed by consultants, training grade doctors, associate specialists and clinical assistants

Nursing establishment

The 20 selected clinics employed between two and 15 nurses. At one end of the scale, two part-time clinics each employed two part-time nurses, while at the other end of the scale, a large full-time clinic employed 14 full-time nurses and one part-time nurse.

- in ten clinics there were between two and four nurses on the clinic establishment. In seven of these clinics all the nurses worked part-time and in the other three clinics both full-time and part-time nurses were employed
- in eight clinics there were between five and eight nurses on the establishment. In two of these clinics all the nurses worked full-time, in two clinics all the nurses worked part-time, while in the other four clinics both full-time and part-time nurses were employed
- in one clinic there were 10 nurses (eight full-time and two part-time)
- in one clinic there were 15 nurses (14 full-time and one part-time)

Three of the clinics each had one nursing post vacant.

Most of the clinics (16) employed both RGNs and SENs. Three had only RGNs in post, while one employed SENs only. Two clinics each had one registered fever nurse, while one had an auxiliary nurse in post.

Thirteen of the clinics employed dedicated GUM nurses, while seven were staffed by nurses who also worked in other out-patient clinics.

The role of the nursing staff in the clinics varied considerably, and is discussed in detail in the following chapters. As a general rule, the nursing staff in the medium to large clinics, which were staffed by dedicated GUM nurses, tended to have greater responsibilities and more of an extended role. (We use the term 'extended role' in relation to nurses throughout this report since it was in current use at the time of the fieldwork, and can be readily understood by readers.) The nursing staff in the small to medium clinics, on the other hand, which were often staffed by general out-patient nurses, tended not to have an extended role. This was by no means always the case, however. The role of the nurse was often dictated by consultant or clinic or hospital policy, while in some clinics, it appeared to be simply a combination of historical reasons which governed whether nurses carried out certain tasks.

Health advising establishment
The number of health advisers employed ranged from none to six. At one end of the scale, four clinics had no health advisers on the establishment and at the other end of the scale, one of the large full-time clinics employed six full-time health advisers.

Four clinics had no health advisers on the establishment:
* in two clinics the health advising was done by the sister
* in one clinic by the medical and nursing staff
* in one clinic there were two HIV counsellors but no dedicated staff for health advising

Eight clinics had one health adviser on the establishment: two full-time posts and six part-time posts. (In one of these clinics a full-time health adviser's post was vacant at the time of the study because of a dispute over its grading. In this clinic, the sister was carrying out the health adviser's role. Another of these clinics had a part-time health adviser on the establishment, but had alternated, over a period of time, between employing a part-time dedicated health adviser and a full-time combined sister/health adviser. At the time of the study, a sister/health adviser was in post.)

Five clinics each had two health advisers on the establishment:
* two clinics had two part-time health advisers
* three had two full-time health advisers (in two of these clinics one post was vacant at the time of the study)

Three clinics had more than two health advisers:
* one had three full-time health advisers (one post was vacant at the time of the study)
* one had three full-time and one part-time health adviser (one full-time and one part-time post vacant)
* one of the large full-time clinics had six full-time health advisers

Overall, six clinics did not have a dedicated health adviser in post at the time of the study. In four of these clinics, a sister was taking on most of the health advising (either permanently or temporarily), in one clinic, both medical and nursing staff were taking on the health advising duties, and one clinic employed two HIV counsellors.

Administrative and clerical establishment
Administrative and clerical staff fell into four main groups;
i) Receptionists with clerical duties
ii) Receptionists with clerical and secretarial duties
iii) Manager/supervisors with reception and clerical duties
iv) Medical secretaries

The establishment of administrative and clerical staff varied widely between the clinics. It might have been assumed that there would have been some relation between the numbers and types of administrative and clerical staff employed and the workload of the clinics, but this was by no means always the case, and, indeed one of the busiest clinics had only one full-time receptionist/clerk, compared with another which had fewer clinic sessions but had nine administrative and clerical staff, albeit including seven part-timers.

One clinic had no administrative and clerical staff
* reception and clerical duties were carried out by the sister and other nursing staff

Four of the clinics had only one administrative and clerical staff:
* one had a full-time receptionist/clerk
* three had a part-time receptionist/clerk

Five clinics had two administrative and clerical staff:
* four had two part-time receptionist/clerks (some with secretarial duties)
* one had a part-time receptionist/clerk and a part-time secretary

Five clinics had three administrative and clerical staff:
* one had a full-time supervisor/receptionist, a full-time receptionist/clerk and a part-time secretary
* one had two part-time receptionist/clerks and a full-time secretary
* three had two part-time receptionist/clerks and a part-time secretary

One clinic had four administrative and clerical staff:
* three part-time receptionist/clerks and a part-time receptionist/clerk/ secretary

One clinic had five administrative and clerical staff:
* four part-time receptionist/clerks and a part-time secretary

One clinic had eight administrative and clerical staff:
* one full-time manager, one full-time and four part-time receptionist/ clerks, two full-time secretaries

One clinic had nine administrative and clerical staff:
* two full-time managers, five part-time receptionist/clerks and two part-time secretaries

One clinic had 13 administrative and clerical staff:
* one full-time manager, eight full-time receptionist/clerks and four full-time secretaries

Three of the clinics had vacant administrative posts at the time of the study. One was short of a part-time receptionist/clerk and two clinics each had a full-time medical secretary post vacant.

The use of 'typologies' of clinics in the report
This chapter has given an overall description of the clinics in terms of location, clinic sessions, patient attendances and staffing and has grouped the clinics into

'types' of clinics according to these criteria. As we pointed out in Chapter 1, it proved very difficult to analyse the data collected solely in terms of these 'typologies', since there were so many individual differences which cut across the types of clinics.

The following chapters therefore mainly present data in terms of analyses of the different staff disciplines, with reference to the different types of clinic as appropriate. Nevertheless, it is important that the four main types of clinic should be kept firmly in mind in reading the rest of this report, with the proviso that individual GUM clinics were dominated by custom and practice and that expected patterns, suggested by 'typologies', did not necessarily ensue.

3   The medical staff and their roles

Medical staff interviewed
We interviewed all the medical staff working in 17 of the 20 clinics. In two clinics where a high number of clinical assistants did one session each, a decision was made to restrict the number of interviews to half of these clinical assistants. In the final clinic, which was by far the largest, we interviewed all the medical staff apart from the SHOs and the academic staff.

Interviews were carried out with a total of 89 medical staff:

- 33 consultants
- 2 associate specialists
- 1 staff physician
- 6 senior registrars (including 1 locum)
- 8 registrars (including 1 locum)
- 2 SHOs
- 37 clinical assistants (20 GPs, 17 others)

Characteristics of medical staff
Overall, we interviewed 56 men (63 per cent) and 33 women (37 per cent). This ratio, of around two-thirds men to one-third women, was also reflected among the different medical grades – consultants, training grades and other medical posts (clinical assistants and non-consultant career grades).

The ages of the medical staff ranged from 26 to 69. As shown in Table 3.1, two-thirds of the consultants were over 45, with an average age of 49.8. The doctors in other career grades and the clinical assistants tended to be rather younger, with 50 per cent of them 45 or younger. However, like the consultants, very few were under the age of 35. Over 80 per cent of doctors in the training grades were, as might be expected, under 35.

Qualifications
94 cent of the doctors had a medical degree; five doctors (6 per cent) had a conjoint qualification *only*, including two consultants and three clinical assistants.

One third of the consultants – all men – had qualified as doctors overseas, while the remaining men and all the women consultants had qualified in the UK.

Table 3.1   Sex and age of medical staff

column percentages

	Total	Consultants	Training grades	Other doctors
Sex				
Male	63	67	63	60
Female	37	33	37	40
Age				
25-35	19	6	81	5
36-45	34	27	19	45
46-55	29	39	-	33
56-65	15	24	-	13
Over 65	4	3	-	5
Mean age	**45.2**	**49.8**	**31.9**	**46.9**
Base: all medical staff	*(89)*	*(33)*	*(16)*	*(40)*

One third of the consultants were Members of the Royal College of Physicians (MRCP), while just over a quarter were Members of the Royal College of Obstetricians and Gynaecologists (MRCOG). Just over a third of them (36 per cent) had a diploma in venereology/genito-urinary medicine.

Two of the doctors in other (non-consultant) career grades had a diploma in venereology/GU medicine.

Ten of the 16 doctors in training grades (63 per cent) held the MRCP and two held the MRCOG. Two also had a diploma in GU medicine.

Around a quarter of the 37 clinical assistants had a Diploma from the Royal College of Obstetricians and Gynaecologists (DRCOG); a similar proportion had a diploma in venereology/GU medicine. Five were Members of the Royal College of General Practitioners (MRCGP).

Length of time in grade

61 cent of the consultants had been in the grade for more than 10 years, just under one third for less than 5 years and three for between 5 and 10 years. The doctors in training grades had all been in their particular grade for less than 5 years.

A quarter of the clinical assistants and other doctors had been working in their particular grade for more than 10 years; a third for between 5 and 10 years. All the rest had been working as clinical assistants for less than 5 years (42 per cent).

Specialty

All the consultants were consultants in GU medicine. Many of the doctors in training grades had decided to specialise in GU medicine, though a few of the more junior doctors, particularly those who were spending an elective period in GU medicine, were undecided about their final specialty.

Most of the clinical assistants 'specialised' in GU medicine. 17 of the 20 GP clinical assistants did sessions only in the GUM clinic in addition to their work in general practice; three worked in other clinics as well as in the GUM clinic. Similarly, most of the other clinical assistants worked only in GU medicine; only four of the 17 worked in other clinics as well as the GUM clinic.

Length of time in GU medicine

Overall, one third of the doctors had worked in GU medicine for less than 5 years (32 per cent), one fifth for 5 to 10 years, and almost half (46 per cent) had worked in the specialty for 10 years or more. Some doctors had worked in GU medicine for considerably more than 10 years, including one consultant who had been working in GU medicine for 44 years!

But there were marked differences between the grades. Around three-quarters of the consultants had worked in GU medicine for 10 years or more (73 per cent); a fifth had worked in the specialty for between 5 and 10 years. Only two consultants had worked in GU medicine for less than 5 years.

The three doctors in other career grades had all been working in GU medicine for more than 5 years. The majority of the doctors in training grades, on the other hand, had worked in the specialty for less than 5 years (88 per cent), including a quarter who had worked in it for less than one year. Only two had worked in GU medicine for 5 years or more.

The clinical assistants' experience in GU medicine varied more widely. Around a third had worked in GUM for less than 5 years, a quarter for between 5 and 10 years, and 41 per cent for 10 years or more.

Why the doctors had entered GUM

We were particularly interested to know what had brought the doctors into this particular specialty. The doctors gave a wide variety of reasons but the single most frequently mentioned reason for choosing to do GU medicine was its relation and closeness to obstetrics and gynaecology, which was mentioned by a quarter of all doctors interviewed (26 per cent).

Many of these doctors had clearly wanted to make a career in obstetrics and gynaecology, but had found this difficult for one reason or another, and had, therefore, decided to work in what they regarded as a related specialty.

There was no doubt that overseas qualified doctors had found it particularly difficult to progress in the highly competitive specialty of obstetrics and gynaecology. A consultant, who had qualified overseas, explained why he had entered the specialty: 'It was not my first choice of specialty. Obstetrics and gynaecology was my first choice. I went for second best due to circumstances beyond my control. It was prejudice to a great extent and coming into the country later. If you join at SHO level, it's easier. I did my SHO post here but I didn't come with the idea of staying. I did my exams within a year but I couldn't get a post in a teaching hospital and you need to if you're going to go up...'

A senior registrar, who had also qualified overseas, told a similar story: 'In my case, I was qualified as an obstetrician. I tried to further my career in O and G but it was not very possible. I started attending GUM clinics as a registrar while I was in O and G, and I quite liked it. It was difficult to progress in obstetrics and gynaecology. I had several options. They offered me an associate specialist in O and G or I could have been a GP. But I preferred this option...'

Others had been working in obstetrics and gynaecology but had found the hours too demanding, especially at a time when they were hoping to have children. A clinical assistant explained why she had chosen GU medicine: 'I wanted to have a family. I was doing obstetrics and gynaecology and I needed to find something less demanding in time. GU medicine fits in with having a family and it's relatively close to O and G...'

The GP clinical assistants had sometimes taken on sessions in GUM because they felt the closeness to O and G helped with their work in general practice: 'I was very involved in family planning and therefore dealing with women and problems relating to sexuality and this seemed a natural extension when the job came up. Being a GP is a bit of a "jack-of-all-trades" and it's nice to be involved in an area you can become a specialist in...'

Around one in six doctors said they had chosen GU medicine because it related to other specialties such as dermatology, immunology, microbiology, psycho-sexual medicine and psychiatry. Doctors who had qualified overseas, like this registrar, were particularly likely to cite the connection with dermatology: 'I'm here for four or five years from India. We practise GU with dermatology. I was a dermatologist back home. I have to treat GU back home. So I came to it from dermatology...'

GU medicine was undoubtedly seen by consultants and those in training grades as a specialty where there were opportunities for career progression. A quarter of both these groups of doctors cited good career opportunities as one of the reasons for working in GUM.

Apart from those who had actually experienced difficulties in progressing in other specialties such as obstetrics and gynaecology, others, like this consultant, had recognised that they might be promoted more quickly in GU medicine than in other specialties: 'The promotion prospects were better than in dermatology and I found the more I did it, the more I liked it. I followed the advice given to me by a senior surgeon - "If you like something and you find the opportunities are there, stay with it"...'

Some of the junior doctors, who had made their specialty choice in more recent years, echoed these views, like this senior registrar: 'I was in general medicine. I wanted to be a physician, but it was very crowded. The future was unsure whereas there were lots of vacancies in GUM. So I swallowed my pride and came...'

GU medicine had also been chosen as a specialty by some doctors because the hours were good and there was no shift work. Others specifically mentioned the fact that there was no on-call work in GU medicine. The hours and lack of on-call duty were mentioned by around one in five of all grades of doctors.

Women were particularly likely to cite the hours as a reason for choosing this specialty. The need for doctors to travel while training and the effect that this has on doctors' relationships and career decisions are recognised and have been well-documented (Allen, 1988). We heard many similar examples from women working in GU medicine about the influences on their specialty choice. A consultant in one large clinic told us: 'I got married to my boyfriend as a medical student. I thought there can't be two of us taking exams. I knew he wanted to go up the ladder. I was interested in skins and gynae. GUM had no on-call, it was sessional and good for women...'

Another woman consultant explained: 'I went into it for all the wrong reasons! I wanted an SHO post and I wanted to stay in the same area. It fulfilled what I was looking for at the time but I found I enjoyed it, and the more I enjoyed it, the more I stayed! It's suitable for married women to do. My husband is a career cardiologist, which is very demanding. If I wasn't married, I'd be in obstetrics...'

And another consultant said: 'It was a "nine to five", no on-call specialty. I was in dermatology but I couldn't see a future in it. Lots of countries in Europe were into dermato-venereology, so I went into venereology, as it was known then. Dermatology was very full, any consultant post was way out of London and I had to be in London for my husband...'

A wide range of other reasons were cited for entering GU medicine, some of which were common to all grades and some of which were specific to certain grades. The consultants, as discussed above, were likely to have entered GU medicine because it was close to obstetrics and gynaecology and because of the good opportunities for career progression. They were also likely to say that they had found the specialty interesting and varied. But it was also interesting to note that around one fifth of the consultants had been attracted to GU medicine because they were able to cure their patients, as this one explained:

> I made up my mind as an undergraduate that I wished to do it. I could see this was a branch of medicine in which you were dealing with young and healthy patients as opposed to senile geriatrics with long-standing conditions I could do nothing about. The young people in GUM had potentially serious conditions that one could cure. It was the success. Also I got a kick from meeting a large number of people each day. Meeting 100 people a day is very exciting, 50 is less exciting and meeting 20 is dead boring. The patients are all different...

It was quite clear that the vast majority of consultants had chosen GU medicine before HIV and AIDS had emerged to have a major impact on the specialty. It is not insignificant that a number of GU medicine consultants entered the specialty because treatment of the STDs was curative. The advent of HIV/AIDS must inevitably have changed at least some of their views about GU medicine. This is discussed in more detail below.

The doctors in training grades were also likely to have entered the specialty because of its closeness to obstetrics and gynaecology and the opportunities for career progression. But it is noteworthy that a third of the training grades chose GUM because they wanted to work with HIV/AIDS patients. This senior registrar worked in a large clinic with a substantial amount of HIV/AIDS related work: 'I chose GUM largely because of the HIV commitment. It's a very exciting branch of medicine. But also, the two sides complement each other well. Young people with defined problems you can cure offsets a specialty with terminal illness...' Some of these young doctors commented that they 'wouldn't have considered GUM if it wasn't for HIV'. GU medicine had also appealed to the doctors in training grades because of the research opportunities available in the specialty.

This distinct difference in reasons for choosing the specialty between a significant minority of the junior doctors and a similar proportion of the consultants has interesting implications. The consultants were attracted by being able to cure patients quickly and sometimes expressed a dislike of working with ill or dying patients, whereas among the younger doctors in training grades there appeared to be quite a different motivation and attraction towards the specialty.

Like the other doctors, many of the clinical assistants had decided to work in GU medicine because of its relation to obstetrics and gynaecology or other specialties. They also said that they had found it interesting and varied. But more than a third said that they had not actively *chosen* the specialty. The clinical assistants had frequently been asked to take on sessions, as this GP clinical assistant explained: 'I was asked to do it. I'll give it a whirl, I thought, and now I love it...' Some had come temporarily to the specialty and found that they liked it.

Other reasons cited by medical staff for entering GU medicine included the fact that the patients were generally young, as well as being healthy; the breadth of patient contact generally; the reward of helping people; a desire to widen their skills and experience; the limited range of conditions, making it an easily mastered specialty; the variety of conditions; health or age reasons for entering a physically undemanding specialty; and a wish to stay in the same locality.

What the doctors liked about GU medicine
It could not be argued that most of the doctors had entered GU medicine as a first choice or with a burning ambition to work in the specialty. However, there was a strong sense in most of the interviews that, once in GU medicine, many of them had found it very much to their liking.

All but three of the doctors said there was something that they particularly liked about working in GU medicine. The single most common reason, cited by a third of all doctors, was the effective and curative treatment. Consultants were especially likely to mention the efficacy of treatment (45 per cent), reflecting the fact that this was one of the main reasons why consultants had entered the specialty. But some added the comment that HIV/AIDS had somewhat changed this view: 'One satisfaction is that we can cure most of the conditions – apart from AIDS that is...'

It was perhaps not surprising that the efficacy of treatment brought other benefits, and a quarter of the doctors specifically mentioned the pleasure they got from helping patients. Reassuring and curing apprehensive and upset patients was said to be particularly rewarding, as this consultant remarked: 'You can treat the condition and patients respond. The patient's reaction at the next visit is, "Doctor, I'm all right". You don't find any problems with your treatment except with AIDS. You get credit and enjoyment...'

The extent of patient contact was also a very popular aspect of the specialty, especially with the consultants and doctors in training grades, a quarter of whom mentioned that it was something they found particularly attractive about the specialty. The consultants also particularly liked the fact that the patients were young (36 per cent) and healthy (18 per cent). One consultant said: 'The youth of the patients. You're more in touch with normal human beings. Because they're not ill, they're not so dependent, they don't think of doctors as God. You can cure their illness...'

Some doctors also found the variety of patients and lifestyles particularly interesting, and there was no doubt that some enjoyed hearing about the rather exotic lives that patients attending GUM clinics occasionally led.

20 per cent of the medical staff interviewed liked the fact that GU medicine was a 'complete' or 'self-contained' specialty. The clinical assistants, who were doing sessional work, were particularly likely to mention this: 'I can completely diagnose, treat and trace contacts and eliminate disease from the community. People can come and ask for help from us and it's all confidential...'

Some doctors said that they found GU medicine generally interesting and challenging, while some, like this consultant, specifically mentioned the social, emotional and psychological aspects of the specialty: 'Even as a consultant, one maintains contact with the patients who are often emotionally upset and one can do an awful lot to allay their fears...'

A wide range of other reasons were given by medical staff for liking GU medicine. Most important as far as the doctors in training grades were concerned was the HIV/AIDS work, mentioned by a quarter of the junior doctors, who also particularly appreciated the absence of on-call duty and the good working hours.

Other reasons mentioned by all medical staff included the continuity of patient care; the affinity of GUM to other interests (such as obstetrics and gynaecology, dermatology and general practice); again, the limited range of conditions making GUM a specialty in which it was relatively easy to develop an expertise; the lack of chronic patients; and the good staff relations.

What the doctors disliked about GU medicine

The doctors liked a great deal about GU medicine, particularly the patient contact. But almost two-thirds (63 per cent) said that there was something they did not like about working in GU medicine. The consultants and the doctors in training grades were much more likely than the clinical assistants to dislike aspects of the specialty. 79 per cent of consultants and 88 per cent of junior doctors said they disliked something about GU medicine, compared with 41 per cent of the clinical assistants.

The consultants were most likely to cite the low status of GU medicine as a specialty and this was mentioned by more than two thirds of those who disliked some aspect of the specialty. This consultant voiced his feelings on the subject: 'I don't like the fact that I'm not as respected as my colleagues are. I *feel* it – as though it's something I'm compelled to battle against. And also I've given up with some of my colleagues because of this. Maybe I'm paranoid. For example, the gynae. department have very little respect for us. I think it's to do with sex, to do with their anxieties about sex. They say, "Why do people want to do GU medicine? It must be because they're gay, or too interested in sex, or have had lots of STDs themselves"...'

This 'paranoid' feeling was not unique to this consultant. Many of the consultants referred to the negative image attributed to GUM and those working in the specialty by others working in the hospital: 'Being considered a second-class consultant by everyone else and being called a second-grade specialty and trying to fight harder to get funds, staff and equipment...'

The perceived low status of GU medicine appeared to be associated with the negative image which the specialty was thought to reflect. A fifth of the consultants said they disliked the stigma attached to GU medicine, a view summarised by a consultant: 'It was a Cinderella service for a long time, though HIV has changed that. The stigma attached to GU concerns me. Our needs get pushed aside or they would be if I didn't push them back. It's not a high profile specialty, the public are not sympathetic...'

This view of GU medicine was said to be widespread, as this consultant remarked: 'There's still a stigma attached to the specialty amongst the public and the professionals as well. It's going gradually, but there's still a stigma...' And another consultant agreed: 'There is a stigma associated with the specialty, even within the medical profession...'

The stigma associated with GU medicine was thought to affect the behaviour of patients visiting GUM clinics. Some consultants disliked what they saw as the aggressive and abusive behaviour of some of the patients. A senior consultant reflected: 'I dislike the change in attitude of the patients. The increase in aggressive behaviour. It's what the Department of Health calls the "increased expectations of patients". But what it boils down to is increasing aggressiveness and argumentativeness and a desire to have everything on their own terms. Sometimes they're physically violent. It happens in other specialties too, but people going to a grand surgeon are very much more humble. They can get an appointment with us right away – it rather devalues us...'

Other aspects of the specialty disliked by the consultants included the limited range of conditions encountered in the specialty and the isolation of GUM clinics: 'The amount of isolation associated with GU medicine. It was originally a Cinderella specialty, but we are also architecturally isolated and the confidentiality aspect further compounds the isolation...'

The junior doctors, on the other hand, were most likely to dislike the routine tasks and treatments involved in GU medicine. Around a third of the doctors in training grades referred to the repetitive nature of their work, like this registrar: 'The job is very repetitive and doesn't intellectually tax you...' The junior doctors also disliked the volume and turnover of patients and the limited range of conditions, which may, to some extent, have exacerbated the routine nature of the work.

The clinical assistants were less likely to dislike any aspects of the specialty, although some mentioned its negative image, the attitudes and lifestyles of the patients and the danger of infection (with HIV or hepatitis).

Had the doctors changed their views about GU medicine?

More than half the doctors (55 per cent) said their views about working in GU medicine had changed since they entered the specialty. But the reasons differed between the different grades.

The consultants found the specialty more interesting and stimulating than they had originally expected. This probably relates to the fact that GU medicine had not been the first choice of many of the consultants who would have preferred to have pursued a career in other specialties such as obstetrics and gynaecology. But many had clearly reviewed their opinion of their second choice specialty, and, like this consultant, were pleasantly surprised to find it more demanding than expected: 'When you enter any specialty, you don't know what it's going to be like. GU medicine is very personally challenging. You're dealing with sexuality and a terminal illness. When you go into it, you don't realise it will be a personal challenge...'

But some consultants had developed a more negative view of the specialty since the advent of HIV/AIDS. Some felt that HIV/AIDS had changed the specialty and, after years of experience of STDs, were finding it difficult to keep up-to-date with the HIV-related work: 'It's changed the type of disease with the advent of AIDS. I'm not really trained to deal with it, only up to a small point. I feel inadequate but you still have to deal with the bread and butter of the clinic...'

Some consultants also felt that the patients they were now seeing were more demanding and questioning than they had been in the past.

The junior doctors' views had changed as they had gained greater knowledge and understanding of the specialty, and some said they now felt more confident about working in GU medicine. And some had a more positive view of the specialty because of HIV/AIDS. This registrar was working in a large clinic with a substantial amount of HIV/AIDS-related work: 'I always thought it would be interesting, even from my student days, and there was very little HIV then. But HIV has changed the specialty. It's more varied than I thought it would be and there's scope for increasing that even more. It's brought variety – in the patients, cases and conditions...'

A senior registrar, who was also working in a large clinic with a high proportion of HIV work, voiced a similar opinion: 'I went into it with my heart in my mouth. I thought, "I hope it's the right thing. I can't go back". But the specialty has changed and is held in high esteem because of HIV. There are now links with infectious diseases and there are the academic aspects, as well as virology and immunology. There are still some people who think of us as "clap" doctors. But I'm surprised I like it as much as I do. I thought it would be a quiet life, but it's not, and the career structure is very reasonable compared with other specialties...'

The clinical assistants were rather less likely to have changed their opinions about the specialty, but those who had were generally more confident about working in GU medicine and felt more positive about the specialty.

Around one fifth of all the medical staff who reported a change in their views of GU medicine said their attitudes towards the patients had changed in that they now had broader and less stereotyped attitudes towards people visiting GUM clinics.

Training in GU-related topics

The consultants had all trained in GU medicine and most of the junior doctors were training in the specialty. Nearly a quarter of the clinical assistants had a diploma in venereology/GU medicine and, as we have seen, many of them had considerable experience in GU medicine. But we were interested in establishing what training all the doctors had had in GU-related topics, such as colposcopy, family planning and HIV/AIDS.

More than 80 per cent of the doctors reported that they had had training in GU-related topics. The junior doctors were rather less likely to have had training (69 per cent) than the consultants (88 per cent) and other doctors (83 per cent).

More than half of all the doctors interviewed had received training in family planning (55 per cent), while just under half had received training on HIV/AIDS (44 per cent). Consultants were rather more likely to have received training on HIV/AIDS but rather less likely to have received training in family planning.

Around 40 per cent of doctors had received training in colposcopy, with consultants, not surprisingly, the most likely to have received colposcopy training (61 per cent of all consultants interviewed).

Over half the doctors who had received training in topics related to GU medicine had attended only one or two courses, but more than a quarter had attended three or four courses, and the rest (16 per cent) had attended more than five courses or study days. Apart from the family planning certificate, which had both theoretical and practical elements, most of the courses lasted between two and five days. The majority of courses were not certificated; three-quarters of the doctors who had received training said they had received no 'qualification' from the training course they had attended. However, more than half had attended a course which resulted in a certificate.

16 of the 89 doctors interviewed had *not* received any training in GU-related topics. This included 4 of the 33 consultants (12 per cent), 5 of the 16 doctors in training grades (31 per cent) and 7 of the 40 clinical assistants and other doctors (18 per cent). The four consultants did not want any training in a GU-related topic now, but all but two of the other doctors wanted further training. The most common request was for training in colposcopy (6 doctors), but four doctors wanted training in HIV/AIDS and two wanted family planning training.

Work in the selected GUM clinics

The aim of the study was to examine the work roles and responsibilities of all staff working in GUM clinics. The above descriptions and analyses give some background to the doctors working in the clinics in terms of their age, sex, qualifications, training and experience, and their reasons for entering the specialty. We now turn to their work in the selected GUM clinics.

Length of time in clinic

Overall, 44 per cent of the medical staff had been working in the clinic for less than 5 years, 16 per cent for between 5 and 10 years, and 40 per cent for 10 years or more.

The consultants and other career grade doctors were the most long-standing members of the clinics. Two-thirds of the consultants and other career grade doctors had been working in the selected clinics for more than 10 years. Two consultants had been working in the clinic for between 5 and 10 years, and nine (27 per cent) for less than 5 years. All the junior doctors, on the other hand, had only been working in the clinic for less than 5 years and nearly two-thirds of them had been with the clinic for less than one year.

The clinical assistants' association with the clinics fell somewhere between the career grade doctors and the junior doctors. They were split almost equally between those who had worked in the clinic for less than 5 years (35 per cent), those who had worked in the clinic for between 5 and 10 years (32 per cent), and those who had worked in the clinic for 10 years or more.

Time spent working in the clinic

Medical staff usually worked in a particular GUM clinic on a part-time basis. Three-quarters of all the doctors interviewed worked part-time in the selected clinics and only a quarter worked full-time.

Among the consultants, around a third worked in the clinic full-time and just over two-thirds worked on a part-time basis. The mean number of sessions worked by the consultants was 5.9, and:

- two-fifths worked in the clinic for 2-4 sessions per week

- one third worked for 6-9 sessions per week
- just under a fifth worked for 10 or 11 sessions per week

Two of the other career grade doctors worked full-time in the clinic and one worked part-time (6 sessions per week).

The junior doctors were much more likely than the other doctors to be working full-time in the clinic and only 5 of the 16 said they worked part-time in the clinic. The mean number of hours worked in the clinic by the junior doctors was 33.9.

The work undertaken by the clinical assistants was very much of a sessional nature. Only one of the 37 clinical assistants worked full-time in the selected clinics. Around a third worked only one session in the GUM clinic, a quarter worked for two sessions and around a third worked for three sessions or more. The mean number of sessions worked in the clinics by the clinical assistants was 2.8.

Table 3.2   Sessions worked by medical staff

			column percentages
	Consultants	Other career grades	Clinical assistants
No. of sessions			
One	-	-	35
Two	15	-	27
Three	12	-	14
Four or five	15	-	10
Six or seven	21	33	3
Eight or nine	12	-	5
Ten or eleven	18	67	3
Don't know	6	-	3
Mean no. of sessions	5.9	8.7	2.8
Base:	(33)	(3)	(37)

Work in other GUM clinics

44 cent of the doctors said that they worked in other GUM clinics in addition to the selected clinic. Three-quarters of the consultants did so, compared with 38 per cent of the junior doctors and 24 per cent of the clinical assistants.

Most of those who worked in another GUM clinic worked only in *one* other clinic, though six doctors worked in two other GUM clinics and one worked in three other clinics. The clinics were generally in the same district or within the same region as the selected clinic. The number of sessions worked in other clinics ranged from one to ten, but the average number of sessions in other clinics worked by doctors was 4.3.

Other work

We also asked the doctors if they did any *other* work, on either a paid or voluntary basis.

The clinical assistants were most likely to do other work (86 per cent). Half of them were general practitioners and spent the greater part of their working week in general practice, while more than a fifth were clinical assistants in clinics other than GU medicine.

61 cent of the consultants were carrying out other work. This was, most commonly, private practice (24 per cent of all consultants), but nearly one fifth of them worked as a medical officer within the prison service.

Junior doctors and the doctors on other career grades were much less likely to do other work, as they were usually working full-time in the selected clinics.

Full-time and part-time working

Overall, 80 per cent of the doctors worked full-time, including their other work. All but two of the consultants worked full-time overall; those who worked part-time worked 9 sessions and 7 sessions. Two of the three doctors in non-consultant career grades worked full-time overall, while all the junior doctors worked full-time. The clinical assistants were rather different in that only 59 per cent worked full-time, while 41 per cent worked part-time.

Working pattern of medical staff

The general pattern of working emerged as follows:

- the consultants tended to work part-time in the selected GUM clinics but often worked in other GUM clinics and did other work, so that virtually all held full-time appointments. The non-consultant career grades followed a similar pattern;
- all the doctors in training grades worked full-time overall, and were most likely to work full-time in the selected GUM clinic;
- the clinical assistants generally worked for one or two sessions in the selected GUM clinic. The GP clinical assistants worked in general practice and tended to work full-time overall, while the other clinical assistants sometimes worked in other clinics and might work either full-time or part-time overall.

Medical staff and the management structure of the clinic

We asked all the staff to whom they reported managerially and professionally. The consultants were, perhaps not surprisingly, often puzzled by the questions, and one third said that they reported to *no-one* in managerial terms. Others, however, referred to the unit general manager or the regional medical officer (15 per cent each), the clinical director of medicine, the director of public health or the district general manager. The vast majority of clinical assistants and junior doctors reported managerially to the clinic consultant (although a few of the more junior doctors said that they reported to the senior registrar or registrar).

The consultants were most likely to say that they reported to *no-one* professionally because they were clinically autonomous (73 per cent). But some said they reported to the *senior* consultant on professional matters (12 per cent). All the non-consultant career grades, all the clinical assistants and the vast majority of the doctors in training grades said they reported professionally to the consultant or senior consultant, while four junior doctors referred to the medical grade above their own (senior registrar or registrar).

Around two-thirds of the consultants said that there were people in the clinic who reported to them. Given the lines of responsibility outlined above, this figure might have been expected to be nearer to 100 per cent. In some clinics, however, the consultants had devolved managerial responsibility for junior members to other senior members of the GUM clinic staff.

The consultants who said staff reported to them managerially were most likely to say that *all* the clinic staff reported to them (or, in some cases, all the clinic staff except the other consultants). Others, however, said their lines of responsibility were confined to the other medical staff.

Few of the other doctors said that staff in the clinic reported to them. In the larger clinics within teaching hospitals, however, the senior registrar or registrar was likely to say they were responsible for the registrars or SHOs.

Given the changes in the health service and the feeling of isolation of GUM clinics which pervaded this study, we were interested in the extent to which the doctors felt they had enough managerial support in their jobs. Overall, more than a third of felt they did *not* have enough support. But the consultants in particular felt unsupported; more than half (55 per cent) felt they had insufficient managerial support. The problems arose from lack of support from staff outside the clinic. Around one fifth of all the consultants considered that their 'managers' in the hospital did not understand their professional needs and requirements, a view summarised by this consultant: 'One manager that I deal with – it would be better for everyone concerned if he was paid to stay at home. He obstructs or delays everything that goes through. I've been waiting since well before he was appointed for somewhere to put my files and teaching equipment and it's still not complete, largely thanks to him. I was required to find the funds myself, even though they exist. You have to find them yourself. It's one of the areas of the health service that's a game. The funds are there but it's up to you to find them...'

In some cases, this problem was exacerbated by the lack of continuity of hospital personnel, as this consultant said: 'In the last couple of years, no, I haven't had enough managerial support. They keep changing, there's no continuity at all. Once you've established a relationship, then they're gone. And they're often young and don't understand what we're trying to do...'

Others said that the changes taking place within the health service had resulted in changes in the management structure of the hospital which meant that some consultants no longer knew to whom they should go with different problems. Some blamed the low status accorded to GU medicine. One consultant said that 'the GUM department was always pushed to the bottom of the priority' and that 'GU consultants were not medically or politically powerful'. This resulted in a general lack of management support for the GUM clinic, as outlined by another consultant: 'They don't give us the things we ask for – extra staff, better premises. When the AIDS money was allocated, we weren't told it was here or what it was. It was all spent before we knew it was here and we haven't seen a penny of it...'

The majority of the clinical assistants (76 per cent) felt they had sufficient management support, but those that did not also complained about the general lack of support for the GUM clinic from staff outside the clinic, although some criticised the lack of teamwork and communication within the clinic.

Six of the 16 doctors in training grades felt that they had insufficient managerial support, mainly from within the clinic, either because of what some staff considered to be poor management ability or because the consultant was so busy that it was difficult to see him or her.

Balance of responsibilities

Overall, three-quarters of the medical staff interviewed considered that the amount of responsibility they were given was about right. But 11 per cent felt they had too much and 11 per cent thought they had too little responsibility.

Again, it was the consultants who were most dissatisfied with the level of their responsibilities. While around two-thirds felt they had about the right amount of responsibility, six consultants (18 per cent) thought they had too little and five (15 per cent) thought they had too much.

The latter generally felt busy and overworked, but specifically cited their high clinical commitment, the lack of administrative support and a feeling of isolation where there was only one consultant: 'With the paucity of facilities, there is too much pressure on the consultant. I still have no secretarial support and I have lengthy clinic times. The patients get very agitated...'

The consultants who thought they had too little responsibility were most frustrated by their lack of control over staffing and budgets and some, like this consultant, felt they had little or no say in decisions that were made about the clinic: 'I don't have enough responsibility in terms of what I can do with the clinic. We shouldn't be lumped with other out-patient departments and lumped with other medical departments. Even the money you get is utilised by others. I'd like to have more independence...'

All the doctors in other career grades and the vast majority of the clinical assistants felt the amount of responsibility they had was about right. Three-quarters of the junior doctors also felt they had the right amount of responsibility, though some, like this senior registrar, thought they had too much for their particular grade: 'I have too much, but it suits my personality. It just doesn't suit my timetable! I have a "consultoid" role. The consultants are tied up and the senior registrars take on decisions that should be taken by the consultant. It happens more so here in this clinic and less so in other places. But at least you know what's going to hit you when you become a consultant...'

Job description

Before looking in detail at the work carried out in the GUM clinics by the doctors, we asked them whether they had a job description. The sample was split fairly evenly between those who said they had one (46 per cent) and those who did not (49 per cent), while five per cent did not know whether they had one or not.

It is perhaps surprising that as many as *half* the doctors did *not* have a job description. Those least likely to have one were the clinical assistants, of whom only about one third said they had one. This compared with just over half the consultants and around two-thirds of the doctors in other career grades and in training grades.

The majority (80 per cent) of those with a job description had *not* been involved in the process of drawing it up. *None* of the clinical assistants or non-consultant career grades had been involved, and neither had all but one of the junior doctors. However, seven of the 33 consultants had drawn up their own job description or had been consulted about it.

The question of what staff in the GUM clinics thought of their job descriptions, if they had one, was of interest to us in this study, since there was clearly such a wide variation in the roles of most staff. It might be thought that job descriptions would help to delineate what was expected of staff and might therefore help to bring some order into what was generally thought to be a rather ill-defined world of roles and responsibilities.

Surprisingly, considering that they had been more involved than others in drawing the document up, the consultants were the least positive about their job descriptions. Some said their job description was out-of-date, while others said it was too broad and general and covered too many responsibilities. Few were satisfied with their job description.

The junior doctors, other career grades and the relatively few clinical assistants who had one were usually satisfied with their job descriptions, even though they were often said to be generally applicable to a particular grade or job, rather than specific to the individual or clinic.

Given the dissatisfaction of the consultants and the fact that some of them felt their job description was out-of-date, we explored the question of whether the descriptions were regularly reviewed. Only one third of the medical staff who had job descriptions said that it *was* reviewed on a regular basis. In these cases, the consultants reviewed the job descriptions of other medical staff, while the consultants' own job descriptions were reviewed by the unit or district general manager, by a senior consultant, or by themselves. Most doctors whose job descriptions were *not* regularly reviewed thought they ought to be, with only the clinical assistants tending to think this was not necessary.

Content of the job

We were particularly interested in finding out what staff felt about the component parts of their work and whether they thought the balance was right. We therefore asked them a series of questions designed to assess whether they wanted to increase or decrease the time they spent on any part of their job, whether there was anything they did not do in their job at present but would like to do, and if there was anything they did which they would prefer not to do.

Increasing time spent on activities

More than half the medical staff (54 per cent) said they would like to increase time spent on particular activities. One in seven of all the doctors interviewed wanted to increase the amount of time they spent on research and publication. The doctors in training grades were particularly keen to develop this aspect of their work, which they said was precluded by the pressure of clinical work. A registrar told us: 'I'd like to do more research. I'm at the point now where I could drop one or two general clinics and do specific research projects. But with the number of staff, it's too busy to do that now. I'm at the point in my career where I should be publishing papers...'

A further one in seven said they would like to spend more time with individual patients. A consultant described the problem in his clinic: 'Time with the patients. We give them ten minutes, but it's not enough, especially for new female patients. By the time you've examined them, there's no time to discuss or explain anything. The Royal College of Physicians recommended an average of 20 minutes per patient...'

The clinical assistants were those most likely to feel pressurised by the number of patients passing through the clinic, and a quarter of them wanted to spend more time with the patients.

Just over a quarter of the consultants wanted to increase the amount of time they spent in the clinic by increasing the number of sessions held. These consultants were generally working in the smaller, part-time clinics.

Five of the 16 doctors in training posts were keen to increase the amount of HIV/AIDS work they did. However, three of them were in one clinic where the HIV/AIDS work was carried out by two members of the medical staff, with little input from the other doctors, and this desire did seem to relate to the particular organisation of this clinic.

The doctors cited a wide range of other activities on which they would like to spend more time, including management or administration of the clinic, counselling generally and psycho-sexual counselling specifically, microscopy, colposcopy and teaching. However, none of these activities was mentioned by more than five doctors in each case, and, as we found throughout this study, there were considerable individual differences among staff in their perception of their ideal roles in the GUM clinics.

Additional activities

Just over half the doctors said that they would like to undertake an activity which they did not do at all at present. The most commonly cited activity was colposcopy; one in six (17 per cent) of all the doctors interviewed said they did not currently carry out colposcopy but would like to do so. The clinical assistants were particularly keen to perform colposcopy, although it was also mentioned by some consultants and some of the junior doctors.

Around one in ten of the consultants wanted to spend time on research and publication but found themselves unable to do so at present because of the pressure of work. The doctors in training posts, on the other hand, wanted to take on more responsibility generally.

The doctors again cited a wide range of other activities which they would like to pursue, including psycho-sexual counselling, contact with other specialties and HIV/AIDS work.

Decreasing time spent on activities

It was interesting that as many as 42 per cent of the doctors, in particular the consultants and junior doctors, said that there were activities they would prefer to do less often. The most common of these was the routine assessment of routine complaints, mentioned by around one in ten doctors. Much of the clinical work was said to involve repetitive tests and treatment. More specifically, some doctors said they would prefer to treat warts less frequently. And some, particularly those in training grades, said they would prefer to do less clinical work generally.

The other main area cited by the doctors was administrative and clerical work. More than one in ten said they would prefer to spend less time on paperwork and form-filling, and clerical tasks, such as 'pulling' and filing notes and looking up patient results. Some consultants also begrudged the amount of time spent attending meetings and committees and the amount of time they felt they wasted either travelling between clinics or waiting for patients.

Few other activities were mentioned, but they included work with HIV/AIDS patients, microscopy, examination of male patients and teaching staff outside the clinic. None of these tasks, however, was mentioned by more than three doctors in each case.

Activities to exclude

Finally, we asked the doctors whether there was anything they did in their job that they would rather not do at all. Only eight of them, spread across all grades, said they would prefer not to do some aspect of their work. Four said they would rather not do administrative and clerical tasks, such as paperwork and writing letters, while a fifth said he would prefer not to do reception work! Other tasks receiving single mentions included microscopy, repetitive and low status tasks, treating non-GU conditions, as well as managing and training clinic staff.

41

Job satisfaction

In general, the medical staff were happy in their work. Around three-quarters (73 per cent) of all the doctors interviewed said they were satisfied with their job, including a third who were very satisfied (35 per cent). One fifth were fairly satisfied with their job and only three, all consultants, were not very satisfied. The clinical assistants were the most positive; four-fifths of them were satisfied, including over 40 per cent who were very satisfied.

We asked the doctors the reasons for their satisfaction or dissatisfaction with their job. This question elicited a huge response; many gave multiple reasons and many cited both positive and negative aspects of their job.

Two-thirds of the doctors gave positive reasons for being satisfied with their job. One in six said they liked the work and were generally happy in their job, while a further one in ten said they found their work exciting and challenging. Others specifically mentioned their enjoyment of the clinical work and the reward they got from helping and curing patients. Around one in ten regarded staff relations as good in the clinic, while others said they had good professional support from other staff working in the clinic. The opportunities for promotion and career development was also cited as a positive aspect of the job, while others said their work in the clinic was pertinent to other work or interests.

A wide range of other comments were made on the 'plus' side, including the good hours and lack of on-call duty, the opportunity for research and the HIV/AIDS related work.

But more than half the doctors mentioned negative aspects of their job, even if they were generally satisfied with it. Most of them mentioned only one aspect, but these varied widely and there was no one major criticism found among all doctors. The consultants were the most likely to be dissatisfied. Around one fifth of them referred to the lack of support they received from hospital management. Others, however, were concerned about their workload and the lack of time in which to carry out their duties, the lack of clerical and administrative support and the long hours they had to work as a result.

Some clinical assistants complained of poor professional support from other staff and low pay. But complaints made by doctors at all levels included the low status, isolation and negative image of GU medicine, the lack of time spent with patients, the routine nature of the clinical work, the poor clinic building, lack of resources and lack of staff. These were issues which recurred throughout the study and were reiterated in one form or another among staff of all types.

An increased role for GUM clinic staff?

We were interested in the views of all staff about the role of other types of staff within the GUM clinics. The staff's perception of the work roles of others in these self-contained, often small and isolated units, was of importance in a study of this kind. We were particularly interested to know whether they thought that particular types of staff could take on extra responsibilities or duties in addition to those they currently performed. In general, we restricted our questioning about the medical, nursing and health advising staff to staff in these particular categories. But we asked all types of staff about the administrative and clerical staff. Our aim was to examine the role of the various types of staff from a number of different angles. We looked first at whether the doctors themselves felt they or their medical colleagues could take on any more responsibilities in the clinic.

Could the medical staff take on more responsibilities?

Only one third of the doctors of all grades thought the medical staff could take on *other* responsibilities in the clinic. The most commonly mentioned task was colposcopy. More than 10 per cent of all doctors said they *could* carry out colposcopy, broadly reflecting the proportion of doctors who said they would *like* to perform colposcopy. The junior doctors were particularly likely to say that they could take it on. One in ten consultants felt they could take on teaching and training of clinic staff, while the same proportion said they could take on research and publication.

The doctors mentioned a wide range of other activities that they, or other medical staff, could take on. Some of these were practical tasks such as examining all new female patients, microscopy, diathermy/cautery and laser treatment. But there was evidence of considerable interpersonal resentment within some clinics, with some doctors considering that other medical staff should fulfil their current responsibilities, improve their communication and carry out their own administrative work.

But what was preventing the doctors from taking on these other responsibilities in the clinic? For the most part, it was simply because they were too busy. Even if they thought the medical staff could take on additional responsibilities more than half of them said that lack of time prevented them from doing so. In some cases, notably where practical tasks were concerned, it was lack of equipment or space which precluded doctors from taking on other activities. But the consultants sometimes commented that other medical staff were reluctant to take on further responsibilities, while some clinical assistants said the consultant was reluctant for them to take on additional duties.

As many as two-thirds of the doctors, therefore, felt that they could *not* take on any more responsibilities. These doctors were almost unanimous in their reasons; three-quarters said they already did enough in their job and there was really nothing else they *could* do, while the remainder said they were too busy and did not have enough time to take on any more responsibilities.

There was a striking similarity in the proportion of nursing staff and health advisers and medical staff who thought that medical staff could take on more responsibilities: just over a third of the nursing staff (37 per cent) and health advisers (36 per cent) agreed with the 34 per cent of doctors on this issue.

Again the nurses mentioned a wide range of potential additional responsibilities for the medical staff, and no single activity stood out. But, like the doctors themselves, the most commonly cited activity was colposcopy, mentioned by 7 per cent of all nurses interviewed. A handful of nurses, from different clinics, thought the doctors could fulfil their current medical duties and ought to spend more time in the clinic and take better care of the patients generally. In one particular clinic, where some medical staff were said not to be examining new female patients, the nurses thought the doctors *should* be examining all new female patients; and some thought the doctors should carry out a pelvic examination of all women attending the clinic.

The health advisers, on the other hand, were more likely to say that the medical staff could take on more patient education and information, more work with HIV/AIDS patients and more training of staff in the clinic.

The nurses and health advisers generally thought the reason why the doctors were not carrying out these responsibilities was because that was the way the clinic was organised. They often said the doctors did not want to take on more responsibilities. But two-thirds of them said that the doctors were too busy and did not have enough time to take on extra responsibilities.

The medical staff

The structure and composition of the medical staffing undoubtedly played a key role in determining the work roles and responsibilities of the other members of staff in the GUM clinics. However, much depended on the personality and interests of the consultants, which, as we have seen, were by no means homogeneous. They came from a wide variety of backgrounds, like many consultants in other specialties, but their traditional autonomy in determining the organisation and structure of clinics which were characterised by their geographical and professional isolation had far-reaching consequences. These can be seen in ensuing chapters on the work roles and responsibilities of other members of the GUM clinic staff, and, indeed, throughout the report.

4   The nurses and their roles

Nursing staff interviewed

We interviewed all the nursing staff working in 19 of the 20 clinics. In the final clinic, which was by far the largest, we made a random selection and interviewed two-thirds of the nurses working in the clinic.

Interviews were carried out with a total of 98 nursing staff;
- 2 clinical nurse specialists
- 14 sisters/charge nurses
- 1 sister/health adviser (combined post)
- 2 acting sisters/charge nurses
- 2 outpatient sisters
- 42 staff nurses
- 32 enrolled nurses
- 2 registered fever nurses
- 1 auxiliary nurse

In our analysis of the work roles and responsibilities of staff and enrolled nurses, one registered fever nurse (RFN) was included with the staff nurses and the other was included with the enrolled nurses because these were the posts they held on the establishment of the clinics in which they worked.

For the analysis, we grouped the 98 nurses in the following way:
- 21 sisters/charge nurses/clinical nurse specialists
- 43 staff nurses (including 1 RFN)
- 33 enrolled nurses (including 1 RFN)
- 1 auxiliary nurse (whom we included with the enrolled nurses in the tables)

Characteristics of nursing staff

Of the 98 nurses interviewed, 14 were men (14 per cent) and 84 were women (86 per cent). The male nurses were predominantly charge nurses and staff nurses, rather than enrolled nurses. A quarter of the sisters/charge nurses/clinical nurse specialists were men, while three-quarters were women.

As shown in Table 4.1 the nurses ranged in age from 23 to 63, with a mean age of 43.7 years. Although the sisters/charge nurses were rather older on average, it was interesting that there was not a lot of difference either in the mean age or in the distribution of ages among the different types of nurses. GUM

Table 4.1   Sex and age of nursing staff

column percentages

	Total	Sisters/ charge nurses	Staff nurses	Enrolled nurses*
Sex				
Male	14	24	14	9
Female	86	76	86	91
Age				
25-35	22	19	23	24
36-45	22	19	21	27
46-55	38	43	37	38
56-65	13	19	12	12
Over 65	-	-	-	-
Mean age	**43.7**	**46.1**	**42.4**	**43.6**
Base: all nurses	*(98)*	*(21)*	*(43)*	*(34)*

*   includes 1 auxiliary nurse

nursing is very much an occupation for middle-aged nurses, according to the figures from the selected clinics.

Qualifications

All but one of the nurses (the auxiliary nurse) had a nursing qualification. 63 were registered general nurses (RGN), while 33 were enrolled nurses (EN). Two had qualified as registered fever nurses (RFN), a qualification which is now obsolete.

All but one of the sisters/charge nurses were RGNs; one of the acting sisters was an enrolled nurse. One sister held both an RGN *and* an EN qualification.

A number of the RGNs had additional nursing qualifications. Six were registered mental nurses and five were registered midwives. Two had a health visitors' certificate and one held a district nursing certificate.

Some of the nurses held certificates from nursing courses they had attended, some of which were ENB courses and some were other certificated courses. These will be considered later when discussing the nurses' training.

The nurses' academic qualifications varied widely. A quarter of them had no academic qualifications, while seven had a school leaving certificate. Two-fifths said their highest academic qualification was GCE 'O' levels (41 per cent), while around a fifth had obtained GCE 'A' levels (19 per cent). A small proportion (five nurses) had a degree.

Thirteen of the nurses said they had other 'professional' qualifications. These included a teaching certificate, typing/shorthand certificates, health administration/management and City and Guilds qualifications in a subject not directly relevant to GU medicine.

Nurse grades

Table 4.2 shows that two-thirds of the *sisters/charge nurses* were on a G grade, while three were on a higher grade (H or I). Another three were on an F grade, while the enrolled nurse who was acting as a sister was on an E grade.

More than half the *staff nurses* were on an E grade while a third were graded D. The remainder (five nurses) were on an F grade. The *enrolled nurses* were mainly on a D grade, although four were an E and three were a C grade. The *auxiliary nurse* was a B grade.

Table 4.2   Grades of nursing staff

				column percentages
	Total	Sisters/ charge nurses	Staff nurses	Enrolled nurses *
I	1	5	-	-
H	2	10	-	-
G	14	67	-	-
F	8	14	12	-
E	29	5	53	12
D	42	-	35	76
C	3	-	-	9
B	1	-	-	3
Base: all nurses	*(98)*	*(21)*	*(43)*	*(34)*

* includes 1 auxiliary nurse

Length of time in grade

Half the nurses said they had been working on their current grade for between 2 and 5 years, reflecting the fact that nurse regrading took place from June/July 1988 and many of the nurse were regraded at this time (ie. 2-3 years before fieldwork for this study). Around a quarter had been on their grade for between 1 and 2 years, and around a quarter for less than one year.

Length of time in GU medicine

The nurses' experience of work in GU medicine varied widely, ranging from less than 6 months to more than 10 years. Overall, 60 per cent of the nurses had worked in GU medicine for less than 5 years, including 19 per cent who had worked in the specialty for less than one year. However, 15 per cent of the nurses had worked in GU medicine for between 5 and 10 years and around a quarter for 10 years or more.

Not surprisingly, the sisters/charge nurses had most experience. Around two-fifths (43 per cent) had worked in GU medicine for more than 10 years, compared with 27 per cent of the enrolled nurses and 14 per cent of the staff nurses.

Why the nurses decided to work in a GUM clinic

One third of all the nursing staff said they had chosen to work in a GUM clinic because the hours were good and there was no shift or weekend work. Male and female nurses were equally likely to cite the good hours as a reason for choosing GUM, and it was the single most common reason mentioned by nursing staff.

A staff nurse described how she had started work in a GUM clinic: 'The only thing really was the hours. I'd never thought of it before. I came off nights after years and years and applied for a day job. They said, "What about the special clinic?" I felt shock, horror! It's not a place you know anything about. The hours were lovely though. They said try one day in the clinic to see if I could do the work...'

One fifth of the nurses said they had chosen to work in a GUM clinic because they found the work interesting and varied, while one in ten had chosen it because they wanted to widen their experience. The same proportion (11 per cent) said they had chosen to work in a GUM clinic because they wanted to work with HIV/AIDS patients. This was mentioned in particular by the nurses working in the largest GUM clinic with the greatest proportion of HIV/AIDS-related work.

Around one in ten nurses had decided to work in a GUM clinic for health reasons. Some of these nurses cited back problems or simply older age, but all considered the specialty to be less physically demanding than ward work, which involved lifting patients and long shifts.

A wide range of other reasons were given for choosing to work in a GUM clinic. These included its relationships to family planning and gynaecological work, the opportunities for promotion and career development, the limited range of conditions encountered, making it an easily mastered specialty, and the patient contact.

However, as many as a quarter of the nurses said they had not *chosen* to work in GU medicine. They had either been asked to do so or had taken it on because they needed a job and a post became vacant in the clinic. Similarly, a further 13 per cent said that they had only come to the specialty temporarily but had found that they liked it and had consequently stayed on. More than a third of the nurses interviewed, therefore, could not be said to have actively chosen the specialty, but had ended up working in GUM almost by chance.

What the nurses liked about GU medicine

Whatever their reasons for entering GU medicine, all but one of the nurses said there was something they particularly liked about working in a GUM clinic, the most popular aspect being the patient contact. Around a third cited the patient contact generally, but others particularly liked the fact that the patients were young (14 per cent) and that the patients were healthy (3 per cent). Some enjoyed the volume of patients passing through the clinic and the variety of different lifestyles encountered, while others liked the continuity of patient care.

One fifth said that they found working in a GUM clinic generally interesting and challenging, while a similar proportion found it particularly rewarding to reassure and cure the patients. One sister explained: 'The patients are very highly strung. They're nervous. It's extremely personal and embarrassing. But it can happen to anyone from any walk of life. I get great satisfaction putting patients at ease and getting them better. It's not easy for patients to enter a GUM clinic – they get very upset. It's satisfying to help and alleviate their problems...'

A further fifth of the nurses referred to the good staff relations within the GUM clinic. Those who had worked in other clinics or on the wards found the GUM clinic refreshingly informal and some particularly liked the lack of staff hierarchy.

Some of the nursing staff (12 per cent) referred to the varied work and extended role of the GUM nurse. Others specifically said they liked the microscopy (9 per cent), while others mentioned counselling and health education. Around one in ten said they particularly liked the hours associated with working in a GUM clinic, which was not surprising in view of the fact that this was the main reason given by nurses for entering the specialty.

What the nurses disliked about GU medicine

Just over a third of the nursing staff interviewed said that there was some aspect of working in GU medicine that they disliked. The sisters/charge nurses were particularly likely to mentioned aspects that they disliked (67 per cent). As with the doctors, the most common of these was the low status and stigma associated with the specialty, mentioned by around one in ten of all nurses, including this sister:

> There's a slight tendency among the hierarchy to overlook us. People shove us into the background. We're offering a good service, we have a huge clientele and our reputation spreads by word of mouth. We're very non-judgemental. But there's a slight tendency to say the day ward comes first, and the abortion clinic and colposcopy come first. They always think, "We'll cope, we'll manage". But there's an obligation on us, as there is with any other clinic, to keep the appointments. We should be brought to the forefront, into the outpatients clinic. We're not a "special" clinic. But we're frowned on, even the administrators frown...

Around one in ten nurses disliked the routine tasks and treatments involved in GU medicine and found the work repetitive: 'The repetition perhaps,

49

especially with something like painting warts. There's a lot of that. You think, "Oh God! Not again!"...

Other aspects disliked by the nurses tended to be specific to the clinic, rather than to GU medicine itself. These included the poor GUM clinic building, poor staff relations, staff hierarchy in the clinic and the nurses' role in the clinic, but none of these was mentioned by more than three nurses in each case.

Training to work in GUM clinics

Only one third of the nurses (32 per cent) had been on any kind of specific training course to work in GUM clinics (other than counselling courses).

The sisters/charge nurses were more likely to have received some GUM training than the more junior nurses: just over half of the sisters/charge nurses compared with around a quarter of the staff nurses and enrolled nurses. Nevertheless, it is surprising that nearly half the sisters/charge nurses, and three-quarters of the other nurses, had *not* had any training courses to work in GUM clinics.

Of the 31 nurses who had had training:

- 16 nurses (16 per cent of all the nurses interviewed) had attended the short ENB one week course on GU medicine (ENB 932)
- 3 had attended the ENB 275 course, the six month course in GU medicine which has now been discontinued
- 7 had attended a general STD course/introduction to GUM organised by a district or regional health authority
- 4 nurses had attended seminars given by the GUM consultant
- 2 had had work experience or training in another GUM clinic

Most of the nurses who had received training to work in a GUM clinic had attended only one course, though four had attended two courses and three said they had attended 'several'.

Nine of the nurses had been on courses that were not certificated and did not result in a letter of attendance. These courses tended to be those organised by the clinics themselves. The ENB courses were said to be certificated, while those organised by health authorities might result in a letter of attendance.

As already noted, two-thirds of the nurses had *not* received any training to work in GUM clinics. But there was little doubt that nurses were crying out for training and three-quarters of those who had not received training in GU medicine said they would like some. (This represented half of all the nurses interviewed.) 24 of them (representing a quarter of all the nurses interviewed), said they would like to attend the ENB 932 course; ten of these nurses had their name down to attend the course, but some had been waiting for a place for some time. Eight wanted to attend the ENB 275 course, or a course of this nature, while nine wanted any course which would provide a general introduction to GU medicine and STDs. Other nurses said they wanted to attend a course on microscopy, an update on STDs and treatments, and a course to upgrade from an EN to an RGN.

There can be little doubt that the extent to which the nurses had received training in GU medicine was very limited and that there was a clear need and a strong desire among the nurses to attend training courses in order to improve and update their skills.

Training in GU-related topics

We also asked the nurses whether they had had any training in GU-related topics, such as colposcopy, family planning or HIV/AIDS (other than counselling). Although a rather higher proportion had received some training in a GU-related topic the figure was again low. Less than half had had specific training in a topic related to GU medicine (45 per cent), and this proportion was broadly reflected across all nursing grades.

Of the 44 nurses who had received training in GU-related topics:

- 15 had attended the one week ENB 934 course on HIV/AIDS (representing one third of the nurses who had had training and 15 per cent of all the nurses interviewed).
- 19 had attended an HIV/AIDS study day or course organised by someone other than the ENB, such as the hospital or a district or regional health authority
- a handful had attended the ENB 934 as well as another course or study.

Overall, 30 of the 98 nurses interviewed had received some training in HIV/AIDS (31 per cent). In addition:

- 11 nurses had received family planning training: two referred specifically to the ENB 901 course, but most said they had attended a course organised by the Family Planning Association
- 4 had attended a course on colposcopy.

Other courses mentioned by one or two nurses included the family planning instructing course, sexuality awareness, fertility awareness, psychosexual medicine and training in midwifery.

Two-thirds of the nurses who had received training had attended only one course, but ten had attended two courses and five had attended more than two. Again, many of the courses were not certificated. Half of the nurses who had had training in a GU-related topic said that they had not received either a certificate or even a letter of attendance from the courses they had attended. However, 19 said they had attended a certificated course, mostly the ENB 934 and the ENB 901/family planning courses.

However, 54 of the 98 nurses interviewed had not received any training in a GU-related subject. Again, we were impressed by the desire expressed by the nurses for training of any kind. More than three-quarters of those who had received no training said they would like some. (This represented 43 per cent of all the nurses interviewed.)

The most common request was for training on HIV/AIDS, made by 21 nurses, representing a fifth of the total sample. Six of these nurses specifically referred to the ENB 934 course. 11 of the nurses wanted family planning training, 11 wanted training in colposcopy and a further 11 said they would be happy with *any* sort of training.

Only ten nurses who had not had any training said they did not want any, mainly because they thought it was too late.

Some nurses had attended other courses in subjects which were not directly relevant to working in a GUM clinic. Six had attended an ENB course in other subjects and eight had attended other certificated courses, including orthopaedics, spinal injuries, care of the elderly, nursery nursing and tropical medicine. Three nurses had a BTA certificate.

Having described the characteristics, qualifications and training of the nurses working in the GUM clinics, we turn now to their work roles and responsibilities.

Length of time in clinic

In general, the nurses had been been working in the selected clinic for less time than the doctors. Overall, around two-thirds of the nurses had been working in the clinic for less than 5 years, including one fifth who had been working in the clinic for less than one year. But 15 per cent had been working in the clinic for between 5 and 10 years, and 20 per cent for more than 10 years.

The senior nurses had usually been in the selected clinics for the longest time. More than half (57 per cent) of the sisters/charge nurses had worked in the clinic for more than 5 years, including more than a third who had worked in the clinic for 10 years or more.

Time spent working in the clinic

We have seen that the doctors generally worked in the selected GUM clinics on a part-time basis, although virtually all of them worked full-time overall. As far as the nursing staff were concerned, the sample was split fairly evenly between those who worked in the clinic full-time (45 per cent) and those who worked part-time (55 per cent). The sisters/charge nurses were more likely than the other nurses to work full-time in the clinics (62 per cent compared with 40 per cent).

All the nurses who worked full-time in the clinic worked a total of 37.5 hours per week. The hours of the part-time nurses varied from less than 5 hours per week to 33.5 hours per week. Across all nursing staff, the mean number of hours worked in the GUM clinic was 25.1 hours per week, the average for the sisters/charge nurses being 38 hours, and for all other nurses 24.3 hours per week.

Work in other GUM clinics

Only six of the nurses worked in a GUM clinic in addition to the one selected for this study: two in one other and four in two other GUM clinics. These clinics were generally in the same district as the selected clinics, but one nurse worked in a clinic in another district and one worked in another region.

Work in other clinics

Almost a third of the nurses said they also worked in *other* clinics (30 per cent). A quarter said they worked in an out-patient clinic within the same hospital as the GUM clinic. In all these cases, the GUM clinic was part of the out-patients department and the nurses were general out-patient nurses who covered a variety of out-patient clinics, including surgical and medical out-patient clinics, gynaecology, dermatology and oncology. Five nurses worked in a family planning clinic in a health centre.

Other work

Around a fifth (22 per cent) of the nurses were involved in other paid or voluntary work. Seven worked as agency nurses, four worked on the wards, while one did paid counselling work, one did health visiting and one was also a practice nurse. Eight nurses did other work on a voluntary basis, including counselling for a voluntary organisation, church work and working as a magistrate.

Full-time and part-time working

When all their work was taken into consideration, 61 per cent of the nurses said they worked full-time and 39 per cent part-time. Nearly all the sisters/charge nurses (18 of the 21 senior nurses) worked full-time overall.

Nursing staff and the management structure

To whom did the nursing staff report managerially? The question elicited a wide range of names and titles. We experienced two main problems in analysing the nurses' response to this question: first, at the time of the study, many of the hospitals were changing their structures and appointing new people, and staff were sometimes unsure who their manager was. Secondly, different titles were used in different hospitals and it was not clear which titles and posts were comparable.

A quarter of the sisters/charge nurses (five respondents) said they reported to the out-patient services manager on managerial matters, while four referred to the (assistant) nursing services manager. Two senior nurses said they reported managerially to the unit general manager, the nurse manager, the clinical nurse specialist and the senior nurse (medicine). Other managers receiving single mentions included the out-patients sister and the outpatients coordinator, the community nurse manager, the business manager and the clinic consultant.

However, the majority of the staff nurses and enrolled and auxiliary nurses reported managerially to the sister/ charge nurse (52 per cent) or the out-patients sister (21 per cent). Five reported to the clinical nurse specialist and two to the *acting* sister/charge nurse. But again, a wide range of other people were mentioned, including the out-patient services manager, the field/community nurse manager, the nurse manager, the (assistant) nursing services manager and the business manager.

On professional matters, more than half (57 per cent) the sisters/charge nurses said that they reported to the clinic consultant, but three mentioned the out-patient sister, two reported to the nurse manager and two to the senior nurse (medicine).

The other nurses were most likely to report professionally to the (acting) sister/charge nurse (74 per cent), to the out-patient sister (14 per cent) or to the clinical nurse specialist (6 per cent). Three of the staff nurses, however, felt they were professionally responsible to the clinic consultant.

But were the nursing staff managerially responsible for other members of the clinic staff? Overall, one fifth of the nurses said that some members of the clinic staff reported to them. Not surprisingly, this included three-quarters of the sisters/charge nurses, though it was perhaps surprising that this figure was not closer to 100 per cent. These senior nurses were managerially responsible for the other nurses in the clinic, the number depending on the size of the clinic. Most, however, were responsible for between one and five members of staff. Two sisters/charge nurses said the health adviser reported to them and two said the receptionists reported to them. In addition, six of the other nurses, five staff and one enrolled nurse, said that other nurses below their grade reported to them.

The question of whether GUM clinic staff felt they had enough managerial support was a recurrent theme in this research. While the majority of nurses felt they had sufficient managerial support (59 per cent), more than a third disagreed (39 per cent). Perhaps not surprisingly, it was the sisters/charge nurses who were most likely to say that they did not have enough managerial support (71 per cent compared with 30 per cent of the other nurses).

The problems lay predominantly in a perceived lack of support from staff *outside* the clinic. The biggest complaint was the lack of support for the GUM clinics from managers within the hospital: 14 per cent of all the nurses interviewed complained about this. It is possible that the lack of support related to the negative image which it was felt that the GUM clinic attracted. Around one in ten of the nurses felt that the clinic had a low status among hospital managers and that managers considered that there was a stigma attached to GUM clinics.

Around one in ten of the nurses also complained of the lack of contact with managers outside the clinic. This was sometimes due to the manager being too busy, but some felt it again reflected the clinic's low status.

The changing structure of hospital management appeared to play a key role in the question of managerial and professional responsibility. Five of the nurses said that they had insufficient managerial support specifically because the management structure was changing and they no longer knew to whom they should go with different problems or who their manager was; or they were concerned at the lack of continuity of their managers.

Amount of responsibility within clinics

Two-thirds of the nurses said the amount of responsibility they had was about right, but almost one third felt that they had insufficient responsibility. This ratio was broadly reflected among both senior and junior nursing staff.

Nearly two-thirds of those who said they had too little responsibility thought that they were quite capable of taking on more, and some said they had had much more responsibility in a previous job. Other nurses said that their role in the clinic was limited and that the amount of responsibility they had was insufficient for their grade and position in the clinic. Three of the senior nurses complained that they had no say in decisions about the clinic and no control over staffing or budgets.

Only three nurses, all enrolled nurses, felt that they had too much responsibility. All three felt that their responsibilities were too high for their grade and position in the clinic, and one was particularly concerned that she was being asked to perform examinations which she thought should have been carried out by the medical staff.

Work roles and responsibilities of nursing staff

We found an enormous variation in the roles and responsibilities of the nursing staff in the 20 GUM clinics in this study – a much wider range of responsibilities than we found among any other type of staff.

Job descriptions

More than half (57 per cent) the nurses said they had a job description, but as many as 39 per cent said they did not, and four nurses were unsure. The sisters/charge nurses were more likely to have a job description than the more junior nurses (76 per cent compared with 52 per cent).

The nurses with job descriptions, however, had not normally been involved in drawing it up. Eight out of ten of these nurses had not been involved or consulted, although the sisters/charge nurses were more likely than others to have had some say in the writing of their job description.

Around a fifth of those who had a job description thought that it was accurate; it will come as no surprise to learn that these nurses were those who had either been consulted about, or who had actually written, their own job description. A further fifth said their job description was adequate. But most of the rest, almost two-thirds of those who had a job description, were dissatisfied with it. Around a fifth of them said that their job description was general to their grade and did not accurately reflect their role in the clinic. Others said it was too broad and general, while others complained that it was out of date.

Only five of the 56 nurses with a job description said that it was regularly reviewed (by the sister, the nursing services manager or by the out-patient manager). More than a quarter were unsure whether it was regularly reviewed (29 per cent), but almost two-thirds categorically said it was *not* (63 per cent), although the vast majority of these nurses believed that their job description *should* be regularly reviewed.

Increasing time spent on activities

We asked all staff about the balance of their activities. Around two-thirds (64 per cent) of the nurses said there were aspects of their job on which they would like to spend more time. In fact, three-quarters of the sisters/charge nurses wanted to increase the amount of time they spent on parts of their job, mainly the amount of patient contact, particularly with individual patients. They also wanted to spend more time on patient education, as well as on the management and administration of the clinic and on training staff in the clinic.

Just under two-thirds of the other nurses wanted to increase the amount of time they spent on various activities. Nearly a quarter of all the staff nurses and enrolled nurses said they would like to spend more time with individual patients. The enrolled nurses were also keen to increase the amount of patient contact in general. But the other aspect of their work which many of these nurses wanted to expand was counselling; over a fifth of all the staff and enrolled nurses wanted to spend more time counselling patients.

Nurses also mentioned a wide range of other activities on which they would like to spend more time, including microscopy; work with HIV/AIDS patients; health promotion; and the overall amount of time spent in the clinic.

Additional activities

Just over half the nurses (54 per cent) said they would like to take on additional activities which they were not engaged in at present. The sisters/charge nurses were rather more likely than the others to want to take on extra duties.

The main thing they wanted to take on was counselling: 13 of the nurses said they did not do any counselling at present but would very much like to do so. Counselling is discussed in more detail in Chapter 10, but it was quite clear that this was an aspect of the work which the nurses enjoyed; 13 of the nurses wanted to *start* counselling and a further 16 wanted to *increase* the amount of counselling they did – a total of 29 nurses, or 30 per cent, of the total nursing sample who were keen to be more involved in counselling patients.

One in ten of the nurses said they wanted to take on more responsibility generally and to widen their role in the clinic. More specifically, seven wanted to do microscopy and six wanted to become involved in HIV/AIDS related work. Others wanted to take on follow-up tests on female patients; giving results to the patients; colposcopy; and contact tracing. None of these was mentioned by more than five nurses in each case. A few nurses wanted more training, while others said they would like to train staff themselves, both inside and outside the clinic.

Decreasing time spent on activities

Almost a third (30 per cent) of the nursing staff said there were aspects of their job which they would prefer to do less often. However, over half the sisters/

charge nurses said they would rather spend less time on aspects of their job, particularly on administrative and clerical tasks, such as paperwork, stocktaking, answering the telephone and attending meetings or committees. They also wanted to spend less time on practical aspects of the work such as venepuncture, wart treatment and microscopy.

Just under a quarter (23 per cent) of the other nurses wanted to decrease the amount of time they spent on aspects of their work, mainly setting up the clinic before it started and clearing up and cleaning after it finished. But some said that they would rather spend less time taking routine tests and giving routine treatments, less time on microscopy, less time examining male patients and less time helping out on reception and answering the telephone. None of these tasks was mentioned by more than three nurses, and none of them were specific to particular clinics.

Activities to exclude

Finally, 14 nurses said there were certain aspects of their job which they would rather not do at all. These nurses included five sisters/charge nurses, four staff nurses and five enrolled nurses. The activities mentioned varied, but five of the nurses (all women) said they would rather not examine and treat male patients, three said they would rather not treat warts, and two did not want to manage and teach staff in the clinic.

Job satisfaction

Overall, two-thirds of the nurses were satisfied with their job, including nearly a quarter who were very satisfied. The staff nurses were the most satisfied with their jobs; more than three-quarters were satisfied (79 per cent), compared with just over half the sisters/charge nurses (57 per cent) and enrolled nurses (54 per cent). There were also differences between clinics; in six of the 20 clinics, *all* the nurses were satisfied with their jobs.

A quarter of the nursing staff were fairly satisfied with their present job, only six said that they were not very satisfied and one was not at all satisfied.

What were the main factors which contributed to job satisfaction among the nurses? One in six simply said that they liked their job and were happy working in the clinic. More specifically, one in ten nurses said they enjoyed the clinic work, particularly the patient contact and curing and reassuring the patients. The nurses also liked the good staff relations and staff support in the GUM clinic. The clinic was also said to offer good opportunities for promotion, while some of the sisters/charge nurses felt it was well-managed and provided a good service to patients.

But nearly two-thirds of the nurses cited negative aspects of their job, a slightly higher proportion than those who cited positive aspects. The single most common cause for dissatisfaction was the clinic building or area; ten per cent were unhappy with the physical aspects of the clinic, while a further six specifically complained about the lack of space. These complaints were generally specific to particular clinics which we also noted were lacking in space or badly laid out. The physical aspects of the clinic will be discussed in Chapter 7.

Around one in ten nurses were dissatisfied with their grading and some had been contesting this since their regrading two years earlier. A similar proportion said they did not have enough responsibility, while others complained about the lack of promotion and training. These complaints were cited by nurses in different clinics and were not specific to just one or two clinics. A wide range of other causes for dissatisfaction included poor staff relations and staff hierarchy in the clinic, shortage of staff, poor management, lack of management support and lack of resources.

The role of the nursing staff

The role of the nurse in GUM clinics is a subject of much debate and one which we were keen to explore in detail. The nurses' role varied greatly from clinic to clinic; in some clinics, the nursing staff had an extended role, while in others they were more or less acting as chaperones. There was also variation *within* the clinics; some nurses had an extended role while others did not.

We asked both nurses and doctors whether they thought the nursing staff could take on more responsibilities in the clinic. We asked specifically about microscopy, cryotherapy, venepuncture and examination of female patients.

Microscopy

First of all, we asked the medical and nursing staff if the nurses in the clinic carried out microscopy. Their responses indicated that nursing staff were involved in microscopy in 12 of the 20 clinics. But it was clear that in some clinics, not all the nurses were carrying out microscopy. In six of them, all the nurses did microscopy, while in two clinics, only the sister was involved in it. One clinic permitted only trained nurses to do microscopy, while in another, only the male nurses did microscopy (for both male and female patients).

It was difficult to establish exactly who was involved in microscopy in the two remaining clinics, which both had a relatively large number of nursing staff. There was some discrepancy among medical and nursing staff as to which of the nurses were involved, but our tentative judgement was that all the nursing staff carried out microscopy.

However, in eight clinics *none* of the nursing staff carried out microscopy. In five of these, the medical staff carried out the microscopy, while three clinics employed MLSOs. We asked the medical and nursing staff *why* the nurses were not involved in microscopy. In seven of the eight clinics, the main reason given by the doctors was that the nursing staff were not trained or qualified to carry out microscopy, although a couple of doctors added that the nurses did not want to do it and three doctors said they preferred to employ MLSOs. In the eighth clinic, shortage of space prevented the nurses from doing microscopy: there was simply nowhere to put the microscope other than in the doctor's consulting room, which was used by the consultant at all times when the clinic was open.

The nurses also cited lack of training as the main reason for not carrying out microscopy, which meant that the medical staff or MLSOs did it. But the nurses in two clinics said that the consultant did not want them to do microscopy, while in the eighth clinic, the nurses agreed with the consultant that lack of space precluded their involvement in it.

We asked all the doctors and nurses in the clinics where none of the nurses did microscopy whether they thought that the nurses *should* do microscopy. (This included 23 doctors and 27 nurses). Two-thirds of the doctors thought the nurses *should* be doing microscopy, if they were trained and were interested. But a fifth of them (5 doctors) felt that it was a waste of a nurse's time and that it was better to employ MLSOs. The nurses' views were broadly the same. More than half thought the nurses should carry out microscopy, if they were trained and wanted to do so. But nearly a third (8 nurses) felt that nurses should not carry out microscopy, either because the MLSOs were better skilled and had more time, or because they thought the medical staff should do it.

Cryotherapy

At least some of the nursing staff carried out cryotherapy in 8 of the 20 clinics. We again tried to establish if some or all of the nurses were involved in this procedure. In two of the clinics, it was clear that all the nurses were involved in cryotherapy. In two other clinics, there was some disagreement among staff, but after speaking to the doctors and nurses we concluded that all the nurses were involved in these clinics as well. In two clinics, only male nurses performed cryotherapy and in the remaining two clinics, the staff told us that only trained nurses were involved.

In 12 of the clinics, therefore, none of the nursing staff carried out cryotherapy. The medical and nursing staff gave three main reasons why the nurses in these 12 clinics did not perform cryotherapy: clinic policy, lack of trained or experienced nurses and lack of equipment. Other reasons included the possibility of tissue damage and the absence of insurance cover for the nurses, as well as lack of time and lack of suitable patients.

The staff sometimes gave more than one reason why nurses were not performing cryotherapy, but we were able to determine the *main* reason why the nurses were not involved in these 12 clinics. The reasons varied from clinic to clinic. In six, the main reason was clinic policy: the consultant believed it was not part of a nurse's role to carry out cryotherapy. In four, the main reason given was that the nurses were not trained or qualified to carry out cryotherapy; these clinics tended to be general out-patient departments, staffed by out-patient nurses. And in two clinics, the main reason was simply lack of equipment; the clinic had no or too few cryoprobes.

Almost two-thirds of both doctors and nurses thought the nursing staff *should* be performing cryotherapy, if they were trained and were interested in doing so. Some added, however, that they should only perform cryotherapy in certain circumstances, such as external warts, or that they should be supervised by a member of the medical staff.

But around a quarter of the medical and nursing staff in the clinics where the nurses were not carrying out cryotherapy said the nurses should *not* be involved in this procedure. These respondents were concerned about the potential danger of this technique and the possibility of damaging healthy tissue and felt that cryotherapy should rightly be performed by medical staff.

Venepuncture

Nursing staff carried out venepuncture in 19 of the 20 clinics. In 15 of them, all the nurses did venepuncture, but in four, it was carried out only by some of the nurses, usually trained staff nurses. Hospital policy prevented enrolled nurses from carrying out venepuncture in some clinics.

One clinic in our sample, therefore, employed nurses who did not carry out venepuncture. These were enrolled nurses who worked in the main out-patient department. They covered the GUM clinic when it was open but had a very limited role. It was hospital policy that they did not carry out venepuncture, and venepuncturists were employed to take patients' blood. When the venepuncturists were not available, then the MLSOs, who were employed to carry out the microscopy in this clinic, took the bloods. The doctors who worked in this clinic thought that nurses *should* do microscopy and venepuncture, but there was no consensus of opinion among the nurses.

Examination of female patients

Finally, we asked the medical and nursing staff a specific question about whether the nurses examined female patients. The responses were difficult to analyse, not only because we asked about the procedure at both initial and follow-up examinations, but also because the definition of an initial examination varied among the clinics and among different members of staff.

Nevertheless, we concluded that at least some of the nursing staff in 14 of the 20 clinics were involved in examining female patients. As a rule, the nurses in these clinics were not examining female patients at their initial visit, but in most of them, there were occasions when a senior or experienced member of the nursing staff *would* make an initial examination of a female patient. This was generally at the request of a doctor or if the patient wanted to be examined by a woman and there were no female doctors available on that day or working in the clinic at all. Alternatively, a nurse might examine a patient if the doctor was late for a clinic or if the patient attended out of clinic hours and was visibly distressed.

We did, however, come across three clinics where some of the nursing staff seemed to be carrying out initial examinations on a more routine basis. In these cases, the examinations were carried out on behalf of certain doctors in the clinic or were performed by the more senior nurses in the clinic.

Follow-up examinations by the nursing staff were more widespread. At least some of the nurses in all 14 of the clinics examined female patients at a follow-up visit. In six, it appeared that all or some of the nurses were carrying out follow-up examinations routinely. But in the other eight clinics, the nurses only examined follow-up female patients on an occasional basis and at the doctors' direction, or they would only examine simple cases, such as follow-up wart patients.

In six of the 20 clinics, however, it appeared that *none* of the nursing staff were examining female patients, either at an initial or at a follow-up visit. These clinics were part of the out-patients department and staffed by general out-patient nurses. It was clinic policy that the nurses did not examine female patients in these clinics; the doctors considered that examination was a medical responsibility, and some commented that nurses were not trained to carry out examinations on women.

We asked all the medical and nursing staff, regardless of whether the nurses in the clinic were involved in examination, whether they thought nurses *should* examine female patients, either at an initial or follow-up examination. Just over half the doctors (55 per cent) and exactly half the nurses (50 per cent) considered there were occasions when nursing staff should carry out examinations on women. But most of these staff felt that examination by nursing staff should be restricted to follow-up visits only.

However, around a quarter of all the medical and nursing staff interviewed considered that there were no occasions on which nursing staff should examine female patients. They considered that examination was a medical responsibility and that every new patient had the right to be seen and examined by a doctor.

Extended roles

We used these four criteria – microscopy, cryotherapy, venepuncture and examination of female patients – to determine whether the nurses had an extended role in the clinics. ('Extended role' for nurses, as noted in Chapter 2, was a term commonly used at the time of the research, and we retain it in this report.) As already discussed, the role of the nursing staff was the most varied in the GUM clinics, with nurses on the same grade having very different responsibilities, even within individual clinics themselves. As a general rule, however, the medium to large clinics were staffed by dedicated GUM nurses who had greater responsibilities and an extended role. The nursing staff in the small to medium clinics, on the other hand, were often staffed by general out-patient nurses who did not have an extended role.

Could the nurses take on more responsibilities?

The medical and nursing staff were asked whether they thought the nurses could take on any *other* responsibilities in the clinic (other than the procedures already discussed).

More than half the nurses interviewed said the nursing staff in their clinic *could* take on more responsibilities. But there were significant differences between the clinics. This was not surprising given that the nurses in some clinics already had an extended role, while the nurses in other clinics had a very limited role. In eight of the clinics, two-thirds or more of the nurses said that the nursing staff could take on more responsibilities.

The most commonly mentioned activity was counselling; more than one in ten of all the nurses interviewed said the nursing staff could do more counselling. This reflects the earlier finding that many nurses wanted to increase the amount of counselling that they did or wanted to take on counselling as part of their role. A further 10 per cent of the nurses said the nursing staff could take on more wart treatment in the clinic, while the same proportion thought the nursing staff could take on more responsibility generally.

A wide range of other activities mentioned by the nursing staff included taking a social/sexual history from patients, taking tests on new and follow-up patients, doing cytology smears, giving test results and providing patient education. None of these activities was mentioned by more than five nurses. The nurses in clinics where only some of the nursing staff were involved in microscopy and cryotherapy thought that *other* nurses in the clinic could take on these tasks.

What was preventing the nurses from taking on these additional responsibilities? Three main reasons were given by the nurses. The first, and most important, was the clinic consultant, who governed what the nurses did, or did not do, in the clinic. The second reason was simply lack of time, and finally, some of the nurses said they were not trained or experienced enough to take on the extra responsibilities.

The views of the doctors were clearly crucial in determining whether the nurses could take on any *other* responsibilities. Only 39 per cent of the medical staff thought the nurses could take on more responsibilities compared with 56 per cent of the nurses. The activities cited by the doctors, however, mirrored those mentioned by the nurses; counselling and wart treatment were mentioned most frequently, but others included more follow-up tests on patients, more patient education and giving out patient results. Some doctors in the clinics where only some of the nurses were involved in microscopy and cryotherapy thought that other nurses could become involved in these procedures.

The doctors agreed with the nursing staff that nurses were not carrying out these additional activities because it was the consultants' policy that they should not do so, but others considered that the nurses were not trained or qualified to take on additional responsibilities and some thought the nurses did not want extra duties.

We did not ask the health advisers specific questions about whether the nursing staff carried out microscopy, cryotherapy, venepuncture and female examination. Instead we asked an overall question as to whether they thought the nursing staff could take on more responsibilities.

More than half the health advisers (13 of the 22 interviewed) thought the nurses *could* take on more responsibilities, mainly in two specific areas: first, patient information and patient education, and secondly, more involvement in the follow-up tests and in treatment, especially wart treatment: 'They could take a greater role in terms of giving information. All they do is lay the trolleys and pass the swabs. And I think they could do a lot of procedures done by the medical staff such as female examinations, wart treatment, follow-ups and smears...'

We wanted to establish a general overview of whether the GUM clinic staff thought the nursing staff *could* take on more responsibilities in the clinics. Overall, 66 per cent of the medical, nursing and health advising staff thought the nurses *could* take on more responsibilities. As many as 71 per cent of all the nurses interviewed thought the nursing staff could take on more responsibilities, compared with 61 per cent of the medical staff and 59 per cent of the health advisers.

It is significant that so many of the GUM clinic staff thought the nurses could take on more responsibilities. In clinics where the nurses were not carrying out microscopy or cryotherapy or follow-up examinations of female patients, there is a need to consider whether they could take on this role. And there is certainly a need to review the opportunities for nurses to counsel patients and to be more involved in patient information and education.

Nurse-run clinics

We asked the medical, nursing and health advising staff whether they thought the nurses in the clinic could run any types of clinic without medical staff being present. Two-thirds of the nursing staff (67 per cent) thought that nurses could run particular clinics without medical staff being present. The sisters/charge nurses were most likely to be in favour of nurse-run clinics (86 per cent).

Over half (55 per cent) of all the nursing staff interviewed said that nurses could run wart treatment clinics. In some clinics, in fact, the nurses were already running wart clinics for patients. Just over a fifth thought that nurses could run follow-up clinics, taking routine tests or tests of cure on patients who had already been examined by doctors.

Eight per cent of the nursing staff thought nurses could run cytology testing/smear clinics, while the same proportion felt that nurses could run the GUM clinic generally! These nurses were generally working in the larger clinics where the nurses had an extended role and were involved in examination, testing, microscopy and cryotherapy. No other types of clinic were mentioned by more than five nurses, but they included clinics for HIV counselling, HIV treatment/routine testing, hepatitis B vaccination and results clinics.

Almost two-thirds (62 per cent) of the doctors also thought that the nurses could run particular clinics. Like the nurses, half the doctors interviewed thought the nurses could run a wart treatment clinic. A fifth of the doctors also thought the nurses could run a follow-up/routine testing clinic. It is interesting that the junior doctors were most likely to say that nursing staff could run a follow-up clinic. This probably reflects the fact that some of the younger doctors disliked the routine and repetitive nature of the work in GUM clinics. No other clinics were mentioned by more than five doctors but they were broadly those mentioned by the nurses themselves; cytology testing/smears, HIV counselling, HIV treatment/routine tests and results clinics.

The health advisers' response to this question mirrored that of the medical and nursing staff. Thirteen of the 22 health advisers interviewed (59 per cent) thought the nursing staff could run clinics without medical staff being present, and wart clinics were again the most frequently mentioned.

The nursing staff

We have seen that the nursing staff had a wide variety of roles and responsibilities in the GUM clinics in this study. There were clear indications that nurses in some clinics who had the same qualifications and training as those in other clinics were carrying out quite different duties and had quite different levels of responsibility. This was even true of nurses within the same clinic. The rationale for this different use of nurses was often difficult to establish, and we again concluded that much of it related to custom and practice in clinics which had been slow to move with the times or to recognise the contribution which could be made by skilled and trained nurses. The lack of specific training to work in GUM clinics was marked among the nurses, the majority of whom were very keen to improve their skills and to extend their roles and responsibilities within the GUM clinics.

5 Health advisers and their roles

Six of the twenty clinics in which we conducted the research did not have a dedicated health adviser in post at the time of the study. Four of these had no health advisers on the establishment, one had no health adviser in post and one clinic employed a sister/health adviser who was interviewed in her main role as a nurse. We interviewed all the health advisers who were working in 13 of the other 14 clinics. In the final clinic, we interviewed four of the six full-time health advisers.

Interviews were carried out with a total of 22 health advisers;
- 5 managers/senior health advisers
- 13 health advisers
- 1 health adviser/health educator fr HIV/AIDS
- 1 health adviser/HIV prevention
- 1 specialist health visitor for GUM clinic/AIDS coordinator
- 1 HIV/AIDS support – infection control

(The last two posts were found in one clinic and both respondents were employed on a full-time basis by the district health authority, funded out of AIDS money. The posts were community-based, but the respondents worked in the GUM clinic, fulfilling the role of health advisers.)

Characteristics and qualifications of the health advisers

All but one of the health advisers were women. Their ages ranged from 28 to 54, with a mean age of 39 years.

Twelve of the 22 health advisers had a nursing qualification: 11 were registered general nurses and one was an enrolled nurse. Four of these health advisers had additional nursing qualifications: three were registered midwives and one was a registered mental nurse. Two of them also had a health visitors' certificate.

Only two of the health advisers had a social work qualification: one had a CQSW, the other was trained in residential social work.

Eight had other 'professional' qualifications. Three had a certificate in health education, but the other five had qualifications as widely varying as hairdressing, librarianship and catering/hotel management.

The health advisers' academic qualifications also varied widely. One had no qualifications, another had a school certificate. Three said their highest academic qualification was GCE 'O' level, while seven had GCE 'A' level. But eight of them had a first degree, one had a Masters degree and one had a PhD.

Grading system and grades
An indication of the lack of common practice in grading of health advisers' posts was given by the varying grading systems on which they were employed. Fifteen of the health advisers were on the ancillary and clerical grading system, including six of the twelve with nurse qualifications. Their grades ranged from grade 5 to grade 7, (four were on grade 5, eight on grade 6 and three on grade 7).

The other seven health advisers were all employed on the nurses and midwives grading system, although one of them did not, in fact, have a nursing qualification. Two were on a nurse grade H, three on a grade G and two on a grade E.

Length of time in grade
In comparison with the medical and nursing staff, the health advisers were mainly relative newcomers to their grades:
- none of them had been on their particular grade for more than 5 years
- 8 had been on their grade for between 2 and 5 years
- 5 had been on their grade for 1 or 2 years
- 9 had been on their grade for less than one year, including 7 who had only been on their grade for less than 6 months.

Salary
It is known that not only the grading but also the salaries of health advisers vary widely. We asked the health advisers for their gross annual salary (collecting whole-time equivalents (WTE) for part-time workers). We also subtracted the London weighting from the salaries of the London health advisers, to allow comparability of salaries.

The gross annual salaries of the health advisers (WTE and excluding London weighting) ranged from £10,000 to £17,500:
- 6 had salaries of between £10,000 and £11,999
- 6 had salaries of £12,000 to £13,999
- 6 had salaries of £14,000 to £15,999
- 4 had salaries of more than £16,000

With London weighting included, the highest salary was £18,700. The health advisers on nurse grades commanded rather higher salaries than those on the administrative and clerical grades.

Length of time in GU medicine
The length of time the health advisers had been working in GU medicine varied widely, ranging from seven weeks to 17 years, but again, their experience in the specialty was generally much shorter on average than that found among medical

and nursing staff, and almost three-quarters of them had been working in GU medicine for less than 5 years:

- 6 had been working in GU medicine for less than 2 years
- 10 had been working in GU medicine for between 2 and 5 years
- 6 had been working in GU medicine for more than 5 years, of whom 2 had worked in GU medicine for 10 years and 1 for 17 years

Why the health advisers decided to work in a GUM clinic

The single most common reason for deciding to work in a GUM clinic was the counselling component of the work, mentioned by six of the 22 health advisers, like this one: 'I've got a nursing background and I wanted to combine medicine and counselling. I didn't know anything about GU medicine. My previous job was in an alcohol and drug-related centre. I thought about social work, but I didn't want to get away from medicine. I saw something on the television about health advisers and then I saw the job advertised. The medical and emotional is a comfortable frame of reference...'

Five of the health advisers said their main reason for deciding to work in a GUM clinic was because they wanted to work more closely with HIV/AIDS patients. This respondent was typical of this group: 'I was nursing before and I wanted a change in career and a change in direction. I was interested in STDs and particularly in HIV/AIDS. And I liked counselling – I'd done it before in my nursing role...'

Three of the health advisers had decided to work in the specialty because they thought it would be interesting and varied, and some said the work of the GUM clinic related to other interests they had, such as sociology, psychiatry or microbiology.

Three health advisers were attracted to GU medicine by the pay and two said they had wanted to work in a hospital. A range of other reasons were given, including the opportunities for promotion and the good hours.

Three of the health advisers, however, said they had not *chosen* to work in a GUM clinic; they had either been asked to do it or had taken it on because they needed a job. Another three said they had come to the specialty temporarily, but had found they liked it and had stayed. More than a quarter of the health advisers, therefore, had not actively chosen to work in the specialty, although once in it they had chosen to stay.

What the health advisers liked about GU medicine

The most popular aspect of the work was the patient contact, which was mentioned by around two-thirds of the health advisers. Some of them specifically liked the fact that the patients were young and healthy: 'I like the challenge of it. There's a young client group, desperately, in some cases, in need of guidance...'

Four of the health advisers found the work generally interesting and varied, while the same number specifically referred to the interest and variety in the patients' attitudes and lifestyles: 'If you're interested in people, the juicier the situation the more interesting it is! It's really novel to work in STDs rather than in hearts, for example. You see lots of people in different situations. You learn a lot about yourself when you're in contact with people in different situations...'

Reflecting the reasons the health advisers gave for choosing to work in GU medicine, five of the respondents said they particularly liked the counselling aspect of the work, while three others specifically liked the emotional and psychological aspects of working in GU medicine.

Some, like this health adviser in a London clinic, particularly liked the HIV/AIDS related work: 'HIV/AIDS has made the job more interesting and stimulating. It's a new disease that has developed and progressed. It's exciting to work in the field. There are constant changes in the work...'

Others liked the opportunity for health education: 'I like reducing the stigma of STDs. I love doing it and I love talking to people. It's health education. You can spend a small amount of time talking to someone and it can be helpful. It gives me a kick...'

Other health advisers liked the lack of staff hierarchy and the good hours, while some, like this senior health adviser, were very enthusiastic about all aspects of their work: 'I love working in GU. I've never found a job so interesting. It's so varied, there's no set routine. There's variation in the patients we see, in the types of patients medically and in the types of social problems. We do clinics, we make visits, we give talks – the range is so great. It makes the job very interesting. I'm independent and I feel confident with the staff. I can get on with it, I'm not continually with the group of staff...'

What the health advisers disliked about GU medicine
However, although all the health advisers interviewed said that they particularly liked some parts of their jobs, two-thirds of them said there were aspects of working in GU medicine which they disliked (15 out of 22).

The HIV/AIDS-related work had brought some health advisers into GU medicine, and some particularly liked working with HIV/AIDS patients. But four cited the stress related to working with these patients. All of them were spending the majority of their time pre-test counselling and giving test results, a significant proportion of which were positive: 'It's very different now compared to when I started. It's very pressurised, very stressful. People are dying and they're dying young. That's the negative side of things...'

Like the medical and nursing staff, some of the health advisers disliked the low status of GU medicine and the stigma associated with the specialty. One well-qualified health adviser had only been working in a GUM clinic for less than a year and the negative image associated with GU medicine had come as a surprise: 'The lack of status, the lack of credibility. It's the fag end, the poor man. People have said, "What on earth have you taken it on for?" I'd not worked in the health service before. I thought it was a challenge. It's the lack of recognition generally, as a service apart from anything else. There is no status, the pay is poor, people can't understand why I did it. I didn't know how it was regarded...'

Two health advisers said they disliked the poor staff relations in the particular clinic in which they were working, while two others felt that their role was not understood either by the other staff working in the clinic or by the general public.

Training to work in GUM clinics

The health advisers had mainly entered GU medicine for the patient contact, the opportunity to counsel patients and because of the HIV/AIDS-related work. But what training had they received?

Only 9 of the 22 health advisers interviewed had, in fact, had specific training courses to work in GUM clinics

- 7 had attended a health advisers' training course organised by the Department of Health or by the health advisers' organisation, SHASTD, usually lasting a week
- 2 had been on a contact tracing course and 1 had been on a health advisers' seminar in STDs (which lasted for three days)
- 1, who had a nursing qualification, had attended the six month ENB course on GU medicine (ENB 275).

Eight of the health advisers had attended only one course and one of them had attended two courses. The health advisers were generally positive about the courses, but only one of them said her course (ENB 275) was certificated.

More than half the health advisers (13), therefore, had not been on a specific training course to work in GU medicine, but 11 of this group said they would like some training. Two of the health advisers, neither of whom had worked in the clinic for very long, wanted a general introduction to GU medicine and STDs, while two others wanted an update on STDs and STD treatment. One was on the waiting list to attend the short ENB course on GU medicine (ENB 932).

A further six health advisers, representing over a quarter of all those interviewed, simply said they would like to attend a certificated course which would be recognised by other professionals.

Training in GUM related topics

The lack of training specifically to work in GUM clinics was therefore marked among the health advisers, but rather more of them had received training in GUM related topics, such as HIV/AIDS and family planning (other than counselling).

Around half of the health advisers (12) reported that they had had training in GUM related topics:

- 10 had received training in HIV/AIDS: 4 had attended the ENB 934 course on HIV/AIDS while the others had attended other courses or study days on HIV/AIDS
- 2 had attended the ENB 901 course on family planning (and one of these was also trained as a family planning instructing nurse)

- 1 had attended a course in psychosexual medicine and one had attended a course on sexuality awareness

Half of those who had received training in GUM related topics had been on only one course, but two people had been on two or three courses and four had been on numerous courses. Once again, the courses were generally not certificated, and only five of the health advisers had received a certificate following a course (the ENB 934 or the ENB 901); the other seven had not received either a certificate or even a letter of attendance.

Ten of the health advisers had *not* had any training in GU related topics, but seven of these said they would like some: five wanted training on HIV/AIDS (with two specific requests to attend the ENB 934); four wanted family planning training and two wanted some training in colposcopy.

Length of time in clinic

As we have seen, the health advisers tended to have worked in GU medicine for a much shorter time on average than the medical and nursing staff. This was reflected in the length of time they had been working in the clinics in which we carried out the research. Only four of the 22 health advisers had been working in the selected GUM clinics for more than 5 years: three for between 5 and 10 years and one for more than 10 years.

Eighteen of the 22 health advisers, therefore, had been working in the clinic for less than 5 years, most of these for between 1 and 5 years, but four for less than 6 months.

Time spent working in the clinic

Thirteen of the health advisers worked full-time in the selected clinics: twelve of them in full-time clinics that were open all day, or almost all day, every weekday. The other health adviser worked in a part-time clinic which was only open (and attended by medical staff) on two days of the week. However, she was employed on a full-time basis and was available to counsel patients outside clinic hours, as well as making home visits and attending to the administration of the clinic.

Twelve of these full-time health advisers were employed on the administrative and clerical grading system: six were contracted to work for 36 hours and six for 37 hours per week. The other full-time health adviser was on the nurses' grading system and, like the nurses, was contracted to work for 37.5 hours per week.

The nine health advisers who worked on a part-time basis all worked in part-time GUM clinics. The number of hours they were contracted to work in the clinic ranged from 3 to 22.5 hours per week.

Work in other GUM clinics

Only three of the health advisers worked in other GUM clinics. Two of them worked only part-time in the selected clinic but were contracted to work in one other GUM clinic in the same district. One worked for three hours a week and the other for 17 hours a week in the other GUM clinic (in both cases, less time than in the selected clinic). The third health adviser worked full-time in the selected GUM clinic, but often worked in a private GUM clinic at the weekends.

Work in other clinics

Only three of the health advisers said they worked in *other* clinics; one in a family planning clinic (1.5 hours per week), one in a haematology out-patients clinic (4 hours per week) and one as a breast care nurse (for 20.5 hours per week). All of them worked in the selected GUM clinic on a part-time basis and none worked in other GUM clinics.

Other work

Ten of the 22 health advisers said they were involved in other paid or voluntary work:

- 2 were involved in health education work outside the remit of their work in the GUM clinic. The post of one of them was split between the health promotion department, where she carried out general health promotion work, and the GUM clinic. At the time of the study, however, this health adviser had been seconded to the GUM clinic on a full-time basis. The other health adviser was involved in other health education work in the hospital.
- the 2 'health advisers' in community based posts – the specialist health visitor for the GUM clinic and the HIV/AIDS support nurse (infection control) – both worked as AIDS coordinators, providing training and education for NHS staff and coordinating the AIDS services in the district
- 5 health advisers were involved in counselling work outside their work in the GUM clinic: 2 in paid counselling work (pregnancy counselling and counselling for breast cancer) and 3 in voluntary work (2 in HIV/AIDS counselling and one in relationships counselling).
- 2 did other paid work – one as a shop assistant on a Saturday, the other as a part-time receptionist, taking telephone messages for a GP practice during the evenings and at weekends.

Full-time and part-time working

When all their work was taken into consideration, 19 of the health advisers worked full-time and only 3 worked part-time.

Health advisers and the management structure of the clinic
Nine of the health advisers reported managerially to staff within the clinic:
- 5, who all worked in the larger, full-time clinics, reported to the senior health adviser
- 4 reported to the (senior) consultant
- 2 reported to the clinic sister

Thirteen of the health advisers reported to staff outside the clinic:
- 6 to the out-patient services manager
- the others to either the director of public health, the business manager, the field/community nurse manager, the assistant nursing services manager or the community physician.

The personnel to whom the health advisers reported on professional matters were less diverse:
- 7 reported to the senior health adviser
- 10 reported to the (senior) consultant
- the other 5 reported to the GUM clinic sister, the community unit physician, the field/community nurse manager and the HIV coordinator.

Only six of the health advisers said they were managerially responsible for other members of staff. Four were senior health advisers responsible for the other health advisers in the clinic, as well as any other staff working with them, such as clerical assistants or the health advisers' secretary. The specialist health visitor for the GUM clinic was managerially responsible for the HIV/AIDS support nurse. And one health adviser was responsible for the clinic receptionist.

There was a fairly equal division among the health advisers on whether they thought they had enough managerial support in their job Ten thought they did but twelve thought they did not. As we found with the medical and nursing staff, the problem lay mainly with managerial staff outside the clinic.

The health advisers complained about the lack of contact with managers in the hospital, as well as their lack of understanding of the health advisers' needs and requirements: 'I get managerial *intervention*... I don't get any managerial support...The outpatient manager doesn't always understand my difficulties. They try and support me but it's not always achieved. I feel I'm managed in a very hierarchical way. Our interdependencies are not always recognised...'

But around a quarter (5) of the health advisers complained about the lack of managerial support within the clinic. The problems were related to their relations with consultants. Some said the consultants had too little time to devote to management, some said the consultant did not support or understand their role in the clinic, and in some cases communication was poor between the health adviser and the consultant.

Balance of responsibility

The question of the staff's view of their balance of responsibilities was crucial to this research. The great majority of health advisers, 18 of the 22, considered that they had about the right amount of responsibility in the clinic. None of them thought they had too much, but three thought they had too little. The main complaint of these health advisers was that they did not have any say in decisions made about the clinic.

Job description

Whereas only around half the doctors and nurses had a job description, *all* of the health advisers we interviewed said they had one. They were also more likely than other clinic staff to have been involved in drawing up their job description; around a quarter of them (5 of the 22) said they had been involved.

A third of them, including all those who had been involved in drawing it up, thought their job description was accurate and were quite happy with it. Another couple thought their job description was acceptable.

But over half were less than happy with their job description. A third said it was out-of-date, while others commented that it was open-ended or covered too many responsibilities and was too broad and general.

Only three of the health advisers said their job description was reviewed on a regular basis. Two-thirds of the rest felt that it should be, with some of them commenting that jobs and roles changed over time and that there was a need to review job specifications.

Increasing time spent on activities

Like the doctors and nurses, the health advisers were asked whether they would like to increase the amount of time they spent on any part of their job. Three-quarters of them (17) said they would like to spend more time on particular aspects of their job.

Five of them wanted to increase the amount of time they spent with individual patients. Like the doctors and nurses, they felt under great pressure to get through the number of patients visiting the clinic. Related to this, five specifically said that they wanted to spend more time counselling the patients, but once again, the number of patients going through some clinics made this difficult.

The pressure of work in one particular clinic precluded other activities the health advisers wanted to develop, such as community outreach work, health promotion and patient education. These activities were pushed into the background, as this senior health adviser explained: 'The problem is, the volume of patients is so great, there's no time to do anything but see patients. There's no time for health promotion. I'd like to spend more time with the patients to discuss health aspects and safer sex. I'd like to produce leaflets and go out into the community and develop the outreach work. But I just can't do it...' Another of the health advisers in this clinic said: 'The health education side, the preparation of materials and leaflets is currently done in grabbed time between the patients. The patients are a priority. If we want a display in the clinic, it has to be done in our own time...'

Individual health advisers mentioned that they would like to spend more time on research and publication, attending conferences, training staff in the clinic and making contact with health advisers in other clinics.

Additional activities

Over half the health advisers said that there were things they would like to do in their job which they did not do at all at present.

Firstly, and most importantly, six of them said that they did not do any community outreach work but would like to do some. Again, these health advisers were based in busy clinics with a large number of patients passing through the clinic and a high proportion of HIV counselling. Another senior health adviser described the problem: 'I would like more access to the community development area. I would like to increase the profile of the clinic. I'd like to go out to schools or to facilitate it to enable others to go out and take that role on. But it's not possible. We're torn between here and out there, and there are queues of people waiting here...'

Secondly, the health advisers in two busy clinics with a high proportion of HIV/AIDS related work said that they would like to see and contact trace a wider range of conditions. The number of requests for HIV tests and the time spent counselling patients in connection with HIV tests meant that 90 per cent or more of their time was spent working with these patients which left little time for other patients. One of the health advisers said: 'The volume of the HIV work means that we don't provide a service for NSU and herpes patients. We just provide the HIV service. All patients should see a health adviser if they want to...'

And thirdly, three more health advisers said that they would like produce or update the clinic's health education material. In addition, the question of research and publication and attending training courses again arose among health advisers who were not currently able to take on such activities.

These two questions, therefore, elicited a number of key areas which health advisers felt were neglected. Pressure of work in some clinics meant that health advisers could not spend as much time with patients as they would have liked, and some had to restrict the patients seen to particular groups. It also meant that other important and preventative work, such as health education, health promotion and community outreach work, was neglected. The opportunities for research and publication were consequently diminished, which was a cause for regret among some health advisers.

Decreasing time spent on activities

Two-thirds of the health advisers said that there were areas of their work which they would prefer to do less often. The most frequently mentioned was administrative and clerical work. Around a third of all the health advisers said they would prefer to do less clerical work, such as filling out forms, paperwork, writing letters, sending appointments and doing the clinic statistics.

One health adviser was spending a considerable amount of time on clerical work: 'We could do with full-time clerical support. The volume has gone up and it's so frustrating. The time could be spent more usefully...' And two others said that they would prefer not to answer the telephone or cover for the receptionists: 'Answering the phone to inane questions, showing people where to find things, showing people the way. I'd like less patient contact outside of our job description, less picking up of other people's problems...'

Four health advisers, all of whom worked in larger clinics with a large proportion of HIV-related work, said they would prefer to spend rather less time on HIV counselling. One said: 'I'd like to do less pre-test counselling. Both of us have total burn-out because of that. We need someone else to ease the pressure of it. Then we could spend more time with patients who are at high risk or who are positive. We're taking on the majority of the pre-test counselling and it's very repetitive. In the low risk cases, the doctor has already been through the spiel with them and then they come to us and we repeat it. Ideally we should see them all but physically we can't do it. There must be some way of weeding them out but it's difficult to set guidelines to re-evaluate it...'

And four disliked certain aspects of contact tracing, especially difficult telephone calls or home visits, and said they would prefer to spend less time on this.

Activities to exclude

One third of the health advisers (7) said that they would like to exclude certain activities from their job altogether. Three of them wanted to drop certain clerical aspects of their job which they felt could be carried out by clerical staff. This health adviser had little or no secretarial support in the clinic: 'Clerical work – writing letters, recall letters, which could be done on a word-processor with my authorisation by a secretary...' And two felt it was inefficient for them to spend time filing notes, which they thought could be carried out by the receptionists.

In one clinic, the health advisers were running results clinics, in which STD results that were expected to be negative were given to patients by the health advisers. They felt that this task was outside the remit of their job and could be carried out very effectively by the nursing staff in the clinic.

Essentially, there were strong indications that the health advisers were involved in administrative, clerical and reception work which they considered could be carried out by clerical or administrative staff, allowing them more time to spend on aspects of their job which were currently neglected.

Job satisfaction

Two-thirds of the health advisers (15) said they were satisfied with their present job, including a quarter who were *very* satisfied (6). A further quarter were only fairly satisfied with their job, while two (both working in the same clinic) were dissatisfied.

Virtually all the health advisers mentioned positive aspects of their work, many saying they enjoyed their job and found it interesting and challenging. More specifically, they enjoyed the patient contact, the good staff relations, the autonomy they had and the opportunities for career development. But almost all of them tempered these views with negative comments about their job. These varied widely and many cited more than one aspect of the job with which they were dissatisfied.

Around a third said they were too busy and had too many responsibilities. This meant they had insufficient time to carry out all their duties and spent less time with patients than they would have liked or only saw certain patients. These health advisers generally worked in the larger clinics, and this health adviser summarised their views: 'Overall, I suppose I'm *fairly* satisfied. It's difficult. I'm very satisfied with the day-to-day work and with the job content and the nature of the work. I'm satisfied with that. But I'm increasingly dissatisfied with the workload. The stress of the job has a cumulative effect. The more you see people with HIV, the more it gets to you. And there *is* more HIV, there's no doubt about that. And there's too much work. It feels as if the clinic is getting busier, especially in relation to HIV, but the resources are the same. And the smooth running of the clinic seems to be deteriorating, which makes it more stressful...'

In some cases, the pressure of work was caused by shortage of staff: five of the clinics were operating with vacant health adviser posts: 'I'm satisfied with the job. I get a lot of joy from the job. It's a job where I don't have to be responsible for anyone. I feel autonomous and I have a lot of leeway to do what I want. But I feel frustrated. There's not enough time and we're one health adviser short. I feel sad about what's happening. Everything comes down to short-term cost without looking at the long-term benefit. I don't think they are being sensible about what they're doing...'

Around a quarter of the health advisers felt that their role and responsibilities were not recognised in the clinic and they were not appreciated. This was sometimes associated with a lack of support from the consultant or from managers within the hospital. In some cases, the staff relations in the clinic were poor and they felt they received little support from other members of the staff, as this health adviser explained:

> I'm not very satisfied with my job. I'd like to see the whole profile of health advisers improved somewhat. It's mainly because of the fact that we're not fully accepted within the clinic. Our work is undermined by the management. We're not undermined by the staff but things filter through. There's a lack of communication across all levels. It's unhealthy. And there's only one health advising room on site, which is small and not soundproof. The patient numbers are increasing but the health advisers' numbers are not. I'm dissatisfied – I'm torn between management and the hands-on work...

And some of the health advisers were dissatisfied with the physical environment in which they were working. In these cases, the clinics were either old and badly laid-out, or there was a shortage of rooms and space for the staff and the patients: 'I'm fairly satisfied with *my* role, but I'm *very* dissatisfied with the clinic for a lot of reasons...The physical set-up of the clinic. I feel embarrassed for people having to come into a place like this. Look at the waiting room and there are only screens in the examining rooms and you can hear the doctors taking the sexual history and there's no toilet for the men. There's no confidentiality...'

Other health advisers complained about the low pay or low grading and the low status of GUM as a specialty: 'I'm fairly satisfied, but I'm spread so thinly across the clinic and the other work. It's the lack of recognition, that GUM is an important aspect of the service. I've not argued with anyone over the money issue but I could do. It's to do with recognition. I'm skilled – I've got a degree, counselling skills, I'm social work qualified and I took a £5,000 drop in salary for the job. There's no recognition that you're doing a good job...'

The role of the health advisers

We were interested to know what the health advisers themselves considered to be the main role(s) of health advisers.

The principal role mentioned was *education*. Virtually all the health advisers talked about patient education and health promotion and safer sex. Those who did not mention patient education referred to patient information about STDs and HIV/AIDS.

Counselling was also seen to be a key role: 16 of the 22 referred to counselling generally or HIV counselling specifically. Those who did not refer to counselling said they 'supported' or 'listened to' the patients.

Surprisingly, only 13 of the 22 health advisers said that one of their main roles was *contact tracing or partner notification*.

The main roles of the health advisers, therefore, were seen to be patient education and information, counselling and contact tracing. But the emphasis the different health advisers placed on these aspects, and on the HIV-related work, varied according to the work of the clinic and the type of work they encountered.

The health advisers in the large clinics, with a considerable amount of HIV work, were more likely to emphasise patient education about safer sex and HIV counselling, like this respondent:

> To provide a pre- and post-test counselling service for HIV. To give information and advice on risk reduction for STDs, including HIV. This will include safer sex, availability of condoms, supplying condoms and how they are used. To see people with other STDs, such as chlamydia and gonorrhoea, to give them information about infection and prevention and to try and identify their sexual partners who might be at risk, and how the patient can inform them, and how they will be tested and treated. And we also give them information about treatment – how to take it and when they'll need further treatment...

But those health advisers who were working in the smaller, more traditional clinics tended to refer to their contact tracing role, patient education and information and general counselling: 'To inform the patients about particular STDs, to give them the low-down, how to control it and to reassure them about coming to the clinic, that there's no stigma, and contact tracing...'

We specifically asked the health advisers if they thought their role was 'preventative', and all 22 of the health advisers interviewed felt that it was. Most importantly, they saw themselves as educating and informing patients in order to try and prevent infection. Some sought to change patients' behaviour, and promoting and providing condoms was also seen as preventative action. And some saw their contact tracing role as being very much a preventative action.

This senior health adviser described how he saw the preventative role of the health adviser: 'Yes, my role is preventative. Very much so. When you pre-test counsel, they may not be at risk but you can do a lot in 15 minutes. You can say, "There's no need to come back if you do this, this and this. You've put yourself in great danger. This is what could happen. This is a condom and this is how you use it." In a short space of time, you can put across the dangers and the risks of infection. If it's gonorrhoea, you stress how silly they've been, how unsafe what they've done has been and that it's potentially dangerous, especially if it continues to occur. You give people information they don't want to hear. We've gone the opposite way. Previously, we didn't mention HIV because we didn't want to scare people. But now it's right up-front, it's developed, it's virtually all we do. It's a big problem. And if people are coming to the clinic, it's better to prevent them than tell someone they're positive because they didn't know...'

Referral of patients

We were interested to know to what extent patients saw health advisers as a matter of course in the GUM clinics. All 22 health advisers said that they did not see *every* patient who came to the clinic.

Three-quarters said that they saw patients who had been diagnosed as having gonorrhoea, while over two-thirds said they saw patients with syphilis. A high proportion of the health advisers saw every patient with chlamydia and all primary herpes cases. But those working in the clinics with a large proportion of HIV/AIDS related work were less likely to see patients with herpes, unless they were very distressed.

As far as HIV/AIDS related work was concerned, two-thirds of the health advisers said that they saw all patients who were considering an HIV test. A third of them also saw patients who were receiving HIV test results, including those receiving a positive result.

More than half the health advisers said that they would see anyone needing additional support or advice or education, while a quarter saw patients who were particularly worried or distressed or who had other problems. A range of other patients and conditions were mentioned by the health advisers. None of these was mentioned by more than five health advisers but they included patients with warts, NSU, psycho-sexual problems, new patients visiting the clinic for the first time and victims of rape or incest. Again, health advisers in the larger clinics dominated by HIV/AIDS were less likely to see new patients or patients with warts.

So who decided whether or not a patient saw the health adviser? Virtually all the health advisers said it was the decision of the medical staff whether to refer a patient to them. But a third said the nursing staff might send someone to them if, for example, a patient was particularly distressed or in need of counselling. And a third of them said they themselves might decide to see a patient. Occasionally the reception staff might refer a particularly distressed patient to the health adviser and sometimes the patient might ask to see a health adviser.

But health advisers in only three clinics reported that there was a consultant or clinic policy about which patients saw a health adviser. In fact, only one referred to a formal and written policy on referral to the health advisers: 'There's a clinic policy. The management group meet once a month and the policy is reviewed occasionally. There's a clinic handbook so that all new medical staff know who should be referred to the health advisers. It's well defined who we see and who we don't see...'

The medical staff confirmed that they did not send every patient to the health adviser, but generally referred patients with gonorrhoea, syphilis and chlamydia, patients considering an HIV test, HIV positive patients and anyone else particularly distressed or in need of advice, education or support.

But did the health advisers consider that every patient *should* see a health adviser? The sample was split equally between those who thought that every patient should (11) and those who did not (11).

Those who thought every patient *should* see a health adviser considered that everyone attending a GUM clinic ought to receive information on safer sex and that all patients should know of, and meet, the health adviser. They thought the health adviser could also help to reduce patients' anxieties about STDs and the procedures involved in testing and treatment.

But those who did not think every patient should see a health adviser often mentioned practical reasons, such as not having enough time to see *every* patient. And in some cases, it was not thought necessary; for example, some people came to the clinic and were treated for conditions such as thrush, which were not necessarily sexually transmitted. In any event, it was thought that patients should be allowed to choose whether they saw a health adviser and that seeing a health adviser should not be compulsory.

Could the health advisers take on more responsibilities?

We asked the medical and nursing staff and the health advisers themselves whether they thought the health advisers in the clinic could take on any more responsibilities in the clinic.

The health advisers' view

One third of the health advisers considered that they, or their colleagues, *could* take on more responsibilities in the clinic, mainly in sex and health education in the community, as well as other community outreach work and liaison with other services and agencies. Other activities mentioned included research and management of the clinic, while one health adviser, who felt that patients were not being referred to her, said she could see more patients generally and wanted to see all patients visiting the clinic in connection with HIV tests.

What was preventing these health advisers from expanding their role in the clinic and, more importantly, in the community? Like the doctors and nurses who wanted to develop their role, the health advisers said they were simply too busy to take on these additional activities at present. Their lack of time sometimes related to lack of staff: many of the clinics were operating with fewer health advisers than were on the establishment.

Lack of time and pressure of work were the main reasons why the other two-thirds of the health advisers said they could *not* take on any more responsibilities. But some said they already did enough and some said they were not experienced enough as yet to take on more responsibilities.

The medical and nursing view

We have seen that only 14 of the 20 clinics had a dedicated health adviser in post at the time of the study. The medical and nursing staff in these clinics were less likely than the health advisers themselves to think that health advisers could take on more responsibilities. Just over a fifth of the doctors (22 per cent) and just under a fifth of nurses (17 per cent) said the health advisers in their clinic *could* take on more responsibilities.

Both doctors and nurses thought that the health advisers could see, contact trace and counsel more patients. This was most commonly suggested by staff working in clinics with a substantial proportion of HIV/AIDS related work. These staff commented that the health advisers were so 'tied up' or 'bogged down' with HIV related work that they had no time for patients with other problems. Many of these staff wanted the health advisers to see patients with a greater range of STDs, particularly herpes patients.

Like the health advisers themselves, doctors and nurses wanted to see the health advisers involved in sex/health education in the community and other outreach work. The doctors referred to a range of other activities which they thought the health advisers could take on, including running an HIV clinic, giving out test results, patient recall, teaching and management of the clinic. Some of the nurses, on the other hand, thought the nurse-trained health advisers could take the bloods from patients requesting HIV tests at the same time as the pre-test counselling.

In some cases, medical and nursing staff thought lack of staff and lack of time prevented health advisers from taking on extra work. In other cases, the health adviser was relatively new to the job or to the clinic and was not yet sufficiently experienced to take on extra work. But sometimes the consultant prevented the health advisers from taking on more responsibilities and sometimes, the doctors said, the health advisers themselves did not want to take on additional activities.

The majority of the medical and nursing staff, therefore, considered that the health advisers could *not* take on any more responsibilities than they had at present for reasons largely reflecting those given by the health advisers themselves: pressure of work, lack of staff and lack of time.

Could GUM clinics operate without health advisers?

We were interested to know whether staff in those clinics with a dedicated health adviser in post thought that the clinic could operate *without* health advisers. We were also interested to know how staff in clinics without a dedicated health adviser in post managed without one.

Looking first at the 14 clinics with a dedicated health adviser in post, around two-thirds of the nurses (69 per cent), almost two-thirds of the health advisers (64 per cent) and more than three-quarters of the doctors (79 per cent) said, quite categorically, that the clinic could *not* operate without health advisers.

In general, the health advisers themselves thought the clinic would run much less efficiently without them. A health adviser working in a clinic with a significant amount of counselling related to HIV/AIDS said: 'Absolutely not. I think the place would fall apart without us. We'd lose patients and the quality of the service wouldn't be there...'

Another health adviser, in a clinic with less HIV/AIDS work, had more of a 'traditional' role and emphasised the importance of the health advisers' role in controlling infection: 'A GU clinic needs a health adviser to do contact tracing. It would be a waste of time treating patients if their contacts were not treated...'

The medical and nursing staff were in agreement that the clinic would operate less effectively without health advisers, and added that other staff in the clinic simply did not have the time to counsel patients or for contact tracing and education: 'Most of the questions the patients have, they ask the health adviser. The doctors just have a medical role. The health adviser fulfils an education role. She also gives proper counselling. Doctors don't have the time...'

Others, like this consultant, also felt the health advisers were in a much better position to counsel and contact trace: 'No, we couldn't operate without them because they take a load of work off our backs, the type of work we don't want to have to do. When they're contact tracing, they can be brutal with the patients. We have to be nice to them because we want them to come back. They can get the information out of them. They're more subtle than we are about getting the information...'

In this respect, many of these staff thought that the health advisers played a vital role in the work of GUM clinics. A clinical assistant, who worked in a large, busy clinic with two health advisers said: 'The whole point is to get contact tracing and reduce the incidence of disease. There's not much point having a GU clinic if there's no health adviser...'

However, there were staff who said the clinic *could* operate without health advisers. Around a third of the health advisers, a similar proportion of nursing staff and one fifth of the medical staff said the clinic could operate without health advisers. But it became clear that many of their answers were rather misleading. Although most of these respondents said that the clinic *could*, in theory, operate without health advisers and other staff *could* do the contact tracing and counselling, many of them added that the clinic would run less efficiently and that the service provided would suffer since counselling and contact tracing would not be carried out.

This sister's comments summarised many of these views: 'It *could* operate without a health adviser but we'd rather it didn't. It could operate with difficulty. We have done in the past, but it takes up the doctors' time, it takes up the nurses' time. It takes away from the other duties and it cuts down on the number of patients because the doctors and nurses have to take on the health advisers' role...'

In fact, virtually all these respondents (including *all* the health advisers) felt that it would not be a good thing for the clinics to operate without health advisers. In this respect, they were very much in agreement with the majority who said the clinic could *not* operate without health advisers. Only four doctors and six nurses felt that the GUM clinic could operate quite satisfactorily without health advisers.

But if this was the case, what was happening in the six clinics without a dedicated health adviser in post at the time of the research? One of the clinics had, over a period of time, alternated between employing a part-time sister *and* a part-time health adviser, and employing a full-time sister/health adviser. At the time of the study, the post was a combined sister/health adviser post, filled by the sister who was in post at the time the decision was taken to try a combined post again. She carried out the contact tracing and counselling, as well as some nursing duties in the clinic. The nursing staff generally thought this combined post worked well, as did two of the GP clinical assistants. But the consultant and another clinical assistant were unhappy with the arrangement and there did appear to be some difficulty when a sister held two posts.

One clinic had a full-time health adviser on the establishment but at the time of the study, the post was vacant and had been vacant for quite some time because of a dispute over grading. While negotiations continued, the sister was carrying out the health adviser's role, with some help from other members of the staff. Although the sister was experienced and well qualified and had carried out the health advising duties in the past, the medical and nursing staff recognised that the situation was not ideal and the sister herself felt she was only 'touching the surface and following up urgent cases...' and that the post should be filled.

A nurse in this clinic, who was interested in the health adviser post with the support of the sister and other staff, commented: 'The job is and is not being done. It's coping OK but it's not ideal. It undermines the whole health adviser's role. We've managed for a year so it begs the question, "Do we need a health adviser? Is it just a question of giving out contact slips?" I don't think it is. I think the patients suffer. I think there should be a health adviser's post here...'

Four clinics had no health advising posts on the establishment. In two of these clinics, the sister carried out the health advising, with some help from the other clinic staff. The medical and nursing staff in these clinics generally thought this situation was acceptable in these small, part-time clinics.

In one clinic, the medical staff did most of the health advising, with some help from the nursing staff. Again, the staff in this clinic were quite satisfied with the situation and saw no need for a health adviser. The consultant commented: 'It works perfectly well without a health adviser. Health advice is offered by the people who should do it, the doctors. What else are we paid to do?...'

In the other clinic, two HIV counsellors carried out most of the counselling in relation to HIV/AIDS, while medical and nursing staff did the health advising work related to other STDs. But the consultants and most of the rest of the clinic staff were unhappy about the situation. One of the consultants told us:

> It operates badly without a health adviser. The doctors and nurses do it and it is done with varying efficiency. The crucial point is that visiting cannot be done. Contact tracing requiring a visit is a very specialised skill and enormous damage could be done by someone doing that who hasn't the skill. So we don't do any contact tracing like that now. I stopped sister going as it was completely inappropriate...

The sister agreed that the clinic would operate better with a health adviser: 'I think we're doing well but we'd operate a damn sight better with one. She or he is the missing piece in the jigsaw. We'd then be a complete unit. They could give a lot more to the patient than we can. They wouldn't be clinically based. All the other things like counselling are being done at present by the doctors and the HIV counsellors. A health adviser would bring in the all-caring side...' At the time of our fieldwork, this clinic had just received funding for a health adviser's post.

Overall, the vast majority of staff in clinics *with* a health adviser considered that the clinic would operate less effectively *without* one, and most thought the health adviser fulfilled a vital function in the GUM clinic. And, with some exceptions, many of the staff in the clinics *without* a health adviser considered that the clinic would be better off *with* one, since they were currently operating only adequately or badly without a health adviser. The two clinics which seemed to be managing rather better without a health adviser were small, part-time clinics.

Do health advisers need a nursing background?
Health advisers can come from a wide range of backgrounds and training. Around half of the health advisers we interviewed (12) had a nursing background while ten did not. Two of those without a nursing background had a social work qualification and the others came from a wide variety of backgrounds. We were particularly interested in the opinions of medical, nursing and health advising staff on how *necessary* they thought it was that health advisers should have a nursing background.

The health advisers themselves were the most likely group of staff to consider that it was *not* necessary for health advisers to have a nursing background; 18 of the 22 health advisers thought it was not necessary (82 per cent). This included all the health advisers from a non-nursing background (10), as well as two-thirds of those with a nursing background (8).

The health advisers who were not nurse-trained considered that some sort of training was necessary, but not necessarily nurse training. Counselling skills and experience were thought to be particularly important, as was training in GU medicine. This health adviser, from a social work background, said: 'Personally I don't think it's necessary at all. As long as you are given initial training in the basics. My interest is in people, I work on a client-oriented basis. I'm good at counselling, I have counselling skills. I've had to learn a lot and I've not had a chance to use all my skills yet. But there are not many health advisers who haven't come from a nursing background...'

But the health advisers with a nursing background considered that, while a nursing background was not *necessary* or essential, it was helpful: 'It's not essential but I think it's very, very helpful. You get a lot of questions that aren't related to GUM and having a nursing background, you can help them. Things like pelvic inflammatory disease and cytologies, explaining to people exactly what happens here...'

Only four health advisers, all with a nursing qualification themselves, thought it *was* necessary to have a nursing background. This senior health adviser told us why: 'At one time I wouldn't have said it was necessary. But now I think it's more than very useful. I think it's essential. I think they should be a registered nurse at least and preferably with HIV work experience. If they're a nurse, they have a knowledge of the NHS and how the hospital works and medical terminology and who the staff are. It can be learnt. Two or three years ago, it was not as important, but now when we're appointing new staff, it's a major advantage if they are a nurse. My thoughts have changed. But I'm only talking about this clinic. It will depend on the clinic and the workload...'

This health adviser was working in a large and busy full-time clinic, with a significant proportion of HIV-related work. But another of the health advisers who thought nurse training was necessary worked in a small, part-time clinic: 'I think it's essential because very often the clients will talk about their other health problems. Without a medical background, you wouldn't be able to help them...'

On the whole, while health advisers did not generally consider a nursing background to be essential, many recognised that it could be useful, although those without a nursing qualification were keen to highlight the usefulness of other types of training, such as counselling or social work.

Medical staff, and the consultants in particular, are likely to make key decisions about the appointment of health advisers. We were particularly interested in their views on the suitability of different backgrounds for health advisers. Like the health advisers themselves, the vast majority (80 per cent) of the doctors considered it was not *necessary* for health advisers to have a nursing background. This proportion was reflected among the consultants (82 per cent). But more than two-fifths of these doctors considered that it was certainly helpful for a health adviser to have a nursing background. A consultant commented: 'I think it's an advantage. They don't have to be, but it's an advantage, definitely. If they know about the diseases and about physiology and health, and they're given training in counselling, you would have the medical knowledge and the social and emotional training, which is the ideal. If it was a school teacher or someone who had worked in an office, then they're ignorant of the terminology and you have to explain. They have to be extra dedicated to learn and to find out...'

A quarter of these doctors went further, commenting that, while it was not *necessary* for a health adviser to have a nursing qualification, it was *preferable*, as this consultant remarked: 'It's not essentially necessary, but it's very helpful. If I had two candidates who were equal, and one was a nurse and one wasn't, I'd choose the nurse...'

But around a quarter of them, including this consultant, thought that the individual's personality and attitude were more important than the background: 'When our health adviser was appointed, we shortlisted five people. There were at least two nurses and a microbiologist. But we chose J... for what she offered. You have to go for what will fit in with the rest of the team. As long as they're intelligent and willing to learn. It's a small set-up here and everybody's weight has to count, every ounce. You can't have a dead duck in the clinic...' And another consultant said: 'I think it's personality that matters more. We used to have people with no training and they were absolutely superb...'

Some doctors, however, emphasised the importance of having training or experience in GU medicine: 'Not a nurse necessarily, but a nurse in STDs is more important. If they've worked as a nurse in intensive care, that's not much use...' And others said that health advisers needed some sort of training, but not necessarily nursing: 'Anything to do with medical care and caring for the human body is very useful. They could be a psychologist. It's interesting to see the variety of backgrounds of health advisers. They provide a range of services. It's the same with doctors – different backgrounds bring different skills to the job...'

However, just under a fifth of the medical staff (18 per cent) considered that a nursing background *was* necessary for health advisers. It was interesting that only four of the 33 consultants thought it necessary (12 per cent), whereas other doctors were rather more likely to think so. One GP clinical assistant told us: 'I think they should have a nursing background. Otherwise they can't explain the disease and the manifestations...'

On the whole, although most medical staff did not think it was essential for health advisers to have a nursing background, they were inclined to say that it was helpful or preferable. But most would employ a health adviser without a nursing background if their personality and training were acceptable. In the words of one consultant: 'I don't think it's necessary although it certainly helps if they've been around medicine. The main thing is to communicate with the patients...You need to know how to handle people. It doesn't matter if you're a nurse or a window cleaner – if you can do it and you've got the right qualifications and training...'

Finally, we asked the nurses what they thought about health advisers' backgrounds. Many of the health advisers we interviewed had come from a nursing background and many of the nurses were keen to expand their counselling role. It was perhaps not surprising that more than a third of the nurses interviewed (37 per cent) thought it was necessary for health advisers to have a nursing background: 'I think they should have a nursing background. Otherwise how can you go into medical things? It's not just counselling skills, you have to know what you're talking about. You need a medical background...'

Nevertheless, more than 60 per cent of nurses thought it was not necessary, but, like the doctors, half of these nurses thought a nursing background was helpful or preferable. A sister in a large clinic said: 'It's not really all that necessary at all. But it's useful to have a background knowledge of different conditions. A trained nurse would know these things so it's useful, but not necessary...'

Again, it was recognised that other kinds of training apart from nursing were useful, and some emphasised the importance of training in GU medicine and STDs: 'A nursing background is not as important as other skills, such as counselling skills or a background in terminal illness or bereavement. You don't need to be a nurse but you need a knowledge of STDs...'

And some felt that personality and attitude were more important than background: 'I would have said it was essential but with our health adviser, she's a special girl. If they've got her calibre, there's no reason why they should be a nurse. There's no legal requirement. She's picked up so much in terms of treatment and anatomy. You've got to have personal qualities to be a good health adviser...'

The health advisers

There can be little doubt that the role of the health adviser was the most misunderstood in the GUM clinics, and that the extent to which health advisers could develop their talents was very much circumscribed by the structure and organisation of the different clinics. The main problem appeared to be in defining the roles of health advisers, which ranged very widely, often reflecting, again, the way in which consultants wished to use them within the clinic. Their work was often dominated by HIV-counselling, even in clinics with little or no work with HIV-positive patients. Their potential role in developing patient education, outreach work, counselling and prevention was seriously underdeveloped in many clinics.

There was a clear need for a rational approach to the development and training of health advisers. Having 'personal qualities' alone was not enough. The health advisers themselves were eager for their potential to be recognised, and wanted far greater professionalism within their discipline. However, given the extent to which much of their work was 'behind closed doors', it was often difficult for them to attract the greater recognition that many of them wanted and to develop their roles and responsibilities.

6 Administrative, reception and clerical staff and their roles

We interviewed all the administrative and clerical staff working in 13 of the 20 clinics. In the remaining seven clinics:

- one had no administrative or clerical staff. (The nursing staff were responsible for reception, administrative and clerical duties)
- one had two part-time receptionist/clerks, but we interviewed only one since the other had worked in the clinic for only one week
- one had three part-time receptionist/clerks who rotated through the GUM clinic and other outpatient clinics on a weekly basis. We interviewed only the receptionist/clerk who was working in the GUM clinic at the time of the fieldwork
- in three, we did not interview the part-time medical secretaries whose roles were mainly confined to pure secretarial work. They had little or no involvement in the general running of the clinic and no patient contact, and were not involved in the statistics or other administrative duties
- in the last and the largest clinic, we interviewed the supervisor and half of the receptionist/clerks (selected at random). We did not interview the medical secretaries for the reasons stated above.

Interviews were carried out with a total of 52 administrative and clerical staff:

- 35 receptionist/clerks
- 6 receptionist/clerk/secretaries
- 6 medical secretaries
- 5 managers/supervisors (with reception/clerical duties)

The receptionist/clerks worked on the clinic reception and were involved in booking in patients, pulling and filing notes, making appointments and other clerical work. Some were responsible for the collection and collation of the clinic statistics.

The receptionist/clerk/secretaries had similar responsibilities but worked in clinics without a dedicated secretary, and were employed to carry out the secretarial work as well.

The medical secretaries were mainly responsible for the typing and secretarial work, but some were also involved with other clerical work in the clinic.

The roles of the managers/supervisors varied. Some were senior receptionists who supervised other receptionists, and some had the role of clinic manager. All of them were involved in the day-to-day running of the clinic in terms of reception and clerical work.

Characteristics of the administrative and clerical staff

The overwhelming majority of administrative and clerical staff were women. We interviewed 50 women and two men, both of whom were receptionist/clerks.

The ages of the administrative and clerical staff ranged from 26 to 66, with a mean age of 45.1 years:

- one third of the staff were aged under 40 years, including five receptionists who were under 30
- almost two-thirds were aged between 41 and 60
- three staff, all receptionists, were over the age of 60

The average age of the reception staff was 44, of the managers/supervisors 48, and of the medical secretaries 49. The administrative and clerical staff, like the medical and nursing staff, were mainly concentrated in the 40-50 age group.

Qualifications

More than one third (38 per cent) of the administrative and clerical staff had no academic qualifications. Seven had a school leaving certificate and one had CSEs. Just over one third said their highest academic qualification was GCE 'O' level (35 per cent). Six had GCE 'A' levels, but none had any higher academic qualifications.

Around half (48 per cent) of the administrative and clerical staff said they had a 'professional qualification'. These were almost all exclusively typing, shorthand or book-keeping qualifications.

Administrative and clerical grades

Virtually all the administrative and clerical staff said that they were on the ancillary and clerical grading system. Six of the receptionists did not know which grading system they were on but it seems likely that they too were on the ancillary and clerical system:

- 33 per cent were on grade 2 of the A and C scale
- 37 per cent were on grade 3
- 5 respondents were on grade 4
- 4 of the staff were unable to give a grade number, but said they were clerical officers or higher clerical officers
- 7 respondents had no idea which grade they were on

The reception staff were on grades 2 or 3, while the medical secretaries and managers/supervisors were on grades 3 or 4.

Length of time in grade

The administrative and clerical staff had usually only been on their present grade for a fairly short period. Half of them had been on their grade for between 1 and 5 years. Just over a quarter (27 per cent) had been on their grade for less than 1 year and only seven respondents had been on their particular grade for more than 5 years. Five staff were unable to say how long they had been on their grade.

Length of time in GUM

The length of time the administrative and clerical staff had been working in GU medicine varied widely:

* around one fifth had been working in GU medicine for less than a year, (including four who had been in GU medicine for less than 6 months)
* almost half had worked in GU medicine for between 1 and 5 years
* one third had been working in GU medicine for more than 5 years (including almost a quarter, 12 respondents, who had been working in GU medicine for more than 10 years).

Why the administrative and clerical staff decided to work in a GUM clinic

Few of the administrative and clerical staff had actively decided to work in a GUM clinic. In fact, many of them had not even known what a GUM clinic was. More than half said that they had simply needed a job and had seen the post advertised: 'I didn't know what it was. I didn't know what a "special" clinic was. It was just a job...' Some had only come to the clinic temporarily and, to their surprise, had found they liked it.

One third of the administrative and clerical staff said that they had chosen to work in the clinic because of the hours which gave them the opportunity of working part-time: 'It was the fact that it was part-time. That was the main thing. It wasn't the type of clinic it was. It was advertised in the evening paper. It was part-time and it appealed to me because I had a young daughter...'

Six of the administrative staff had simply wanted to work in a hospital or for the NHS and five had wanted to have contact with patients.

A part-time receptionist summed up the circumstances under which some of the administrative and clerical staff had joined the GUM clinic: 'It was nothing to do with GU medicine. The advert didn't state it was GU medicine. What drew me to it was the hours – they were what I wanted. I wasn't worried about the salary, though it's not very good. It just said "clinic receptionist". At the interview, the first thing they said was, "Do you know you'll be dealing with AIDS?" It wasn't in the advert. But I wanted to work in a hospital or in a caring field...'

Seven of the respondents thought it would be interesting work: 'I like meeting people and being with people. I liked the idea of working in a hospital. I'd heard this was a nice hospital to work in and there were nice people. I saw the job advertised and I applied and I got it. I knew what GU medicine was. I thought it would be interesting, I liked the idea...'

What the administrative and clerical staff liked about GU medicine

Nearly 90 per cent of the administrative and clerical staff said there was something they particularly liked about working in GU medicine. The most popular aspect was the good staff relations. Almost half the administrative and clerical staff said they liked the other staff in the clinic and remarked on the good atmosphere and friendliness of the clinic: 'I like the team, it's a real team here. And because it's confidential, we're more of a unit. We're a team pulling together...' Members of the administrative staff referred to feeling 'part of a team' time and time again, and some referred to the lack of hierarchy in the clinic.

The administrative staff also liked the patient contact – 40 per cent of them said they liked working with people: 'I like dealing with the general public. It's very rewarding. I deal with them first hand. I'm their first stop. I'm not in uniform so I'm more approachable. If there's trouble, it's easier for me to step in. I'm a member of the public. I'm not the establishment. They can relate to me and I can allay their fears. I'm a bridge between the inside and the outside...'

Some staff found the variety of patients and their different lifestyles and attitudes particularly interesting, but some also liked the fact that they got to know the patients attending the clinic. Many of them found working in the GUM clinic generally interesting and varied and it was clear that they derived great pleasure from helping and reassuring the patients.

What the administrative and clerical staff disliked about GU medicine

However, although half the staff said there was *nothing* they disliked about working in GU medicine, 44 per cent cited features which they disliked.

Firstly, there was the negative image associated with the GUM clinic, mentioned by around 10 per cent of all the staff. One receptionist said: 'It's the stigma. It's from the people themselves, quite a lot of people, the patients and other people and others working in the hospital. When staff have to come here, we have to hide them. I would too. But lots of cases are not sexual naughties. We all get them...'

And a medical secretary described similar reactions from her friends: 'I don't like other people's attitudes. They take a backward step. They're interested when you say you work at the hospital, but when you say which clinic, they step back. It's from everyone. It's something that could never happen to them, it's other people...'

Secondly, around ten per cent of the administrative and clerical staff said that they disliked having to deal with aggressive and abusive patients. Members of the medical, nursing and health advising staff recognised that the receptionists were in the 'front-line' and there was no doubt that difficult situations sometimes arose. A receptionist in a London clinic described the problem:

> I don't like the fact that some of the patients are obnoxious. We have to put up with the flak. You get it in other departments but not every day like in here. Because it's an appointment system, you've got to be strict and there's a staff shortage so we can't put too much work through to

the doctors. You have to be firm. But there are problems every day. It's because it's taboo – the patients are not happy coming here. They might have been told to come here by a contact slip. They can get very stroppy and nasty. Generally people don't want to come here. They rant and rave...'

And the supervisor in the same clinic told a similar tale: 'Some patients are very aggressive. I have been beaten up badly. It takes your pride away. It took me a long time to get over it...'

Thirdly, around ten per cent of all the administrative and clerical staff said they disliked the physical aspects of the clinic. The staff in one particular clinic complained about the clinic area itself. One explained: 'I don't like the fact we're so closed in, we're so short of space. We're falling over one another...' while another said: 'I don't like six of us in a small room as well as all the equipment. It's hot and people get in the way, they're bending down or you get an elbow in your face. You try not to let it enter your voice but the room is too small. The fact we're short-staffed helps because there's less people but then the phone's always ringing. And then it's bad for the patients. It's cramped in the waiting room and the door opens onto the main hospital corridor and there's no tea room or drinks machine and there's always a wait...'

The medical staff and health advisers worked closely with the patients and referred to the stress of the HIV/AIDS related work. But the administrative and clerical staff were not immune. Three of the receptionists, all working in clinics with a high proportion of HIV/AIDS related work, referred to their feelings about working with HIV and AIDS patients: 'It's very stressful. A lot of people have died recently. There have been quite a few deaths. You get to know the people. It's not so much the death as watching people deteriorate. They're not friends but you can get close and you get to know them. It's quite stressful. You can't get involved, you can't go under but you have to maintain your sensitivity. But you also get a lot out of it...'

Other aspects mentioned by the administrative and clerical staff included the long hours, the low pay, the lack of training and the shortage of staff but none of these was mentioned by more than three members of staff in each case.

Training to work in GUM clinics

Working in the 'front-line' in a GUM clinic and dealing with enquiries from worried and upset patients, either on the telephone or in person, requires personal skills from administrative staff. Many of the staff we spoke to were involved in giving out results, either positive or negative, and many talked about comforting and reassuring patients, as well as giving advice when they were able. We were therefore interested in knowing whether they had had any specific training courses to work in GUM clinics.

Only *four* of the 52 administrative and clerical staff we interviewed said they had had specific training to work in a GUM clinic: two receptionists, one medical secretary and one office manager. Three of them had been on one course but one of the receptionists had attended three courses.

The office manager had attended a first line management course organised by the hospital. One of the receptionists had attended a short course on 'how to deal with patients and how to word things', organised by social services. And the medical secretary had attended a weekend training course on 'counselling' in order to participate in an AIDSline organised by a local voluntary organisation. None of these courses was certificated.

The other receptionist had attended three counselling courses: one general counselling course, one on counselling for an AIDSline and one on bereavement counselling. One of the courses, organised by a local university, was certificated. This receptionist was highly motivated and had made arrangements herself to attend these courses.

But the vast majority (92 per cent) of the administrative and clerical staff had not had any training. We asked them if they would *like* any training to work in the GUM clinic. Two-fifths of them said they did not want any training now, generally because they had been working in the clinic for quite some time and felt it was unnecessary or too late for training.

However, more than half of all the administrative and clerical staff interviewed (56 per cent) felt they needed or wanted training at the time of the fieldwork. A quarter of all staff wanted a general introduction to GU medicine and to STDs. This, they felt, would help them with their work and might enable them to answer some of the simpler or more factual questions posed by patients. This did not seem an unreasonable request.

15 per cent of the administrative and clerical staff said they would like 'something to help me deal with the patients', while a further four receptionists specifically said they would like training in counselling to help them deal with the patients. Five of the staff wanted to attend a computing or word-processing training course.

Length of time in clinic
One third of the administrative and clerical staff had been working in the clinic for more than 5 years, almost half for between 1 and 5 years and one fifth for less than one year.

Time spent working in the clinic
Three-quarters of the administrative and clerical staff worked in the clinic only on a part-time basis. This is not surprising given that so many of the GUM clinics were only open on some days of the week. But even the larger, full-time clinics, which were open all day every weekday, were often staffed by larger numbers of part-time staff, with hours ranging from 2 to 32 hours per week.

One quarter (13) of the administrative and clerical staff worked full-time in the GUM clinic. They included all five of the managers/supervisors, six receptionist/clerks and two medical secretaries. All these staff were working in large, full-time (or almost full-time) clinics, with hours ranging from 35 hours to 37.5 hours, usually 36 or 37 hours per week. The average mean number of hours for which the administrative and clerical staff were contracted to work in the selected GUM clinics was 23.2 hours per week.

Work in other GUM clinics
Only one of the administrative and clerical staff worked in another GUM clinic. A receptionist working in a part-time clinic went with the consultant and the health adviser, one morning each week, to another GUM clinic in the same district as the selected GUM clinic.

Work in other clinics
Five of the administrative and clerical staff – four receptionists and one secretary – worked in other clinics. They were all working in GUM clinics which were part of the out-patients department, and all of them worked in other out-patient clinics in the hospital.

Other work
More than a quarter (15) of the administrative and clerical staff were involved in *other* paid or voluntary work: two were voluntary counsellors and ten did other voluntary work. Only four respondents did other paid work, generally secretarial, clerical or reception work.

Full-time and part-time working
More than a third (38 per cent) of the administrative and clerical staff worked full-time overall, when all their work was taken into consideration, but the majority (62 per cent) worked only part-time overall.

Administrative staff and the management structure of the clinic
The five managers/supervisors reported *managerially* to different people; two to the (senior) consultant, one to the business manager, one to the out-patient department supervisor and one reported to the office manager.

The six medical secretaries also reported to a range of different people including the clinic sister, the (senior) consultant, the clerical/secretarial supervisor and the (assistant) business manager.

The people cited by the 41 receptionists, however, ranged even more widely. Some of the hospitals were undergoing changes in the management structure at the time of the study and some of the staff said that their manager or their manager's title had changed. Some staff working within the same clinic and in the same role often said they reported to different people, in spite of the fact that they should have reported to the same person. And different hospitals used different titles for staff with similar roles and responsibilities, making it difficult to assess who was managerially responsible for staff.

More than a third (39 per cent) of the receptionists, however, said they reported to the senior receptionist, the clerical/secretarial supervisor or to the clinic/office manager. But six reported to the out-patient department supervisor, five to the out-patient services manager and four to the medical records officer.

A range of other personnel were also mentioned by the receptionists, including the sister/charge nurse/clinical nurse specialist, the nursing services manager, the personnel manager, the (assistant) business manager, the manager of the medical directorate and the unit general manager.

The lines of responsibility were rather less varied when we asked the respondents to whom they reported *professionally*. Nevertheless, we still elicited a wide range of responses, especially from the receptionists:

- 2 of the 5 *managers/supervisors* said they reported to the (senior) consultant
- the other 3 reported to the medical records officer, the out-patient services manager or the (assistant) business manager
- all 6 of the *medical secretaries* said they reported professionally to the (senior) consultant
- more than one third of the *receptionists* reported to the senior receptionist, clerical supervisor or office manager
- around a quarter reported to the sister/ charge nurse/clinical nurse specialist
- a quarter reported to the (senior) consultant
- 3 receptionists reported to the health adviser
- 3 receptionists referred to a member of staff outside the clinic: the medical records officer.

Only five of the administrative and clerical staff had responsibility for any other clinic staff: four managers/ supervisors and one receptionist/clerk/ secretary. They were all responsible for the (other) reception staff, while one of the managers said she was also responsible for the medical secretaries and other clerical staff.

Just over half (56 per cent) of the administrative staff felt they had sufficient managerial support in their job . The managers/supervisors were particularly likely to say they had enough managerial support (80 per cent).

But a third (35 per cent) of the respondents, mostly receptionist/clerks, felt they did *not* have enough managerial support. The medical and nursing staff and the health advisers had mainly complained about poor managerial support from managers *outside* the clinic. But the administrative and clerical staff were fairly equally divided between those who also complained about managerial support from outside the clinic and those who said they had insufficient support *within* the clinic.

The receptionist/clerks complained mainly about the lack of managerial support for the GUM clinic from managers outside the clinic. But some were concerned about lack of contact with hospital managers, who were also said to lack understanding for the receptionists' needs.

The receptionist/clerks who felt they did not have enough managerial support from managers within the clinic complained about a variety of aspects of the clinic management including lack of teamwork, the poor relationship and poor communication with managers, the lack of understanding of their needs and poor management ability generally.

Level of responsibility

On the whole, the administrative and clerical staff were satisfied with the level of responsibility they were given, and three-quarters of them said they had about the right amount. The six respondents who felt they had too little responsibility said they were capable of more and some commented that they had had more in a previous post.

But seven of the respondents (13 per cent) felt that they had too *much* responsibility for their grade, salary and role in the clinic. The receptionist/clerks from one clinic were particularly concerned about allocating diagnostic coding: 'Too much responsibility. I wouldn't mind doing the diagnoses if I felt sure I knew what I was doing. But I don't and I worry about it. Even the doctors have trouble but we get pulled up if it's wrong. I'm not happy about having to do it...'

But the concern about having to allocate the diagnostic codes was not confined to one clinic only. A receptionist from another clinic had similar worries: 'Too much responsibility. There's one area where we look in the notes every day, we look in the notes for a diagnosis, we have to try and figure out a diagnosis. That's a bit difficult for someone who's not a medical person. Sister usually puts the codes in but, if not, we have to look through the notes, see if the tests are positive or negative and allocate the codes...'

The issue of diagnostic coding is discussed in more detail in Chapter 8, but was clearly a matter of considerable concern, not only for the clerks who were struggling with the coding, but also in terms of work roles and responsibilities.

Job description

Two-thirds (65 per cent) of the administrative and clerical staff said they had a job description, with the managers and medical secretaries more likely to have one than the receptionist/clerks. But the majority of those who had a job description had not been involved in drawing it up; only a quarter had been involved or consulted.

Just under half the administrative and clerical staff with a job description thought it was accurate or adequate. But around half of them made negative comments about it, mainly because it was too broad and general and was open-ended. Staff often said their job description was general to their grade or job, rather than specific to the GUM clinic or to them personally. Two receptionists said their job description was out-of-date. Only two of the administrative and clerical staff, one manager and one receptionist, said their job description was regularly reviewed, but the vast majority of the rest thought their job description *should* be reviewed on a regular basis.

Increasing time spent on activities

We asked the administrative and clerical staff whether they would like to increase the amount of time they spent on any part of their job. Exactly half of them said they *would* like more time to fulfil their current responsibilities, and there was little doubt that they interpreted the question in terms of having more time to do their job properly rather than in shifting the balance of their work.

The managers/supervisors were particularly keen to spend more time on managing the clinic, with more time for clerical work and more time to train staff. The secretaries wanted more time for all their responsibilities, particularly their typing and for computer data entry. And the receptionists wanted to spend more time on the management of the clinic, on typing, data entry and clerical work, and more time for their responsibilities generally. They also wanted to spend more time on training courses.

Additional activities

Just over one third of the staff said that there was something they would like to do in their job which they did not do at all at present. The receptionists were particularly keen to expand their work.

Some of the administrative and clerical staff simply said that they wanted to take on more responsibilities generally within the clinic, but others were more specific. More than ten per cent of the reception staff wanted to start counselling patients, and a similar proportion were keen to give patients information about diseases and treatments and to give patients their test results. This receptionist described the situation in her clinic:

> Yes, I would like to do things I don't do now, but I would need training. When I came here, I was a stranger to the medical field. People would enquire about their results and ask general questions, like, "What is this infection?" and "What is herpes?" and "What are STDs?". When I was new, it didn't warrant a doctor's or nurse's time, but I was not given guidance to deal with it myself. The nurse-in-charge has recently put a stop to us giving any positive results. At first, we could give a general yes or no, but patients want to know more and we might give the wrong information or insufficient information so she decided no positive results can be given. We can give negatives but I feel some positives could be given. I would be happy...

Although the receptionists mainly wanted to expand their patient contact, they also mentioned a range of other activities including training, computer data entry and typing.

Decreasing time spent on activities

Almost half of the administrative and clerical staff said that there were activities which they would prefer to do less often. All five managers wanted to spend less time on reception and answering the clinic telephone, and on administrative and clerical tasks generally.

Two-fifths of the receptionists (41 per cent) said they would prefer to spend less time on particular aspects of their job. A third of them wanted to spend less time pulling and filing notes, but other aspects mentioned included computer data entry, answering the clinic telephone, looking up and giving patient results, collation of the KC 60 return and administrative work generally.

Activities to exclude

Only eight respondents, four receptionists, two secretaries and two managers, said there were aspects of their jobs they would rather not do at all, including pulling and filing patient notes, setting up the clinic and clearing up afterwards, the KC 60 diagnostic coding and other administrative or clerical tasks.

Job satisfaction

Two-thirds (67 per cent) of the administrative and clerical staff were satisfied with their job, including more than a quarter who were *very* satisfied (29 per cent). Virtually all the rest were *fairly* satisfied with their job (31 per cent). Only one, a receptionist, was not very satisfied with her job.

Almost two-thirds of the respondents cited aspects of their job and their work which they liked. Many of them just said they were happy in their job, but aspects mentioned specifically included the good staff relations, the patient contact and the good management of the clinic.

But 40 per cent of the respondents mentioned aspects of their job with which they were not happy. The most common of these were the low pay and the physical aspects of the clinic, such as lack of space and poor lay-out. But a range of other aspects were also cited including poor staff relations, lack of promotion or training, lack of management support and generally lack of time to carry out their responsibilities.

Could the reception staff take on more responsibilities?

We asked all the staff interviewed whether they thought the *reception staff* could take on more responsibilities. Three-quarters of the administrative and clerical staff considered that the receptionists could *not* take on any more responsibilities than they had at present. In 11 clinics they were unanimous, or almost unanimous, that the receptionists could not take on more for three main reasons: first, and most important, it was said that the receptionists already did enough and there was nothing else they *could* do; secondly, they were too busy and did not have the time to take on other responsibilities; and thirdly, some of the receptionists said that it was not appropriate for their grade to do more.

But a quarter of the administrative and clerical staff – including 11 receptionists and 2 secretaries, working in eight clinics – thought the receptionists *could* take on more responsibilities. The extra responsibilities included the clinic statistics, giving patients their test results, typing and secretarial work, and sending out recall letters. It was said that receptionists were prevented from doing these things through lack of time, lack of training or because the consultant did not wish them to do so.

But other staff in the clinic were less likely than the administrative and clerical staff to think that reception staff could take on more responsibilities. Less than one fifth of the medical staff and the health advisers and less than one in ten of the nurses said they thought they could do so.

A wide range of activities were mentioned by these respondents including the clinic statistics, more work on the computer, processing laboratory results, pulling/filing notes, secretarial work/typing and general paperwork, support/reassurance for the patients and patient information. However, some said the receptionists should fulfil their current responsibilities before considering doing any more. Involving the receptionists in the clinic statistics was the most commonly mentioned activity.

The medical, nursing and health advising staff who thought that, in principle, receptionists could take on more responsibilities usually said that, in practice, they did not have enough time to carry out additional duties, or could not take on more because the clinic was short-staffed. However, some said the receptionists were not trained or qualified or competent to take on extra responsibilities.

It was quite clear that the vast majority of the medical, nursing and health advising staff considered that the receptionists could *not* take on more responsibilities than they currently had, mainly because they already had enough to do and did not have the time to take on extra duties.

Sufficient staff on reception

Given that so many of the respondents thought that the receptionists could not take on any more responsibilities because they were too busy, we were interested in assessing whether there were enough staff working on reception. There was a wide diversity of opinion among staff on this topic. There were variations not only between clinics, but also *within* clinics, both between different types of professional and also within the different professional groups.

The administrative and clerical staff and the nursing staff were the most likely to consider there were sufficient staff working on reception (79 per cent of the administrative staff and 73 per cent of the nursing staff).

But almost half the doctors (46 per cent), a third of the health advisers (32 per cent) and just over a fifth of the nursing staff and administrative and clerical staff (23 per cent and 21 per cent respectively) said, quite categorically, that there were *not* enough staff working on reception. The problems seemed to be greatest in three clinics in particular, all of which were large, full-time clinics.

Respondents commented that the reception staff were extremely busy and that the clinic sometimes did not run very well and work was not done, particularly when staff were off sick and there was no cover, or at times when the clinic was particularly busy. Even staff who felt there were enough receptionists said there were problems when the clinic was busy and other staff had to help out.

What was the solution? It was not simply a question of employing more receptionists. In fact, in six of the clinics, including two of the busy clinics where there were significant problems relating to a shortage of receptionists, staff said there was actually no room for more receptionists. More often than not, staff said more staff or more hours were required for carrying out *clerical* work, as this was the aspect of the work that was neglected when the clinic was busy and patients needed booking in at reception. This often resulted in a backlog of clerical work. Others said that cover was required at times when receptionists were not available, for example at lunchtimes or when receptionists were on holiday or off sick. Only too often, it appeared, nursing staff or whoever else happened to be near the telephone or near reception helped out as necessary. This was sometimes thought to be an inefficient use of a nurse's (or doctor's or health adviser's) time.

A GP clinical assistant described the problem in the GUM clinic in which he worked and how he thought it could be resolved: 'No, there are not enough staff on reception. If we're busy, she's running around, she's at the window and then the doctor will want something and then people have to wait and then she starts pulling her hair out. There should be a clerical job and a receptionist. Nurses have to get involved and do the receptionist's job. There should be two people, two posts – a receptionist and a clerk or a secretary...'

The use of temporary staff on reception

The staff sometimes said there were problems when receptionists were ill or on holiday. Our pilot work had indicated that temporary staff were sometimes used on reception. We wanted to know how common this practice was and what clinic staff thought about the use of temporary receptionists.

Again, there was some diversity of opinion about whether temporary staff were used on reception. Overall, it appeared that temporary staff were sometimes used in 12 of the 20 clinics, while in the other 8 clinics, other clinic receptionists or other staff covered reception when required.

In some cases the practice of using temporary staff was thought to be acceptable because the temporary member of staff worked within the hospital, or because the same person was used each time. But many of the staff were unhappy about the practice. One of the main problems was that the temporary receptionist did not know enough and could only do limited tasks which reduced their usefulness and meant that the clinic did not run as well as it did normally.

One supervisor described her experience of using temporary staff: 'The quality of staff is often not very good. And by the time you've taught them things, they're off again. They're often not much help. If I'm off, then no paperwork is done. I was off sick for seven weeks on one occasion and nothing was done. If people are off and we have a temp. in, I have to come in early to get the work done or it doesn't get done at all...'

But using temporary staff was also thought to compromise the confidentiality of the GUM clinic and it was said that temporary staff did not always have appropriate attitudes towards the patients. This receptionist told us about one of the temporary staff her clinic had employed:

> We sometimes use temporary staff but it happens very rarely. I don't like it. It's very difficult to cover for us. There was one girl in particular, she was only 17, and she was really giggly. All the patients had "VD" or they were "promiscuous" or had been "naughty". And she wouldn't open the male window. She was the wrong sort of person. Someone in the hospital should be trained to cover for us. Your neighbour could come in so you have to be very careful...

Temporary staff recruited from agencies came in for particular criticism. One clinical nurse specialist said: 'We have used temporary staff but we have been disappointed in the quality of the staff we've had. You wonder what these agencies think of as a "receptionist". They just sit there. But their role is much larger. There's a lot of paperwork. One looked through the drawers and said, "Oh, I know someone there". That was very difficult as the clinic was about to start. Some clinics rely on agency staff but in our experience, it doesn't work very well...'

This clinic seemed to have been particularly unlucky, as a receptionist from the same clinic said: 'They are useless. They don't have a brain, they can't pick it up. They sit doing their nails. One said she wouldn't do something for a nurse because she was doing her nails!...'

Nevertheless, staff often recognised that the use of temporary staff was unavoidable and they were sometimes referred to as a 'necessary evil'. This clinical assistant was resigned to the use of temporary staff: 'Yes, we use temporary staff on reception. But as Cardinal Hume said, "What can one do?" It's inevitable. You've got to use temporary staff...They might be used to booking in patients but they haven't got the skills to deal with upset and aggressive patients. People can just walk in off the street. The reception area is your showroom. Like a hotel, it should be welcoming, but of all areas, it's the one under a lot of stress...'

The role of the other administrative/clerical staff

All the reception staff we interviewed were involved, to a greater or lesser extent, in clerical work and some were also involved in secretarial work. But we were also interested in the *other* administrative and clerical staff working in the clinic: the medical secretaries, health advisers' clerks and any other staff without reception duties. As already noted, we did not interview all of these staff, unless they had a particular role in patient contact. Ten of the clinics did not have any other administrative or clerical staff, other than those working on reception. But ten employed medical secretaries, and two of these clinics also had a health advisers' clerk.

The vast majority of the staff in these clinics considered that the other clerical staff could *not* take on any more responsibilities, mainly because they had enough to do already, were too busy and did not have time to take on extra work, especially if the clinic was short-staffed.

Only seven doctors (from three clinics), one health adviser and two administrative staff (from one clinic) thought the medical secretaries *could* take on more responsibilities in general, although specific suggestions included sending out recall letters, working for the health advisers and expanding their secretarial role. But they were prevented from taking on more responsibilities either because of lack of staff and lack of time, or because the consultant did not wish them to take on extra work.

The administrative, reception and clerical staff

The roles of the administrative, reception and clerical staff varied widely among clinics. Staff in smaller clinics were usually more satisfied with their roles and responsibilities than those in larger clinics, often because they felt themselves to be part of a team. However, there was evidence that many clinics had too few administrative, reception and clerical staff, which led not only to overload for these staff but also to inappropriate use of professional staff, particularly health advisers, in carrying out their functions. There was also evidence that some clerical and reception staff were used inappropriately and given too much responsibility, for example in allocating diagnostic codes with little or no support or supervision from medical staff.

There was a clear need for more training of GUM clinic administrative, reception and clerical staff. The receptionists in particular were often under pressure from patients who could be anxious and aggressive. The need for tact and diplomacy in front-line staff performing such tasks was paramount, but there often appeared to be little recognition of the difficulty of the job nor of the need to enhance the skills of those carrying out the role by proper training.

7   Location and physical characteristics of GUM clinics

There can be little doubt that the location and the physical characteristics of GUM clinics can have a major impact on many aspects of their work. The traditional view of an STD clinic is of a clinic with rundown accommodation, often isolated from other facilities in the hospital or community. The upgrading of GUM clinics in terms of accommodation has been a concern of the Department of Health for some years, and recent recommendations have been adopted and guidelines laid down (Department of Health, 1990).

In our review of work roles and responsibilities, we were interested in exploring to what extent the actual physical characteristics of the clinic had an effect on the working conditions of the staff. We were particularly interested in examining whether the lay-out or facilities helped or hindered the development of the roles and responsibilities of the various categories of staff.

The researchers spent between four days and three weeks in the clinics, the length of time depending on the size of the clinic and the numbers of staff interviewed. During this time, detailed notes and records were kept on the location and the physical aspects of the clinics.

Location of the clinics
It is useful to summarise briefly the information on location given in Chapter 2:
- 18 of the clinics were based in a hospital:
  - 11 of these were in the out-patients department, with 8 sharing accommodation with other out-patient clinics and 3 having separate and dedicated GUM accommodation;
  - 7 were not part of the out-patients department but had separate buildings or areas used only by the GUM clinic.

- 2 were based in the community:
  - one shared accommodation with other 'out-patient' community clinics;
  - one was based in a community health centre in an area used exclusively by the GUM clinic.

The researchers noted the geographic location of the hospital/clinic in relation to the town/city, and the location of the clinic within the hospital. In terms of location, six clinics were rated good, ten fairly good, but two were thought to be in a fairly poor location and two in a poor location.

The two clinics in a *fairly poor* location were not part of the out-patients department but had separate dedicated GUM clinic accommodation. However, their location within the hospital was less than satisfactory. One was located some distance away from the main hospital buildings and the other was tucked away at the back of the hospital. Both were rather difficult to find and, in both cases, it seemed that the clinic was somewhat isolated and 'out of the way'.

The two clinics in a *poor* location were both part of the out-patients department, and shared accommodation with other out-patient clinics. In both cases, other clinics were running concurrently with the GUM clinic. The reception and waiting areas were very public and there was a danger that patient confidentiality might be compromised.

The researchers considered that 11 of the clinics were clearly sign-posted from the entrance to the hospital, but nine were *not*. Consequently, nine of the clinics were not easy to find; the researchers often had to ask their way to the GUM clinic (an experience that might be embarrassing to a potential patient) and they sometimes got lost. We found it a matter for some concern that the clinics were so difficult to find by highly motivated researchers, doing a job, and looking hard for the clinic, often with a car. We were afraid that patients who might not have the same level of motivation, and who were more likely to be diffident about asking for directions, might easily be deterred by the difficulties put in their way.

Accommodation and facilities of the clinics
Entrance, reception and waiting rooms
Five of the 20 clinics had separate male and female entrances while seven had separate male and female reception desks. Most of the clinics were accessible to disabled people, but seven were not. These clinics had stairs, narrow doorways or were poorly laid-out.

We considered that ten of the 20 clinics had reception areas which allowed confidential conversation and booking in. But the other ten were less than satisfactory, the main problem being that patients booking in could be overheard or overlooked. But there were also problems with poor soundproofing and some clinics were very close to other outpatient clinics.

Eight of the clinics had separate male and female waiting rooms, while the other 12 had waiting rooms which were shared by patients of both sexes. Most waiting rooms had magazines, pictures and information leaflets, but only half had plants and only a third had children's toys. Very few had a coffee or drinks machine and only one had a public pay-phone.

Most of the clinics kept the patient notes in reception, but some kept them in the consultant's, sister's or health adviser's office and some kept them in a basement or back room. Seven of the clinics kept the notes of HIV/AIDS patients *separately* from other patients' notes, usually in a different drawer or shelf or filing cabinet. Two clinics had separate HIV/AIDS clinics where HIV/AIDS notes were kept.

In 11 clinics, the nursing staff took the patient's notes to the doctor, but the receptionists were responsible in six clinics. Sometimes both nurses and receptionists were involved in taking notes to the doctor, and in one clinic, doctors routinely collected patient notes from reception.

Consulting, examination and treatment rooms

14 of the clinics had consulting rooms which were also used for examination
- 10 had consulting/examination rooms for male patients
- 4 had consulting/examination rooms for female patients
- 4 had consulting/examination rooms which could be used for either sex

14 of the clinics had separate consulting rooms:
- 10 had separate consulting rooms for female patients
- 3 had separate consulting rooms for male patients
- 5 had consulting rooms which could be used for either male or female patients

14 clinics had separate examination rooms:
- 12 had separate examination rooms for female patients
- 9 had separate examination rooms for male patients
- 4 had examination rooms which could be used for either sex

Only six of the clinics were thought, by clinic staff and the researchers, to have consulting/examination rooms which were all, or almost all, soundproof; a further six had *some* which were soundproof but problems with other consulting/examination rooms. And eight were thought to have more serious problems with soundproofing of consulting and examination rooms.

The soundproofing of a room is related to whether the room is fitted with a door or has only a curtain. Only one clinic had curtains only around *all* the examination rooms, but as many as seven had *some* examination rooms fitted with curtains only.

Eleven clinics had separate treatment rooms: six had treatment rooms for male patients, three had treatment rooms for female patients and six had mixed sex treatment rooms. In five of these clinics, the treatment rooms were said to be soundproof, but there were problems with soundproofing in the other six clinics, sometimes because the rooms only had curtains, but more often because of the material of the clinic walls.

Health advising rooms

Eleven of the clinics had separate, dedicated rooms for health advising. These included health advisers' offices (for the sole use of the health adviser) and counselling rooms. Six of these clinics had soundproof rooms for health advising. But four had health advising rooms which were *not* soundproof and one clinic had some rooms which were soundproof and others which were not.

Nine clinics did not have dedicated health advising/counselling rooms. In some cases, the health adviser shared a room with the sister, while in other cases, the sister's room was used for counselling. Sometimes the consultant's office was used for counselling and sometimes counselling took place in the reception area. And in one clinic, the health adviser counselled wherever she could: in the corridor, in the canteen or in her car.

Separate offices

Fourteen of the clinics had separate offices for staff but six did not. The consultants were the most likely to have separate offices, although in some clinics, where space was at a premium, the consultants shared an office. We visited one clinic where four consultants shared a relatively small office. Senior registrars occasionally had an office but it was rare for more junior doctors to have one.

The sisters/charge nurses usually had their own office, although in some clinics it was shared with the health adviser or the clinic manager. Some clinics had a separate office for the health advisers, as well as counselling rooms. The clinic/consultants' secretary and the medical secretaries usually had their own rooms.

Lavatories

All the clinics had lavatories available for use by the patients. In one clinic, however, the male lavatory was being used as a store room because of lack of space in the clinic. It was not, therefore, available for use by patients.

Total number of rooms

The mean number of rooms occupied by the clinics was 13.1. But this masked huge differences between the clinics:

- 3 had five rooms or less
- 8 had between six and ten rooms
- 6 had between 11 and 15 rooms
- 3 occupied more than 25 rooms in total

Other facilities

Virtually all the clinics had tea and coffee-making facilities for staff but only half of them had a refrigerator for milk and food. Five clinics had a toaster and two had a microwave oven. Around half the clinics had a staff room, a staff changing room and staff toilets.

Overall impression of the physical characteristics

The researchers assessed the physical aspects of the clinic using two criteria: the size of the clinic (in relation to the number of staff and the number of clinics held) and its soundproofing/confidentiality.

Size

Overall, four of the clinics were considered to be of a good size and one of a fairly good size. These clinics were spacious, with adequate facilities for both staff and patients.

However, nine were assessed as being fairly poor and as many as six were said to be poor in terms of their size. In some cases, these clinics were actually quite large clinics. But in relation to the number of staff using the clinic, the number of clinics held and the number of patients passing through, they were inadequate. There was often insufficient room for patients to wait, so that patients had to stand or queue, sometimes in public corridors. These clinics often had too few rooms, with counselling rooms and separate offices being in shortest supply. Rooms were often multi-functional.

Soundproofing and confidentiality

Only one clinic was considered to be good and six fairly good in terms of soundproofing. Five clinics were said to be poor and eight were fairly poor.

The main problems in these clinics were that booking in could be overheard by other patients or by other clinics, the walls of consultation and examination rooms were too thin, and examination and treatment rooms were fitted with curtains only.

The physical aspects of many of the clinics, therefore, left something to be desired, according to the observations and assessments of the researchers. However, we were particularly interested in the views of the GUM clinic staff themselves, and we asked all the staff interviewed whether there was anything about the location or the physical characteristics of the clinic which affected the way they did their job.

Effects of the location and physical characteristics on staff

Medical staff

Almost three-quarters (72 per cent) of the medical staff said that there was something about the location or physical aspects of the clinic which affected the way they did their job. Problems arose in as many as 15 clinics; only in five clinics did all, or at least a majority of the doctors interviewed, have no complaints about the clinic's physical characteristics.

By far the biggest problem mentioned by medical staff was lack of space and rooms for the staff and the patients, as well as lack of space for equipment and storage. This was cited by all, or by a majority, of the doctors, in ten clinics. These corresponded to those which the researchers had assessed as being inadequate in terms of size.

Lack of space meant that sometimes there were insufficient rooms for consultation or for examining and treating patients. One consultant said: 'The location is fine but we're desperately lacking in space, from all points of view. We need another consulting suite and a separate treatment room and we need a health adviser's room. We just have to find space where it's available. Yesterday, there was nowhere for the health adviser to go until the clinic had finished. At the other clinic, she has to use one examination room while I use the other examination room for both men and women. And there should be a separate place for microscopy so the nurses can do it. At the moment I have to do it all because the only place for the microscope is in my consulting room...'

Often there was no staff room and a shortage of offices for clinic staff. In some cases, medical staff had no office at all, as this junior doctor explained: 'My only complaint is that the clinic is a bit too small. The consultant has an office but the registrar and SHOs don't have an office. It's too small for the number of doctors. There's nowhere to go to work, to develop questionnaires. You can work in the library but it's nice to have access to the clinic information...'

And in some cases, offices were shared. One consultant worked in a full-time clinic and shared an office with three other consultants: 'The location's OK but it's disastrous in terms of the physical aspects. It's cramped and it's totally inadequate space-wise. And there's no possibility of expansion. There's no room for a colposcope. And the ventilation is terrible. It can reach 90-100 degrees in summer and 80 degrees in winter. It's just too hot and there's no daylight. It's like working in an inadequate aircraft carrier or submarine...'

Some clinics were criticised by the doctors for being badly laid out. The medical staff in one clinic were particularly critical of the clinic lay-out, especially as it had been purpose-built for the GUM clinic.

The location of the clinic was criticised by some doctors, and the medical staff in one clinic particularly disliked the fact that the clinic was some distance from other departments and services. The consultant said: 'I would have preferred the new clinic to be adjacent to the main out-patients but it was not possible. There is a disadvantage in getting general hospital case notes and X-rays and supplies from the pharmacy. There are minor difficulties. And I'm conscious that in the evening, the clinic is isolated...'

The medical staff in another clinic were particularly dissatisfied with the shared premises. One of the consultants described the problems that this caused: 'It's appalling. This is temporary accommodation and we're sharing with various other physicians so access is limited regarding time and sometimes the clinic over-run each other and there's no provision for GU patients to sit anywhere. This has been going on since before 1975 and there's no improvement. I have attempted many discussions, correspondences and meetings with no effect...'

A wide range of other aspects were mentioned, including heating/ventilation problems, poor lighting or lack of natural light, as well as poor soundproofing and lack of privacy for patients.

Effects on nursing staff

The nursing staff were even more likely than the medical staff to say that there were aspects of the clinic that affected the way they did their job (82 per cent). Like the medical staff, the nursing staff were particularly critical of the size of the clinic and the lack of space for staff and patients.

The sister in one clinic said: 'It's really congested, it's a very, very congested clinic and it affects the way we all do our job. It's too small generally, throughout the whole clinic. We desperately need a new building to give our patients a better service and to comply with the Health and Safety regulations. There's no room, no place to implement other procedures. Procedures are being carried out in congested places. It's not an ideal environment. We're treating STDs and cervical biopsies together. The constraints of the building are enormous. We can't take on any more staff because we can't contain them...'

In some clinics, there was no doubt that the lack of space prevented the nurses from taking on more responsibilities, such as examining follow-up patients and microscopy.

Some nurses were also critical of the clinic lay-out. This was particularly a problem in three of the clinics. A nurse in one said: 'It's like a maze or a submarine. It's very crowded and very small. We get flustered and irritated and have arguments. It could be better but there's no room to improve it...'

Another clinic was said to be like a 'rabbit warren' while in another, there was no access between the male and female sides of the clinic, other than through the female waiting room. One of the male nurses said: 'It's badly designed. It's not big enough. It's too small for what we're trying to do. And you've got to go though reception to get to the staff room which can be very difficult if there's a girl in tears. We wanted a door between the male and female side, but it wasn't financed...'

The nurses were rather more likely than the doctors to complain about lack of privacy for patients and poor soundproofing and they were also more likely to complain about the location of the clinic within the hospital. The nurses also referred to the other problems cited by the doctors, such as poor heating and lighting and shared premises.

And some, like this nurse, were disparaging of the clinic generally: 'It's bloody awful. It's multi-coloured and it's out at the back, isolated from the hospital. It looks awful. They've tried to create a better image, but it's farcical. It's got seagulls painted on the outside!! It's a typical clap clinic – small, dingy and out of the way. It's totally inadequate in size as well...'

Effects on health advisers

Around two-thirds (64 per cent) of the health advisers said there was something about the location or the physical aspects of the clinic that affected the way they did their job. Like the medical and nursing staff, they were dissatisfied with the lack of space: 'There's no space, there's no rooms. There are too many staff and too many clinics for the size of the clinic. We're all tripping over each other for space. I have to do pre-test counselling in an office which is not soundproof...'

In some cases, the health adviser simply did not have a room to use for counselling: 'At this clinic and the other GUM clinic I go to, I have to counsel patients in my car. I haven't got a room. I sometimes see people in a treatment room. I can use the consultant's room but then the secretary is in and out getting things ready or looking for notes. There are no facilities. I have no room of my own. It's not ideal. If someone's distressed I've got nowhere to take them...'

Problems with space were sometimes exacerbated by poor lay-out: 'When I see a male patient, I have to take him outside, walk outside the clinic, and bring him in through the back door, or else I have to take him through reception and through the women's waiting room. If I do that, I ask the reception staff first, but reception is a very small area and there are usually patients in the female waiting room. So I have to explain to the patients where I'm taking them. And when there's a patient to be seen, we have a bell system. But if I'm with someone or if I'm caught in an interview, I sometimes forget the bell and the patients wait for a long time. It's awkward...'

Five of the health advisers complained that the clinic was on more than one floor or site. One clinic had a counselling room away from the clinic, causing problems with security: 'One of the health advising rooms is off-site. One patient, a male, tried to make a pass and there was no way of raising an alarm. The room's all right but from the security angle, it's appalling...'

And around a third of the health advisers said there were problems with soundproofing and lack of privacy for the patients: 'The health advisers' room is a converted store room without a window or heating. It's cold and uncomfortable and it's not relaxing and it's not soundproof...'

Effects on administrative and clerical staff

Just over half the administrative and clerical staff reported that there was something about the clinic that affected the way they did their job. They too complained about lack of space and lack of rooms for staff and patients.

The reception areas in three clinics were particularly small, as this secretary pointed out: 'I don't know how the receptionists move - the reception area is appalling. I don't know how they work in it. I spend part of the day in there and there's notes around, the health adviser, doctors. It's the centre of the clinic, the most important aspect and it's terrible. But it's all terrible. It's a pox joint. It's like a lavatory. It's totally out of date and cramped. It's the architect's idea of what a V.D. clinic should look like...'

The administrative and clerical staff were also particularly concerned about the lack of soundproofing and privacy for patients. This was a particular problem in one of the large, full-time clinics. One of the secretaries told us that 'the soundproofing is bad. You can hear through the air conditioning', while a receptionist said: 'There's no privacy at all on the female side. You have to be very careful what you say. From the waiting room, they can see the new patients coming to book in. We have music to try and disguise it...'

Administrative and clerical staff also complained about heating, ventilation and lighting problems, and lack of space for equipment and storage.

Clinics

The main problems with the physical characteristics of the clinics related to location, size, lay-out, soundproofing/privacy and shared premises. We had wondered whether the different categories of staff might express different views on the clinics, but there was little doubt that the problems experienced by different types of staff were common to the clinic in which they were working, rather than to the type of professional.

By far the greatest problem was lack of space, which appeared to be a problem in at least thirteen of the 20 clinics. When we asked a general, open-ended question at the end of the interview about how staff would change or improve the way the clinic operated in general, around one fifth of all GUM clinic staff said that they would increase the size of the clinic or the number of rooms.

But if size was the main constraint on the work of staff in GUM clinics, poor lay-out was also a major problem in five clinics. Location and access were thought to be less of a problem, but there were problems of soundproofing and privacy in six clinics.

Many of the clinics had individual specific problems. But some clinics had a multitude of problems, encompassing size, lay-out and soundproofing. Four of the 20 clinics, all large, busy full-time clinics, were thought to be particularly poor in terms of their physical characteristics.

Patient confidentiality

Many of the staff spontaneously referred to problems with soundproofing and privacy when we asked them about the location and physical aspects of the clinic. But we also asked a specific question about whether the physical lay-out and organisation of the clinic ensured patient confidentiality.

The medical staff were rather less likely than other staff to consider or admit that there was a problem, but the views of the other staff were remarkably similar. Overall, 42 per cent of the doctors, 53 per cent of the nurses, 55 per cent of the health advisers and 54 per cent of the administrative and clerical staff thought the physical lay-out and organisation of the clinic did *not* ensure patient confidentiality.

Once again, there significant differences between the clinics. Three of the 20 clinics were clearly quite satisfactory in terms of patient confidentiality, and very few, if any, of the different types of staff complained. A further six received relatively little criticism from staff about confidentiality.

But the remaining 11 clinics were all criticised by a substantial proportion of the clinic staff. Four of these attracted a considerable amount of comment and criticism on the subject of patient confidentiality from all types of staff. Two of these were also included in the four which were said to be particularly poor in terms of location and lay-out.

The main complaint centred around poor soundproofing. The problems occurred in more than half the clinics, but three in particular were said to suffer from major soundproofing problems. The poor soundproofing might occur in any or all parts of the clinic. In some cases, staff complained about the reception area and waiting rooms. Some staff specifically mentioned that the booking in of patients could be overheard: 'If patients are talking in the waiting room, you can hear them in reception and vice versa...' And some staff said that patients could be overlooked by other patients: 'When the patients are booking in, there's a whole queue. People can see your names and addresses on the notes....'

In some clinics staff told us that the consulting and examination rooms were not soundproof. Sometimes this related to the general soundproofing and thickness of the walls, as this secretary rather graphically described: 'The walls are made of plasterboard. It's terrible. You've got to have a very quiet voice to maintain confidentiality. Some of the doctors, if they think the patients don't understand they shout' "It's your willy!" really loud...'

As already noted, some clinics had only curtains around the examination and treatment beds so that everything could be overheard, and sometimes the counselling rooms were said to have poor soundproofing.

The staff unanimously denounced the lack of soundproofing in those clinics where there was a problem. Many staff expressed concern and thought the situation was unacceptable, especially if it made the patients anxious and inhibited. In many cases, staff said they tried to overcome the problem by talking quietly or by playing music. This no doubt helped to some extent, although the staff in one clinic were clearly unhappy about the type of music played.

One receptionist said: 'It's hopeless. We have to play lousy music all day because we can hear everything the doctor says to the patient if we don't play music. It wasn't designed to be a clinic but a hallway. The walls are thin and some walls don't reach the ceiling. I wouldn't like to be a patient coming here...' And a nurse in the same clinic said: 'The walls are not soundproof. We can hear the doctors. We have music but it should be more varied and suited to the patients. It's Barry Manilow! Sometimes we hear Barry Manilow 20 times a day!...'

But apart from the soundproofing, there were other problems related to confidentiality. The staff in three clinics in particular referred to the lack of privacy in the examination rooms. They not only referred to the lack of soundproofing and use of curtains, but also to the fact that the doors of the examination rooms opened directly on to the waiting room, leaving patients feeling vulnerable and in danger of being exposed.

The problems with confidentiality in counselling were not only related to a lack of soundproofing in the counselling rooms. Some clinics did not have a counselling room at all, which meant that counselling sometimes took place in public places, with a considerable risk to confidentiality.

The waiting rooms in some clinics also came in for criticism. Some staff considered that mixed sex waiting rooms hardly ensured confidentiality, while others said that the waiting room was too public, or was shared by other clinics, or that the clinic was generally too close to other clinics and services. In some clinics, telephone conversations taking place in reception could be heard by patients attending the GUM clinic or other clinics.

Access to patient notes presented a problem in some clinics. Most clinics kept patient notes in reception, but problems sometimes arose with the notes of patients waiting to be seen by a doctor. In some clinics, notes were left in areas or in places accessible to patients or non-GUM clinic staff.

Overall, to a greater or lesser extent, the physical lay-out and organisation of *all* of the clinics in the study were not conducive to ensuring patient confidentiality, and we had no doubt that they all needed to take a fresh look at their practices as far as patient confidentiality was concerned. Some clinics were much better than others, but some were particularly bad, with confidentiality compromised to some extent in a variety of ways.

Staff were, of course, aware of the problems and, as we have seen, were quite willing to express their objections and concerns. In many cases, staff went to great lengths to overcome the problems, but in some cases, they said there was nothing that could be done in practical terms, and some thought the only answer was a new clinic building. It was interesting, however, that, even in those clinics which had been purpose-built, there were problems with soundproofing and lay-out that compromised confidentiality, and there appeared to be a great need for the guidelines on design and confidentiality that have recently been issued (Department of Health, 1990).

8 Workload and statistics

One of the aims of this study was to look at the effects of changing workloads on GUM clinics. The increase in HIV infection, and the apparent accompanying increase in the demand for treatment and counselling at GUM clinics, was one of the reasons for setting up the Monks working group (Department of Health, 1988). In this study we set out to examine the balance in the workload between patients with different types of condition, with particular reference to whether this balance had changed in the previous year or so.

We collected statistics from the clinics about clinic sessions, patient attendances and the incidence of different conditions, with a view to establishing the actual workload of each clinic. The statistics on clinic sessions and patient attendances collected through the KH 09 returns were discussed in Chapter 2. The present chapter looks in more detail at how these statistics were collected and collated and relates them to the statistics on diagnoses of different conditions collected through the KC 60 returns. It summarises the problems associated with both sets of statistics and makes recommendations for a further review.

Incidence of conditions

But, first, we take a closer look at the statistics on the incidence of conditions collected through the KC 60s and then compare them with the views of the staff when asked about their workload in relation to the various conditions.

We collated the KC 60 figures which had been collected by the clinics for the period covering the whole of 1989 and the first two quarters of 1990. We concentrated on the statistics for six main conditions: syphilis, gonorrhoea, chlamydia and NSU (non-specific urethritis), herpes, warts and HIV/AIDS. Graphs illustrating the figures for each clinic are given in the Appendix.

Essentially, the statistics indicate that there was no sudden upsurge in the number of conditions diagnosed in the clinics. Only a gentle upward trend could be seen in some clinics, while in others, the actual overall trend was slightly downwards. The overall trends were relatively stable, with only minor quarterly fluctuations in the number of diagnoses of different conditions.

Chlamydia/NSU and warts were the most frequently diagnosed conditions in all clinics apart from the largest one, in which the numbers of HIV/AIDS cases were higher than warts diagnoses in three of the four quarters for which figures were available from the clinic (Chart VI).

In most clinics, the incidence of gonorrhoea and herpes was considerably lower than that of warts and chlamydia/NSU. Syphilis was mostly rarely diagnosed, with only a tiny number of clinics having more than two or three cases a quarter and some having none at all during the 18-month period.

The incidence of diagnoses in connection with HIV/AIDS was similarly very low in most clinics over the period, apart from one clinic, which had by far the highest number of HIV/AIDS cases in the sample. Even in the other larger clinics, none had had more than 30 HIV/AIDS diagnoses in a quarter and most recorded single figures for each quarter. In some clinics, no diagnoses of HIV/AIDS were made during most or all quarters in the 18-month period.

The views of staff on changes in workload

For a variety of reasons, which are discussed in some detail in the second part of this chapter, the statistics which go to make up the workload of the clinic are perhaps not as robust as they might be in describing the complete picture of workload in the GUM clinics. We were aware of some of the discrepancies in recording and interpretation of workload statistics from our pilot study. We decided at the outset therefore to ask all categories of staff a series of questions about different conditions. Their responses gave their *perceptions* of how the workload and the balance of their work had changed. Although these perceptions provided rather 'softer' data than the statistics, in many ways they give a more accurate picture of what was going on in the clinics in which we carried out this research.

HIV/AIDS related work

We first asked all staff whether they thought there had been an increase, a decrease or no change in the last year in the number of people coming to the clinic with, or in relation to, HIV and AIDS. We had originally intended to ask about people with HIV positive infection and AIDS, but it soon become clear that, although the spread of HIV infection was said to be one of the main reasons for the increase in workload in GUM clinics, many of the clinics, in fact, had little or no experience of HIV positive or AIDS patients. Even among clinics with a relatively large number of such patients, one of the main reasons for the apparent increase in work connected with HIV infection was an increase in pre-test counselling and support.

As Table 8.1 shows, more than half the doctors, nurses and administrative and clerical staff thought the number of patients coming to the GUM clinics with, or in relation to, HIV/AIDS had *increased* in the past year. Few of them thought the HIV/AIDS related work had decreased. Around one fifth of the doctors and nurses thought the number of patients had remained about the same, while a similar proportion felt unable to comment. The administrative staff felt least able to comment on the number of HIV/AIDS patients.

More than three-quarters of the health advisers thought the number of patients attending the clinics with, or in relation to, HIV/AIDS had *increased* in the past year. These respondents were most likely to be working with these patients, and were perhaps in the best position to comment. But the demands that these patients put on the health advisers, in terms of time and emotion, may have caused them to overestimate the increase in demand, although the statistics we collected seemed to support their estimates up to a point. It is quite clear, however, that the KC 60 returns do not present an accurate picture of the work carried out in GUM clinics in connection with HIV and AIDS, and this is discussed in more detail later in this chapter.

Table 8.1   Changes in HIV/AIDS related work

column percentages

	All staff	Medical staff	Nursing staff	Health advisers	Admin. & clerical
Increase	57	58	52	77	54
Decrease	4	1	5	9	6
No change	20	24	22	9	12
Don't know	20	17	20	1	29
Base: all	*(261)*	*(89)*	*(98)*	*(22)*	*(52)*

Many of the respondents commented that the number of patients requesting an HIV test increased during or following health education campaigns, and much of the increase related to an increase in HIV testing, rather than to patients who actually had HIV infection or AIDS.

Viral conditions

We then asked the respondents whether they thought there had been an increase, a decrease or no change in the last year in the number of people coming to the clinics with other viral conditions, such as herpes and wart virus.

As Table 8.2 shows, around half the doctors and administrative and clerical staff and 61 per cent of the nurses thought that the number of patients with other viral conditions had *increased* in the past year. The increase was said to be largely due to an increase in patients attending with warts. The nursing staff were commonly treating warts and this might account for their rather higher estimate of the number of patients attending with viral conditions.

Few of the GUM staff said these conditions had decreased but around one fifth thought there had been no change in the number of patients attending with other viral conditions.

More than two-fifths of the health advisers and administrative and clerical staff were unable to comment on the number of patients. Most of the health advisers in the larger clinics with a greater proportion of HIV/AIDS work said that they did not see patients with other viral conditions, since their time was spent solely or mainly on HIV counselling and contact tracing of traditional STDs. The health advisers who felt able to comment, however, generally agreed with other staff that the incidence of viral conditions had increased.

Table 8.2   Changes in viral conditions

column percentages

	All staff	Medical staff	Nursing staff	Health advisers	Admin. & clerical
Increase	54	56	61	32	48
Decrease	3	3	4	5	2
No change	22	29	23	18	8
Don't know	20	11	11	45	42
Base: all	*(261)*	*(89)*	*(98)*	*(22)*	*(52)*

Traditional STDs

We also asked the respondents what trends they had noted in the last year in the number of people coming to the clinics with traditional STDs, such as gonorrhoea and syphilis.

Table 8.3   Changes in traditional STDs

column percentages

	All staff	Medical staff	Nursing staff	Health advisers	Admin. & clerical
Increase	33	31	30	55	31
Decrease	16	20	17	14	10
No change	32	38	40	18	12
Don't know	19	10	13	14	48
Base: all	*(261)*	*(89)*	*(98)*	*(22)*	*(52)*

As shown in Table 8.3, around one third of the doctors, nurses and administrative and clerical staff, and more than half of the health advisers thought the number of patients attending the clinics with traditional STDs had *increased* in the last year. This was often said to be due to an increase in the incidence of chlamydia, but some said there had been an increase in the incidence of gonorrhoea, particularly in homosexual men, an indication that some were failing to practise safe sex. Some staff thought that this was due to younger generations of homosexual men who had missed the main sweep of AIDS advertising or who thought they were safe if they only had sex with other young men. But some said that homosexual men were becoming less motivated about practising safe sex.

Respondents sometimes commented that there were seasonal fluctuations in the incidence of gonorrhoea, and many said that the incidence of gonorrhoea, and especially syphilis, was low in any case. One third of the staff thought that the incidence of traditional STDs had remained about the same, while around one in six thought it had decreased. Half the administrative and clerical staff were unable to comment.

Workload

Finally, we asked the GUM staff if the actual workload of the clinics had *increased* in the last year. A majority of all the GUM staff thought it *had* increased. As Table 8.4 shows, this was particularly true of health advisers, around three-quarters of whom thought the workload had gone up.

However, around a quarter of the staff did not think the workload had increased while around one in ten felt unable to comment. Some staff commented that there were seasonal variations in the workload of the GUM clinics.

Table 8.4   Increase in workload

	All staff	Medical staff	Nursing staff	Health advisers	Admin. & clerical
					column percentages
Yes	61	61	55	73	65
No	27	34	29	14	19
Don't know	12	6	16	14	15
Base: all	*(261)*	*(89)*	*(98)*	*(22)*	*(52)*

Effect on the work of GUM staff

We were interested in exploring how any of the changes in the actual workload or in the balance of the different conditions had affected the work of the GUM clinic staff.

Effect on work of medical staff

One fifth of the doctors (21 per cent) said that the changes had not had any effect on their job. A further 7 per cent felt unable to comment as they had been working in the clinic for less than one year, and 6 per cent said there had been no changes in the incidence of conditions or in the workload in the past year. But two-thirds of the doctors said the changes in the workload or the balance of conditions **had** affected their job.

The main effect of the change in the balance of conditions was an increase in the time medical staff spent in counselling. One fifth of the doctors (22 per cent) said they did more counselling. This was most commonly in relation to HIV, and was usually pre-test counselling and counselling of the 'worried well'. Related to this, one fifth of the doctors (22 per cent) said they spent more time with individual patients, usually in relation to HIV/AIDS, but occasionally in relation to other conditions.

The doctors cited a number of other ways in which their job had changed. Around one in ten (13 per cent) said more tests were being carried out in the clinic. This increase was accounted for by an increase in HIV tests, in the number of tests on HIV positive patients, and in the number of tests and procedures such as cytology and colposcopy, carried out in relation to other viral conditions. The same proportion (13 per cent) said that more treatments were now carried out. These treatments corresponded with the increase in the number of patients attending the clinic with wart virus.

One in ten doctors said there were now more medical consultations than there had been one year before. Related to this, the same proportion of doctors felt there had been a fall in the quality of the service provided by the GUM clinic, since they were having to spend less time with patients than was recommended.

Overall, taking all the changes into consideration, one quarter of the medical staff (24 per cent) said they were busier than they used to be and had to work longer hours.

Effect on work of nursing staff

Just over a quarter of the nurses (28 per cent) said that the changes had not had any effect on their job. A further 6 per cent felt unable to comment as they had been working in the clinic for less than one year, and 5 per cent said there had been no changes in the incidence of conditions or in the workload in the past year. But three-fifths of the nurses said the changes in the workload or the balance of conditions *had* affected their job.

One fifth (19 per cent) of the nurses said they were carrying out more tests on patients. The nurses, like the doctors, said that they were taking more bloods for HIV tests, they were carrying out more cytology tests for other viral conditions, and were also carrying out more tests for other STDs, which meant there were more slides to read. Around one in ten said that the increase in patients attending the clinic with wart virus meant that they were carrying out more treatments for warts.

A fifth of the nurses (19 per cent) said they were busier than they had been in the past and were working longer hours. Some of the staff nurses and enrolled nurses felt more stressed (7 per cent).

The nurses cited a number of other ways in which their jobs had changed. Some said they spent more time with patients, some said they gave more information, some did more counselling and some felt the quality of the service was not as good as it once was. Each of these changes were mentioned by around 5 per cent of the nurses.

Effect on work of health advisers

Only three of the 22 health advisers said that the changes had not had any effect on their job (14 per cent). One health adviser felt unable to comment as she had been working in the clinic for less than one year. But 18 (82 per cent) of the health advisers said the changes in the workload or the balance of conditions *had* affected their job.

More than half (13) said they were doing more counselling, almost always in relation to HIV. They were doing more pre-test counselling, more post-test counselling, more counselling of the worried well and more counselling of HIV positive patients. Related to this, nearly a quarter of the health advisers said they were spending more time with patients discussing HIV infection. There were also more telephone calls from patients worried about HIV.

The increase in the number of patients attending the clinic with HIV or AIDS meant that some of the health advisers spent more time liaising with other services or departments, which entailed more letters and other paperwork.

Around a fifth of the health advisers said they were now doing more contact tracing, usually associated with an increase in chlamydia or gonorrhoea.

While some health advisers said that the increase in HIV-related work had made their job more interesting, the demand these patients made on their time in terms of counselling meant that they felt busier and worked longer hours than they had in the past (32 per cent), and felt more stressed (23 per cent).

As many as a quarter of the health advisers considered that the quality of service offered to patients by the GUM clinic had deteriorated, mainly, as we found with the medical staff, because there were more patients attending the clinic and they had less time to spend with individual patients.

Effect on work of administrative and clerical staff

Around a quarter of the administrative and clerical staff (27 per cent) said that the changes had not had any effect on their job. A further 6 per cent felt unable to comment as they had been working in the clinic for less than one year, and 2 per cent said there had been no changes in the incidence of conditions or in the workload in the past year. But two-thirds of the administrative and clerical staff said that changes in the workload or the balance of conditions *had* affected their job.

A quarter (27 per cent) said they were busier than they used to be and had to work longer hours. The managers/supervisors were particularly likely to say they were busier. Around a fifth of the staff (19 per cent) said there were more letters and more paperwork than there had been in the past. The secretarial staff were most likely to refer to the increase in paperwork.

The increase in workload meant that there were more telephone calls being dealt with by the staff, and the receptionists said there were more patients requiring appointment and more processing of test results. The managers also referred to the increase in computer data entry and in statistical analyses.

Statistical (Korner) returns from GUM clinics

GUM clinics are required to make two statistical returns to the Department of Health:

1. The KH 09 is returned on a monthly basis and provides workload information on the number of clinic sessions held and the number of visits by patients to NHS GUM clinics (threshold crossings). All out-patient clinics are required to complete the KH 09.
2. The KC 60 is specific to GUM clinics. It is returned on a three-monthly/ quarterly basis and provides epidemiological information on the number of new cases of conditions seen in NHS GUM clinics in each quarter (diagnoses).

The KH 09 return

The KH 09 form provides the following information:

(i)   clinic sessions held
(ii)   clinic sessions cancelled
(iii)   referral attendances seen
(iv)   referral attendances DNA (did not attend)
(v)   consultant initiated attendances seen
(vi)   consultant initiated attendances DNA (did not attend)
(vii)   GP written referral request
(viii) private patient attendances
(ix)   contractual arrangement attendances

Referral attendances

These were the 'new' patients attending the GUM clinic. There were two types of 'new' patient:

a) patients who were totally new to the clinic in that they had never attended before;
b) patients who had attended the clinic in the past but were reattending with a new condition or a new episode of a previously treated condition. These patients were sometimes called 'rebooks' or 'reregistered' patients as they already had a set of clinic notes.

Referral attenders (new patients) generally had longer consultations than the consultant initiated (follow-up) attenders as a patient history and tests had to be taken and a diagnosis made.

Consultant initiated attendances

These were the patients who returned to the clinic for a 'follow-up' consultation after an initial visit. Consultations for consultant initiated attendances (CIAs) were generally shorter than referral attendances as patients were generally simply receiving results and treatment.

Total attendances (referral plus consultant initiated referrals)

The total number of attendances in a year is not a count of the total number of patients attending a clinic in a year as a person is likely to attend a clinic on more than one occasion in each episode and may have more than one episode or condition per year.

Problems associated with the KH 09

Clinic sessions

There was considerable variation in the way in which information on clinic sessions was recorded.

Discrepancies arose where there were separate male and female sides to the clinic. Some clinics recorded one clinic session for each occasion the GUM clinic was open (eg. morning/afternoon/ evening), regardless of whether male and female clinics were running concurrently. Others recorded two sessions when a male and female clinic were running concurrently.

Example Two GUM clinics both had a male clinic and a female clinic open from 9.00-12.00. One clinic recorded this as one clinic session on the KH 09; the other recorded it as two sessions.

There was also variation in the length of time of a session. Some clinic sessions were as short as one and a half hours; some were as long as three and a half hours. But both would be recorded as one session.

The KH 09 only provided a measure of the number of clinic sessions held. It did not reflect the number of doctors who were present. One clinic might have only one doctor per session, another might have up to 5 doctors per session. But both would record this as one session.

Some clinics recorded sessions held by nursing staff or health advisers, while others did not.

Clinic sessions cancelled

The main confusion about this category was whether or not clinics not held because of statutory/bank holidays should be recorded as 'cancelled' clinic sessions.

Referral attendances

The main confusion about this category was whether patients who only saw a health adviser or a nurse (eg. for HIV pre-test counselling) and did not see a doctor were recorded as an attendance. Some clinics recorded these patients; some did not.

Referral DNAs

DNAs (patients who Did Not Attend) were only recorded in those clinics that had an appointment or partial appointment system. Clinics which did not have an appointment system but operated a 'walk-in' or 'drop-in' system did not, by definition, have any non-attenders. But even clinics which did have an appointment system did not always record the DNAs. And some clinics recorded the *total* number of DNAs, rather than recording referral DNAs and consultant initiated DNAs separately.

Consultant initiated attendances

The main ambiguity about this category was in defining what constituted a consultant initiated attendance. Patients actually attending the clinic on a follow-up visit were recorded. But some clinics also included certain telephone calls to the clinic as an attendance. For example, if a patient telephoned asking for results and was put through to a doctor or a nurse, that patient might be recorded as an 'attendance' because the amount of time taken might be equal to that of a personal visit. But telephone calls of a similar nature handled by the receptionist or lengthy telephone conversations by doctors or nurses with patients who had never *attended* the clinic were *not* recorded.

Some clinics, therefore, included certain telephone calls in the statistics (including one which had obtained permission from the Region to do so) while other clinics definitely did not. There also appeared to be some variation between clinics as to which calls were included and which were not.

An additional ambiguity lay in the inclusion of letters in the attendance statistics. One clinic included certain letters sent out to patients as a 'consultant initiated attendance'. It was not known whether permission had been obtained for this practice.

And, like the referral attendances, some clinics recorded patients seen only by a health adviser or nurse; others did not.

Consultant initiated DNAs

As with the referral DNAs, only clinics with an appointment system recorded this information. But even then, these clinics did not always do so and did not always split the information into referral and consultant initiated DNAs.

Collection and collation of the KH 09 statistics

In 16 of the 20 clinics, the responsibility for collation of the KH 09 lay with a member of the administrative and clerical staff. In the majority of cases (12 clinics), a receptionist or a secretary took responsibility for collating these statistics, but in 4 clinics, generally the larger clinics, the office manager/clinic supervisor/senior receptionist took on this responsibility. In only 4 clinics were the KH 09 statistics collated by someone other than a member of the administrative staff – in 3 by the sister/charge nurse/clinical nurse specialist and in 1 by the health adviser.

Computers

Only 7 of the 20 clinics had a computer in the clinic. These computers were relatively new to the clinics – all had been acquired within the previous five years.

Five of the clinics used the computer for data entry and subsequent collation of the KH 09 statistics; the receptionists entered patient details at the front desk and the computer collated the data on patient attendances. One of the other clinics with a computer planned to introduce this system of data collection and collation.

Overall, therefore, only a quarter of the clinics produced the KH 09 statistics with the aid of a computer, while three-quarters recorded and collated the information manually.

Form used

Some clinics submitted information directly on the KH 09 form; others had their own clinic form which they submitted to the hospital/district. It was in the cases where the KH 09 form was *not* used that certain types of information were not collected (eg. DNAs, GP referrals), while additional information might be collected (eg. wart patients, HIV patients, telephone calls etc.)

Submission of KH 09 statistics

Different clinics submitted the KH 09 statistics to different departments or personnel within the hospital. These included the information unit, hospital statistics department, medical records, the patient services officer and the out-patient clinic manager. Four mentioned the district statistics department.

We encountered one clinic which did not appear to submit information on clinic sessions at all. Enquiries within the clinic, within the hospital and within the district all failed to produce information of this nature.

District health authority – information/statistics department

In some clinics, the statistics were not collated on a monthly basis. Data were submitted to a hospital department on a weekly basis, where they were collated before being sent to the district.

Discussions with a number of district information units revealed some of them to be very out-of-date in terms of the staffing of the clinics as well as the way they were run. For example, when collecting statistics from one district, the DNAs were seen to be missing. The researcher queried the omission and was told the clinic operated a drop-in system and this category was not applicable. In fact, the clinic had been operating an appointment system for many years. The same district reported that the drop in attendances was due to a consultant leaving and not being replaced. The consultant was, in fact, still working in the clinic.

Summary of problems associated with the KH 09

The total picture was one which, at first sight, might appear to be straightforward with all the statistics in good order. But on closer scrutiny, in reality our research on the GUM clinics found that the statistics were full of inconsistencies. They often did not reflect the real situation in the clinics, and statistics from different clinics were not directly comparable. Given that the KH 09 is completed by *all* out-patient departments, it is possible that similar inconsistencies are occurring in other out-patient clinics.

Our findings lead to the conclusion that closer attention should be given to the way in which the form is completed. The responsibility for collecting and collating the KH 09 statistics most frequently lay with a receptionist or a secretary. The task was generally carried out to a high standard and we encountered few difficulties in obtaining the information we required. But there does seem to be some problem with supervision, consistency and responsibility for the accuracy of the statistics.

There also appears to be a need to review the information collected on the KH 09 form and for clear guidance to be produced in *one* document by the Department of Health. This document would then be available for reference by whoever was responsible for collecting these statistics. There is also a need for the consultant to take overall responsibility for ensuring that the statistics are completed correctly and that administrative staff have sufficient training and supervision.

A document with guidance on completion of the KH 09 statistics in GUM clinics should address and clarify the following points:

i) What is a clinic session? Does it simply cover the times when the clinic is open or does it cover the different types of clinic? Should it relate to the number of doctors on duty? Should sessions held by health advisers/nursing staff only be included?

ii) Should clinics not held as a result of statutory/bank holidays be recorded as cancelled clinic sessions?

iii) What is an attendance? Should telephone calls be included? What about letters? Should patients seen only by health advisers/nursing staff be included?

On the final point, there is a need for a decision to be taken on what 'counts' as an attendance in order to ensure comparability of data. Discussions with consultants revealed the importance of patient attendances and the 'numbers game', particularly where there were a number of GUM clinics in the area.

It was the policy of one clinic *not* to give out any results of any STD, whether positive or negative, over the telephone. It was said that this particular clinic was very busy and could not have coped with the number of telephone calls with the current level of staffing. It was also said that the policy was introduced to ensure patient confidentiality. But some members of staff in the clinic felt that it was unreasonable for patients to have to make a second visit to the clinic, wait to be seen, sometimes for a considerable period of time, only to be told that they had tested negative on all counts. Clearly, a second visit gave the clinic a second opportunity for health education, but one member of staff speculated that the real reason for asking patients to return for negative results was to keep the numbers up. We cannot judge the reasons, but the result certainly was that attendances were proportionately higher in this clinic than in clinics where results were given over the telephone and telephone calls were not recorded as an attendance on the KH 09.

The KC 60 return

The KC 60 is a record of diagnoses. It provides information on the number of new diagnoses made in GUM clinics in any given quarter. It does not give a count of the number of patients seen, as a patient attending a clinic with more than one condition will be counted for each of these conditions on the KC 60. Conditions are counted whether or not treatment is required and whether or not the condition is sexually acquired.

Neither the KH 09 nor the KC 60, therefore, provides a count of the number of *people* attending a GUM clinic. Information is provided on the number of threshold crossings and on the number of new conditions seen. Perhaps the number of actual *people* attending the clinic is not important to the Department of Health. The clinics kept a record of all patients' names, addresses and diagnoses in a 'confidential register' but information on the number of patients was not normally collated.

The figures recorded on the KC 60 are an aggregate of all the diagnoses attributed to all patients in a given quarter. Each diagnosis has a KC 60 diagnostic code. It is important to highlight who allocates the codes and at what stage.

Staff involved in diagnostic coding

Medical staff were involved, to a greater or lesser extent, in the attribution of diagnostic codes in 18 of the 20 clinics. In one clinic, the sister was attributing codes to all diagnoses, and in one clinic, the sister and receptionist were coding.

When a doctor had examined a patient and taken the necessary tests, he or she made a (probable) diagnosis. The doctor generally recorded the diagnosis on the patient records. Some doctors also recorded the appropriate diagnostic code on the patient records, either at the time of the consultation or at a later date. Not all the doctors working in a clinic were involved in recording diagnostic codes however. The consultant(s) were invariably involved, but many of the clinical assistants and some of the junior medical staff did not record diagnostic codes.

In many clinics, however, other staff were also involved in allocating diagnostic codes. And in many of these clinics, other staff were, in fact, mainly responsible for the diagnostic coding, with medical staff only being consulted where there was a query about a code. Some medical staff allocated codes only to the most commonly occurring diagnoses, for which they knew the appropriate code, leaving all other coding to another member of staff. But it was quite difficult to ascertain who was involved and who was mainly responsible for the diagnostic coding.

In at least four clinics, the sister/charge nurse/clinical nurse specialist allocated the codes, health advisers were involved in at least three clinics, while

125

MLSOs allocated the codes in one clinic. But what was particularly worrying, both to some of the respondents concerned and to the researchers, was the extent to which administrative and clerical staff were involved in allocating diagnostic codes. In at least five of the 20 clinics, receptionists or secretaries were involved in the KC 60 coding. Some were clearly unhappy about the task, considering it to be a form of diagnosis and therefore a medical duty. Some felt they had little or no training in the procedure and became flustered when researchers queried what conditions they put into individual categories. In one clinic, two receptionists were using diagnostic codes in different ways and it was only when the researchers asked questions that the consultant and the receptionists picked up errors and inconsistencies.

The worst case we came across was a clinic where the clinical assistants did not record the diagnostic codes on the patient records. Not only did they not record the codes, but in some cases they failed to write the diagnosis in long-hand. In these cases, the receptionists were reading the notes to discover what the patient's symptoms were and what treatment had been given in order to come up with a diagnosis to which the receptionist could then attribute a code.

Quite clearly, consideration needs to be given as to whether this is really the best way in which important epidemiological statistics are produced and, if not, whether guidance should be produced as to who should record the diagnostic codes and what training and supervision they should receive.

Point at which diagnostic codes are allocated
The point at which the diagnostic codes were allocated and fed into the records was another area of variation between clinics. It was a problem because it resulted in the 'double counting' of some conditions in some clinics.

For example, it was not always possible to make a definitive diagnosis on the day the patient attended the clinic.

Example A patient attended a clinic and received epidemiological treatment of suspected chlamydia. This was recorded and entered in the notes, together with a C4e code. Tests were sent off to the laboratory and came back several days later with a positive result for chlamydia. In some clinics, the C4e code was changed to one of the codes for confirmed chlamydia (eg. code C4a). But in other clinics the code was added so that two codes appeared for the same episode of the same condition for the same person.

Some clinics made efforts to ensure that double-counting did not occur. In some clinics, diagnostic codes were not allocated until confirmatory results came back from the laboratory, while in other clinics, diagnostic codes were not entered until the patient had been discharged. But this was not always the case, and medical and nursing staff told tales of the practices in other clinics in which they had worked. Again, it appeared that the 'numbers game' came into operation in some clinics. Double-counting was sometimes seen as a good thing as it made the clinic appear busier than it really was.

Anomalies in code allocation

There were many inconsistencies in the specific code allocation between the clinics. Many of the anomalies occurred in the D (other conditions) and E (HIV and AIDS) categories, but staff also had comments to make on other aspects of the return.

D3 category - *other conditions not requiring treatment*

D3 was a 'bucket' or 'catch-all' category into which any number of 'conditions' or situations might be placed. The most important of these were HIV pre-test counselling and negative HIV tests. The research found a number of variations on a theme. Some clinics allocated this code to patients who were pre-test counselled and had an HIV test which came back negative. Some allocated this code to patients who were pre-test counselled but did not go ahead and have an HIV test, the logic being that pre-test counselling took just as long whether the patient went ahead and had the test or not. But other clinics did not allocate any code to patients who received pre-test counselling and then chose not have an HIV test.

D2 category - *other conditions requiring treatment*

D2 was also a 'bucket' category. Some clinics used this category (and not the D3 category) for patients who were pre-test counselled and had an HIV test with a negative result. One clinic used it for the attendances of HIV patients who were receiving AZT. Other clinics used it for anyone who was given treatment for a condition not covered elsewhere in the KC 60 categories, for example colposcopy or non-GUM conditions.

D2 and D3 categories

Apart from the inconsistencies in the way in which these codes were used, the most worrying aspect to the researchers was the way in which important information on HIV pre-test counselling and testing was included in a 'catch-all' category, which could not be disentangled and therefore became meaningless.

The researchers heard a great deal from medical staff and health advisers about how their workload had increased because of requests for HIV tests and the sometimes considerable amount of time spent in pre-test counselling. It is generally acknowledged that the KC 60 does not measure actual workload in spite of the fact that theoretically it is designed to be a workload measure. However, many of the staff were using it to try and represent their workload. In some clinics, a health adviser could spend two or three hours pre-test counselling one patient. If the patient then decided not to have a test, nothing at all was recorded on the KC 60. The health advisers felt this aspect of their work ought to be reflected in the statistics.

The researchers agree that this aspect of the work of the GUM clinic should be recorded, if not on the KC 60 then somewhere else. Records were not readily available on the number of patients receiving pre-test counselling, the number of patients who went ahead and had HIV tests and the number of patients who tested negative. We even had problems in some clinics trying to establish the number of HIV positive patients ever registered. Given that this aspect is such an important part of the work of some GUM clinics, and that it is likely to become more important in other clinics, there does seem to be a need to adapt the KC 60 to reflect the HIV-related work more clearly, or for clinics to collect this information separately. In any event, there is a need to clarify the coding of patients attending for HIV pre-test counselling and testing in order to eliminate the inconsistencies currently present.

D4 category - *other conditions referred elsewhere*
This category was relatively high in some clinics, sometimes being used for referrals to colposcopy clinics. But in other clinics, the category was zero because the staff responsible for coding had not noticed the introduction of the category and had been recording patients as D2 or D3 before they were referred.

HIV/AIDS related codes
E1a - asymptomatic HIV infection, first presentation
This category was used for patients who were diagnosed as HIV positive in the clinic. It was possible, and in fact comments from staff indicated that it was probable, that a patient might already have had an HIV test in another clinic or might go on to have another HIV test. There is a possibility, therefore, that double counting of positive HIV diagnoses might occur at a national level with aggregated KC 60 statistics. Discussions with the Communicable Disease Surveillance Centre (CDSC), however, indicate that the degree of double-counting is minimal, as birth dates are taken into account when collating national HIV and AIDS statistics which are based on specific individual reports by laboratories responsible for the tests.

E1b - asymptomatic HIV infection, subsequent presentation
Some clinics used this category every time a patient with HIV but without symptoms visited the clinic. Others recorded these patients under the D2 or D3 category, depending on whether they were receiving AZT or not. And some used it for patients who had been diagnosed positive elsewhere but were attending this particular clinic for the first time.

E2 - symptomatic HIV infection, first presentation
This category was used either for patients who were tested for HIV for the first time and who had symptoms, or for patients who were already known to be HIV positive but who had progressed to a phase of the infection with symptoms manifesting.

E3 - AIDS, first presentation

Like the E2 category, this code was used either for patients who were tested for HIV for the first time and were diagnosed as having AIDS, or for patients who were known to be positive but who had now developed AIDS.

Other comments on HIV/AIDS reporting for the KC 60

A criticism of the KC 60 made in a number of clinics was that there was nowhere to record AIDS patients' subsequent visits to the clinic. It was commented that at the very time the patient took up a considerable amount of time in terms of counselling, treatment and referral to other professionals, the form did not make allowances for this. Clinics often recorded these patients under the D2 and/or the D3 category, which included a wide range of other conditions. Again, it is recognised that the KC 60 is not designed to measure actual workload, but this information on AIDS patients has great significance and should be recorded separately on the KC 60 or elsewhere.

The classification of whether conditions were homosexually acquired was sometimes recorded in a misleading way. In some clinics, if the number of people with homosexually acquired HIV infection was not known, this was recorded as zero. This clearly has implications for the national statistics on HIV infection and transmission. And some clinics recorded cases of women who had acquired the HIV virus from bisexual men as being homosexually acquired. This might result in an overestimate of the number of homosexually acquired cases of HIV and, more importantly, in an underestimate of heterosexually acquired HIV.

Other comments on the KC 60 codes

Some staff referred to the increasing importance of performing smears and colposcopy in GUM clinics and were concerned that this was not a part of the KC 60. Another query mentioned was to which code the condition 'yaws' should be allocated.

Collation of the KC 60

As with the KH 09, the main responsibility for collation of the KC 60 lay with administrative and clerical staff. In 13 of the 20 clinics, clerical staff collated the KC 60. Other staff involved in the other clinics included the health adviser (in 3 clinics), the sister (2), the consultant (1) and the MLSO (1).

Six of the 20 clinics used a computer to collate the KC 60 - the remaining 14 collated the data manually. There was no doubt that computerisation aided collation but there was also no doubt that a significant amount of time was spent entering patient details and diagnostic codes. In one clinic, KC 60 data were not available for the previous six months due to a backlog in entering data because of staff shortages and problems with the computer.

Submission of the KC 60 statistics

The KC 60 statistics were generally submitted directly to the district health authority. Half the clinics also submitted the KC 60 directly to the regional health authority, while three said they sent the information directly to the Department of Health. Some clinics sent copies to other departments or personnel within the hospital (for example, medical records, out-patient manager).

Summary of problems associated with KC 60

It is clear that there was considerable variation in the way in which diagnostic codes were allocated and there were huge inconsistencies both between and within clinics. Some of the problems arose because staff were trying to use the form to reflect their workload. While it is recognised that the KC 60 was designed to provide epidemiological information, the nature of the work of GUM clinics has changed and if clinics, health authorities and the Department of Health are to understand the nature and amount of HIV/AIDS related work in clinics, then it seems to be essential either to modify the KC 60 to accommodate the additional information or to introduce additional data collection on HIV/AIDS related work.

It is recognised that there have already been a number of changes and additions to the KC 60 as it replaced the SBH 60 and that further changes may not be welcome. It is also recognised that additional data collection may be unwelcome, particularly in clinics which are already short of administrative and clerical staff.

Nevertheless, we recommend that there is a review of the KC 60 to determine the nature of the information required and that guidance should subsequently be made available to clarify the aims of the return and the use of the component codes. Some guidance has already been produced by the Department of Health but few staff appeared to have seen it. Therefore, as with the KH 09, it seems essential that further guidance on the completion of the KC 60 is provided in *one* document, together with guidance on who should complete the diagnostic coding and at what stage. In this way, it is hoped that accurate and comparable information will be available on the conditions seen by, and treated in, GUM clinics.

9   HIV and AIDS

The balance of the work of the medical staff and the split between traditional STDs and HIV/AIDS related work are clearly related to the numbers of patients with HIV infection or AIDS who attend the clinics. It was generally agreed that such patients took more time than patients with traditional STDs, and it was also agreed that work with patients in connection with HIV/AIDS, for example, those seeking tests, took more time than other work, since many of these patients needed more reassurance and counselling. But how many people were we talking about? How many patients with HIV infection or AIDS attended the clinics?

Number of HIV/AIDS patients
These were not easy questions to answer. In the last chapter we discussed the problems associated with collecting information on diagnoses. During our pre-piloting work, we were advised by staff working in GUM clinics that they could not supply the number of HIV/AIDS patients *currently attending* the clinic as some of those registered had not attended for some time. They did not know whether these patients had died or were attending another clinic or even if they were attending a clinic at all.

We were, therefore, advised to collect the number of HIV/AIDS patients who had *ever* registered with the clinic and the number who were known to have died. However, even this information was difficult to collect from some clinics, not because of confidentiality, but because it was not collected in a readily accessible form. Some clinics had a hand-written register, which was not always kept up-to-date. We were concerned that the data supplied might not always be reliable, but, essentially, they were the best available.

It can be seen from Table 9.1 that the number of HIV patients ever registered with the majority of the clinics was very small. Two-thirds of the clinics had registered fewer than 20 patients with HIV infection and the majority of these had registered fewer than 10 patients. Two of the clinics had never had an HIV-positive patient.

The larger, full-time clinics based in cities, particularly those in the south, had had a greater number of patients with HIV infection, but as the figures show, only one third of the clinics in the sample had ever registered more than twenty HIV-positive patients, and only two had had more than 100.

Only two of the clinics had ever had more than 10 patients with AIDS, and indeed, six clinics of the twenty had never had a patient with AIDS.

It was not surprising, given most clinics' limited experience with AIDS patients, that eight of them had never registered a death of a patient from AIDS, while a further ten had registered fewer than 10 deaths. Again, only two clinics had registered more than ten deaths from AIDS, and it was the large clinic with over 600 AIDS cases ever registered which had also recorded over 300 deaths from AIDS.

Two of the clinics which had never registered the death of a patient with HIV/AIDS referred their HIV positive or AIDS patients to another department and were therefore ignorant as to the outcome of treatment.

Table 9.1   Number of HIV/AIDS patients registered with clinics

numbers

	No. of HIV patients ever reg.	No. of AIDS patients ever reg.	No. of HIV/AIDS patients died
No. of patients			
None ever	2	6	8
1-10	9	12	10
11-20	2	-	1
21-40	2	-	-
41-60	3	1	-
100-150	1	-	-
300-400	-	-	1
600-700	-	1	-
More than 1000	1	-	-
Base: all clinics	*(20)*	*(20)*	*(20)*

The figures presented in Table 9.1 have a number of significant implications. One of the most important in interpreting the results from this survey is that, although the number of HIV/AIDS patients was very low in most of the clinics studied, work in connection with HIV was said to take up quite a lot of the time of the clinic staff in many clinics. There were two reasons for this: one was the fact that HIV positive or AIDS patients were said to take up more time than patients with other sexually transmitted diseases, for a variety of reasons; and the second reason was that HIV testing, and pre-test and post-test counselling were also said to take up a great deal of time.

We were particularly concerned that, given the way the statistics are collected at the moment, there is no reliable way in which this type of work connected with people who may or may not have been at risk of HIV infection can be measured. We have already discussed some of the difficulties staff had in recording this kind of activity. We will discuss the activities of staff in pre-test and post-test counselling in the following chapter.

In this chapter we look at the balance of work between HIV/AIDS and traditional STDs reported by the doctors, and discuss some of the implications of the impact of work connected with HIV/AIDS on the clinics. However, it is very important to bear in mind the very limited experience the majority of clinics had with HIV/AIDS patients. Most of the work described in connection with HIV/AIDS is related to negative testing or to advice, education or information about HIV/AIDS

Balance of work

We asked the medical staff to give estimates of how their time was divided between traditional STDs and HIV/AIDS related work. It was not surprising, given the balance of conditions encountered in most of the clinics in this study, that the vast majority of the doctors spent most of their time on traditional STDs.

Nine out of ten doctors said that more than 60 per cent of their time was spent working with patients with traditional STDs, and eight out of ten said that more than 70 per cent of their time was spent on traditional STDs. Four doctors, three clinical assistants and an associate specialist, said that they *only* worked with STDs and did *no* HIV/AIDS related work at all.

Looking at the amount of time spent on HIV/AIDS related work therefore, we found that less than one fifth of the medical staff (17 doctors) spent more than 30 per cent of their time working on HIV/AIDS related work.

Of these, 9 doctors said that they spent between 30 and 50 per cent of their time on HIV/AIDS work. Four doctors said they spent roughly equal amounts of time on STD work and HIV/AIDS related work. Two of these were consultants in two of the largest clinics, while the other two worked in peripheral clinics – one in a training post and one as a clinical assistant.

Only four doctors, all working in the same large full-time clinic with a substantial proportion of HIV/AIDs work, said more than half of their work related to HIV/AIDS. Two doctors, both in training posts, said they spent around 60 per cent of their time on work related to HIV/AIDS, while a consultant spent around three-quarters of his time on HIV/AIDS. This clinic also had responsibility for the in-patient care of HIV/AIDS patients and junior medical staff rotated through the GUM clinic and the ward. One of the doctors we interviewed was based on the ward at the time of our fieldwork and *all* his time was spent working with HIV/AIDS patients.

Of the eight doctors who spent 50 per cent or more of their time working on HIV/AIDS related work, three were consultants, four were in training grades and one was a clinical assistant. As we have seen, five of the eight were from one big clinic.

A number of doctors commented that the time ratio tended to distort the numbers of patients they saw in connection with HIV/AIDS, since these patients took up more time on average than patients with other conditions.

We asked the doctors what they felt about the balance of their work. Around a third of them simply said that the balance reflected the workload of the clinic, while 42 per cent felt the balance between STD and HIV/AIDS work was about right and were happy with it. The majority of the medical staff (73 per cent), therefore, had no complaints about the balance of their work.

But around a fifth of the doctors (18 per cent) were somewhat unhappy with the balance. All but one of them said they did not do as much HIV/AIDS related work as they would like. The doctors in training posts were particularly likely to say they did insufficient HIV/AIDS work.

There were two reasons why these doctors were not working with HIV/AIDS patients as much as they would have liked. Firstly, in half the cases, it was simply because there were no patients, or few patients, with HIV/AIDS. One registrar, who spent 90 per cent of his time on traditional STDs, said: 'I'd like to spend more time on HIV. Basically, because I'm learning and we've not got that many HIV patients, I don't see many...'

But it was not only because there were few people with HIV infection in the locality that HIV/AIDS work was limited. Sometimes the GUM clinic had few HIV/AIDS patients because they were being seen by doctors in other specialties, as this consultant explained: 'I only do about 2 per cent HIV/AIDS work. It's a mistake. I personally think it shouldn't be hived off. I think it's very unfortunate what's happened here. When patients get AIDS, they go off to infectious diseases. The haematologists didn't want the homosexuals. So infectious diseases had the patients and their lovers came in. That happened until he was overburdened and then we got a connection going. The consultant in infectious diseases is a man on the make. HIV is an STD. It is part of GUM and we should ensure that our junior staff are well-trained in AIDS and HIV...'

The second reason why some medical staff were not doing as much HIV/AIDS work as they would have liked was because other members of the GUM staff were doing the majority of the HIV/AIDS related work, leaving them with little or none. One junior doctor working in a clinic with a relatively high proportion of HIV work spent more than 90 per cent of her time on traditional STDs. She said: 'The registrar and the consultant mainly do the HIV work. I'd like to do a bit more HIV. I'd like to gain more experience of handling and managing HIV patients. It's a new condition. It would be nice to get the confidence in dealing with all the problems they have...'

Only one doctor felt he did *too much* HIV/AIDS work. He worked in a busy teaching hospital with a high proportion of HIV/AIDS patients and spent around two-thirds of his time on HIV/AIDS related work. However, the doctor from this clinic who was working *only* with HIV/AIDS patients on the ward to which they were admitted was not unhappy with this balance as he recognised it was only a temporary arrangement and that his rotation would take him back to the GUM clinic.

Do HIV/AIDS patients make different demands?

We were initially interested in examining whether patients with HIV infection or with AIDS made different demands on GUM clinic staff from other patients attending the clinic, but it quickly became apparent that patients attending the clinic for HIV testing, who may have had negative results, also made different demands on staff. We therefore examined with all staff the question of the demands made both by HIV/AIDS patients and those who consulted the clinic about HIV infection.

Around three-quarters of the doctors and the health advisers (79 per cent and 73 per cent respectively), two-thirds of the nurses (66 per cent) and half of the administrative and clerical staff (48 per cent) said that HIV/AIDS patients or patients attending the clinic in relation to HIV *did* make different demands from other patients attending the clinic.

The main difference was that these patients took more time, for a variety of reasons. Firstly, staff commented that these patients needed more counselling, which inevitably took more time than a consultation for a patient with warts, for example. This health adviser described some of the differences: 'They definitely make different demands. They take more time for a start. You can spend hours with people and they make more emotional demands. You have to give more personally. With gonorrhoea, it's just, "This is how you got it and this is the cure". With HIV, there's so many questionmarks...'

Patients who were worried that they might have HIV and who wanted to be tested, as well as those who had actually been tested positive, tended to be more anxious than other patients attending the clinic and therefore needed more reassurance from clinic staff. The medical staff, as well as the administrative and clerical staff, were particularly likely to mention this. A clinical assistant said: 'People are very anxious. They see the advertisements on the television and then they go abroad. They don't have sex, but they get a pimple and they want a test. There's a total ignorance in some people and it floods the clinic. But you have to take a rational approach. You have to talk to them and counsel them to see if there's a logical basis for taking the test...'

Patients who were HIV positive or who had AIDS were also said to need more emotional support. The health advisers were particularly likely to cite the need of these patients for emotional support , and some found this emotionally demanding on a personal level. One said: 'It's a physical and mental drain compared to other situations. It just depends on how you're feeling on the day. If you feel OK, then you feel satisfied. But if you're hassled and then you see someone who's positive who has nowhere to sleep, you deal with it but your enthusiasm and motivation are not the same each time...'

But some patients who were *not* HIV positive were also emotionally demanding. Staff referred to patients who were convinced they were positive even though they had been tested, sometimes several times, and had received much counselling. These patients were thought to be particularly difficult to deal with, as a senior registrar explained:

> There's a proportion of worried well who you've counselled about their risk. There was a hard core of patients who thought they had cancer. They had a phobia and they were difficult to reassure. It flushes out a psychiatric element. It's brought out with HIV. Those people who thought they had cancer now think they have HIV. You know you have to get through a waiting room full of people, the nurses are on your heels and someone is trying to split hairs with you about the sex they had in Lanzarote. They've had two tests, both negative, and they still want to go through the risks and they say they don't feel well...

Consultations in connection with HIV/AIDS also involved giving not only more information but also more detailed and complex information. Many of the respondents said that patients with HIV/AIDS were often quite articulate and well-informed and questioned staff about tests, treatment and support. One consultant said: 'They need more time. They're generally well educated and so they ask pertinent questions that need thoughtful answers. They don't accept advice without questions. They also involve you in non-medical problems. The demands are reasonable but doctors aren't used to dealing with those types of demands...'

Some staff, particularly the medical staff, referred to the fact the patients who were HIV positive either wanted or needed immediate attention. Most staff were quite happy to give open access to these patients, but there was a minority who felt that patients with HIV/AIDS were being given special treatment at the expense of other patients.

The medical and nursing staff also said that patients with HIV/AIDS required more tests, and more complicated tests, than other patients, as well as requiring more treatments, some of a very different nature from other treatments administered in the clinic.

The medical staff and health advisers referred to HIV/AIDS patients' need for other services, such as benefits, housing and legal services. This required these staff, particularly the health advisers, to liaise with, and refer to, other services, departments or agencies. One health adviser said: 'There are often more social problems associated with them. Some people ask for an HIV test because there are other problems going on. So you're more involved in referring people to other departments or to other people. They have more baggage generally...'

Patients with HIV/AIDS also differed from other patients seen by the health advisers in that they required on-going care.

The staff interviewed accepted the fact that patients with HIV/AIDS *did* make different demands from other patients attending the clinic. This was seen to be appropriate in that these patients generally required extra care and treatment, and it was usually seen to be part of their jobs. HIV/AIDS patients were said to be much more time-consuming than other patients, and some staff, particularly the health advisers, felt that caring for these patients had made their jobs more interesting. But as many as half the health advisers said that working with HIV/AIDS patients was more stressful than working with other patients: 'It's very stressful, especially when you're doing it all day, every day. It's one after the other and it's tiring. It's a relief when you see someone with gonorrhoea...'

Some doctors said there was a danger of becoming more emotionally involved with HIV/AIDS patients, so that the doctor-patient relationship became rather less professional. One consultant said: 'In some areas, the professional barrier is lost. Colleagues attend funerals and yet with other patients we don't get emotionally involved. That doesn't mean we're not sympathetic. We like to get good care for them but we mustn't get emotionally involved...'

A small minority of all types of staff felt that patients with HIV/AIDS made too many demands and that the care of other patients suffered as a result. One consultant said: 'They can be demanding and somewhat manipulative. They require more time and they want it on their terms and when it suits them. Their demands are perforce of a different nature. For example, we may refer them to a chest physician, but again they want it on their own terms. I'm not sure whether that's due to the type of people, homosexuals or drug addicts, a certain type of personality, or whether it's due to the stress that any person would have. On the whole, I'd say it was more the type of person rather than the way others would react...'

Some felt that other patients within the GUM clinic were overlooked – 'they take staff away from non-HIV work' - but others referred to HIV/AIDS in relation to other terminal illnesses. A health adviser said: 'They are a demanding group and occasionally you feel you're being picked up and put down by them. You might have lots of contact and then nothing. You don't know whether things are working out for them. I also have this lingering feeling about all this money being ploughed into HIV/AIDS. Patients with other conditions deserve facilities too. For example, women with breast cancer need health advisers too. Health advisers used to be contact tracers but their position has developed. They could help other conditions too...'

Specialist staff working with HIV/AIDS patients

Given that many of the staff working in GUM clinics thought that patients with HIV/AIDS made different demands from other patients attending the clinic, we were interested in establishing whether they thought there should be staff who work *only* with HIV/AIDS patients. There were only two clinics where there were, in fact, staff who worked only with HIV/AIDS patients. One clinic had an HIV services nurse and an HIV receptionist and another clinic had HIV counsellors.

Around one fifth of the medical and administrative and clerical staff, and just under one fifth of the nursing staff, thought there *should* be staff who worked *only* with HIV/AIDS patients in GUM clinics. Only two of the 22 health advisers, however, agreed with them.

There were two main reasons why these respondents thought there should be staff who worked only with HIV/AIDS patients: firstly, because the professionals involved would become more skilled and knowledgeable about

HIV/AIDS; and secondly, they would have more time to deal with these patients. Some also said that separate specialist staff would provide continuity of care and support for patients with HIV/AIDS.

We were interested to know whether these respondents thought there were particular categories of staff who should be working only with HIV/AIDS patients. On the whole, they thought it appropriate to have specialist health advisers working only with HIV/AIDS patients, but most also thought there should be specialist medical and nursing staff. The nursing staff themselves were most likely to say that there should be specialist nurses who worked only with HIV/AIDS patients. All types of professional thought it was much less important that there were specialist administrative and clerical staff. But many of these respondents considered that separate staff could be justified only if there was a high number of patients with HIV/AIDS.

However, around three-quarters or more of each type of GUM clinic staff considered there should *not* be separate staff who worked only with HIV/AIDS patients in GUM clinics. The health advisers were the most likely to be opposed to separate and specialist staff.

One of the main reasons given by all categories of staff was that HIV *is* a sexually transmitted disease and, therefore, part of the remit of the GUM clinic. Related to this, many staff considered that *all* GUM staff should understand and work with HIV/AIDS patients. A senior registrar said: 'They should be combined. HIV is only a small minority of the work and it's part of the STDs. The majority of people get HIV because of their sexual practice and so heterosexuals and homosexuals should be screened for STDs. Those with HIV should be screened for STDs and STDs lead to HIV. So we should screen for both...' And a registrar commented: 'It's better for staff to have broader experience. HIV is a new thing but in 20 years time, it will be just another STD. So everyone needs the experience...'

On the other side of the coin, some staff said that patients with HIV/AIDS sometimes had other sexually transmitted diseases, and that all staff should understand STDs. One sister told us: 'You're still getting HIV positive patients coming in with sexually transmitted diseases and HIV/AIDS does come under the venereal act...' And a consultant said: 'At least part of the concern with HIV is concerned with sexuality. You need experience in GUM to be conversant with those aspects of their care. We've had gay men with syphilis where it hasn't been detected because staff caring for them have only attended to the HIV side and didn't look for other things. You really need a broader experience...'

The medical staff also felt that working only with HIV/AIDS patients would be too narrow and specialised and that there was a danger that this practice might split the specialty, which some said was already fairly small. One respondent said: 'I think it would split the specialty down the middle. I don't think we need specialised people...'

One of the ways in which HIV/AIDS patients differed from other GUM clinic patients was that some staff found it more stressful and more emotionally demanding working with terminally ill patients. This was another reason why some staff, particularly the doctors and health advisers, were opposed to the idea of staff who only worked with HIV/AIDS patients. It was feared that staff working under these conditions would soon suffer from 'burn-out'.

A senior registrar working in a clinic with a large proportion of HIV work said: 'I think having staff who only work with HIV/AIDS is a bad idea. If you do nothing but HIV, you're likely to get burnt out. Oncology splits the clinic work and other work for that reason. You'd get burnt out. It's a bad idea – I actively feel it's a bad idea. It's do-able if you split the job with a research job but if you do HIV clinically *all* the time, it's a nightmare. You couldn't do it. You feel as though someone's had you for breakfast! I've done it, before we had the policy on pre and post-test counselling with the health advisers...'

Some doctors also thought working only with terminally ill patients would be too depressing. One senior registrar said: 'People get drained by HIV work alone. It's good to go into an ordinary STD clinic and feel you've cured them and they've gone away happy. You need that for yourself. You get feedback from HIV patients but it's still a terminal illness...'

Some respondents were also opposed to the idea of separate staff because this would separate and segregate patients with HIV/AIDS and might lead to their further stigmatisation. In many cases, these staff were concerned about the protection of the patients with HIV/AIDS. One health adviser said: 'From the point of view of stigma and stereotype, it's good to mix GUM and HIV as a specialty. People feel safer within an STD centre because of the VD Act. They feel safer. There are not that many guidelines with HIV...' And another said: 'Politically, if they're different or special, it could have a negative effect on things. It could add to the stigma already associated with it...'

But some, like this staff nurse, felt there should not be separate staff because there should not be 'special' treatment for patients with HIV/AIDS: 'I don't really think they need special staff all the time. I don't really believe in all the preferential treatment they get actually. There are a lot of people who are a lot worse off and who get very little help. I do think they expect preferential treatment...'

A range of other reasons were cited, including the view that separate staff would create elites, would not be able to cover the GUM clinic when it was busy, and would find it boring or monotonous working only with HIV/AIDS patients.

We have already seen that the majority of the clinics in fact had very few HIV/AIDS patients. This was another main reason why many of the staff did not think there should be separate staff working with HIV/AIDS patients: they considered the small number of patients with HIV/AIDS was insufficient to justify separate staff.

Voluntary organisations and HIV/AIDS patients

Most of the clinics were aware of or involved with local voluntary organisations which worked with HIV/AIDS patients. These included local 'gay' support groups, local drug groups/needle and syringe exchange and locally based HIV/AIDS groups. Clinics also referred to local branches of national organisations, such as Body Positive, as well as local or regional AIDS Helplines. Even where there were no local voluntary organisations, staff referred to regional branches of Body Positive and regional AIDS Helplines.

Clinics in and around London cited more voluntary groups including the Terrence Higgins Trust, Mildmay Hospital, London Lighthouse, Body Positive, Positively Women, Landmark, Mainliners, Blackliners and Black HIV and AIDS Network (BHAN).

The extent of involvement between GUM clinics and the voluntary organisations varied widely and is discussed below. But it was rare for staff from voluntary organisations to work within GUM clinics; only three clinics reported that staff from voluntary organisations sometimes came into the GUM clinic. These included a gay group, a drugs group, an HIV/AIDS group and an organisation for victims of male rape.

We asked the medical, nursing and health advising staff about their views on the ways in which voluntary organisations worked with the clinic's HIV/AIDS patients.

Perhaps the first thing to note is that few of the doctors had much experience of working with voluntary organisations. The activity sheets completed by doctors indicated that only half of them had *ever* liaised with voluntary organisations and most of these did so relatively infrequently. The consultants were most likely to have had direct experience of working with voluntary groups; the clinical assistants were least likely to have done so.

More than a third of the medical staff, therefore, felt unable to comment on the ways in which voluntary organisations worked with the clinic's HIV/AIDS patients. These doctors usually said that they themselves had no contact with the voluntary organisations, but some said that there were no local groups and some said they had no HIV/AIDS patients.

Those who commented, however, were mainly positive about the voluntary organisations, which were said to offer a service which complemented the service offered by the GUM clinic. Their existence was thought to offer patients a variety of service, and one of their main advantages was that they provided on-going support to patients with HIV/AIDS. In this respect, some doctors said that the voluntary organisations provided a service which the GUM clinic could not, and a few said they would not be able to manage without the voluntary organisations. One senior registrar who worked in a large, full-time clinic with a significant amount of HIV/AIDS work said: 'They work extremely well and we use them very heavily. There's so little provision otherwise. The pressure on our team would be enormous otherwise. Their back-up is enormously helpful. However, the fact that we rely on them so much points out the inadequacies of a purely government funded system...'

But some doctors had negative views of voluntary organisations. They were criticised by some doctors as being opposed to conventional medicine, and were said to provide conflicting advice to patients. One consultant said:

> They can be of great help but they can sometimes be a hindrance in that voluntary organisations tend to be pressure groups and therefore tend to be biased...The pressure groups caused the problems with HIV testing. They were obsessive about confidentiality because they were worried about the return of discrimination and that it would lead to irrational behaviour. A lot of the arguments against HIV testing in medicine are amazingly devious. For example, when it was essential that a patient had an HIV test as a medical procedure, the local voluntary organisation said he shouldn't have it. They came out with convoluted and irrational arguments. People were brainwashed by what was said at the beginning. But it is *now* worth knowing that you're HIV positive from the patient's point of view. You can be helped. Their argument was that if everyone behaved as if they were positive, then they didn't need to know or have the test. That's not true now because we can help them and we know that positive people don't always behave as the pressure groups think they do...

Others said that voluntary organisations were aimed only at certain groups of patients, such as homosexuals or drug users. Support for other patients, such as heterosexual men with HIV infection for example, was said to be limited.

Nursing staff had very limited experience of working with voluntary organisations in relation to the clinic's HIV/AIDS patients. The majority had no experience at all. Only a third of the nurses recorded on their activity sheets that they had ever liaised with voluntary organisations. Most of these had only limited experience; only eight, mostly sisters or charge nurses, indicated that they had had direct experience of working with voluntary organisations, while enrolled nurses had generally not had any contact.

More than half of the nursing staff, therefore, felt unable to comment on voluntary organisations. Like the medical staff, however, those who were able to comment generally had a favourable view of voluntary organisations which were said to provide support for patients and services which the GUM clinic could not.

A minority of the nurses held negative views, although these tended to be nurses with little or no experience of working with voluntary organisations. One of the main concerns was the level of confidentiality maintained by voluntary organisations; around ten per cent of the nurses were worried about the possibility of patients being identified. One sister said:

> Not having them on my doorstep, it's a bit difficult to say. I'm not anti but I'm a bit sceptical about people who want to do voluntary work. You've got to know their background. I'd have to vet anyone who came here...I think it's difficult until you get rid of the stigma outside. People may talk. I'd like to think they've got a use but they must have some professional accountability along the line, especially on the confidentiality side of things. It's different in a small town, London is

very different. In a small town, people know things, you can't escape it. So you'd have to be very careful who you gave the information to. Do these people keep notes? Where are the notes held? Things like that...

The health advisers were the most likely to have had contact with voluntary organisations and the most likely to have views on them. Virtually all had liaised with voluntary organisations at some time, and as many as half of them indicated that they had had direct experience of working with voluntary organisations, making contact with such groups at least once a week.

Again, most of those who expressed an opinion made positive comments about voluntary organisations, saying that such groups provided a service which the GUM clinic could not, thereby offering a complementary service. One said: 'They offer services we can't, like befriending. They fill in the gaps in the service. They can provide a service that is good. They tend to be mainly gay men and that's useful because a lot of my clients are gay...'

Voluntary organisations were also said to provide ongoing support to patients. This comment was made most frequently by health advisers working in clinics with a high proportion of HIV/AIDS related work, who spent a considerable amount of time pre-test counselling but had little time for ongoing support of patients. A health adviser in one such clinic said: 'We couldn't do without them. We don't provide ongoing, long-term, emotional and psychiatric support, or at least we very rarely do. It would be impossible to see every patient I've seen who's tested positive on a long-term basis. We don't run support groups for patients and the voluntary groups can offer a lot to some people. They are so good, so important. It's very good for people to get support out of hospital. They may not be sick, their health may not be the major problem...'

Only three health advisers made negative comments about voluntary organisations. These comments were generally quite specific to a particular local voluntary organisation. One health adviser said: 'It depends on the voluntary group... It's a lot to do with personalities and motives... The local voluntary group seem to think they're the experts... They've got an ego. The consultant doesn't rate it highly... I don't trust them. I don't trust them to keep confidentiality. A couple of them are Fundamental Christians; they're good samaritans but they have bad attitudes to homosexuals. I wouldn't refer anyone to them...'

Overall, contact with voluntary organisations was limited. Health advisers were most likely to be involved in liaising with, or referring HIV/AIDS patients to, voluntary organisations, although a number of the consultants also had direct experience of working with such groups.

Most of those who offered an opinion made favourable comments about the way in which voluntary organisations worked with the clinics' HIV/AIDS patients. There was, however, a significant minority who had cause for concern about voluntary groups, some of which seemed to be based on beliefs about voluntary organisations rather than on hard experience. But there was no doubt that some respondents had observed poor practice by voluntary organisations and some had poor relationships with groups.

A minority of the medical and nursing staff were concerned about the amount of money that was being invested in HIV/AIDS. Some, like this consultant, questioned whether the money was being well spent: 'On the whole, the voluntary organisations are quite good. Not everybody who's HIV positive will want their help...I have a feeling that a lot of government money that's gone into HIV coordinators etc may have been wasted. People are doing counselling but it's difficult to get any feedback to see how useful it is. How useful is it? All this money has gone into it. It's politics on two levels – government and homosexuals. The government had these campaigns and said we've got to do these campaigns. The homosexual lobby got up on its hind legs and said, "We're going to be persecuted and pushed back into the closet". They behaved responsibly and it was a new situation. Personally I don't think it's meant that young heterosexual people have changed their lifestyles. How do we get to young people and show them the risks? Also I cannot see that homosexuals are going to change their sexual behaviour...'

And others were concerned that patients with HIV/AIDS were receiving a disproportionate amount of resources compared with other terminally ill patients. One nurse said: 'Any voluntary organisation that's able to help is good. But overall I feel that a lot of money is being put into AIDS at the expense of other things. For example, women with cancer of the cervix – where's the counselling to them? I feel that cancer and women's health is being neglected. There's no counselling there. Why should HIV patients be getting that at the expense of other areas of medicine? Cancer is terminal too...'

Partner notification/contact tracing

Contact tracing in connection with traditional sexually transmitted diseases has, of course, long been the responsibility of GUM clinics. However, the extent to which the nature of contact tracing has been changing over the past ten years or so would perhaps have gone unnoticed had it not been for the advent of HIV infection. The question of whether contact tracing or partner notification in the case of HIV positive infection is necessary, desirable or an intrusion into privacy has been the subject of much debate within the GU medicine specialty, although it has only recently hit the newspaper headlines.

We explored the views of GUM clinic doctors, nurses and health advisers on the question of contact tracing or partner notification in connection with both HIV/AIDS and in relation to all STDs. We found a broad spread of opinion, both within the groups of professionals and across the disciplines, and the results are presented in tabular form in Tables 9.2 and 9.3 for ease of reference. It can be seen that some respondents gave more than one answer, especially with regard to HIV/AIDS.

These questions elicited long and detailed answers, and few respondents were prepared to say that they were completely in favour of contact tracing in all cases, without adding some proviso. The days of 'knocking on doors' were frequently said to be over, whatever the condition. Partner notification in

Table 9.2   Views on partner notification/contact tracing in connection with HIV/AIDS

column percentages

	Doctors	Nurses	Health Advisers
Should be active PN/has to be done	22	18	5
Would encourage patients to take responsibility/voluntary basis	22	20	41
Active PN only with patients' consent	18	13	5
PN entirely up to patient	12	16	9
Mixed feelings/complex question	11	16	14
Would be difficult in practical terms	10	14	16
Would drive patients away/reduce no. tests	6	7	23
Haven't made up mind/in two minds	4	5	14
Should not be a legal requirement	3	0	9
Opposed to it	2	4	14
Opposed to it while no cure	1	2	14
Base: all respondents	*89*	*98*	*22*

connection with HIV/AIDS was thought to be a much more delicate and complex matter than contact tracing with other STDs.

Partner notification/contact tracing with HIV/AIDS
Table 9.2 shows that just over one fifth of the doctors, nearly one fifth of the nurses, but only 5 per cent of the health advisers thought there should be active partner notification with HIV/AIDS and that it had to be done. This contrasted sharply with two-thirds of the doctors and nurses and over half the health advisers who thought there should be active contact tracing with other STDs (Table 9.3).

Very few respondents took the unequivocal view of this consultant on HIV/AIDS partner notification: 'It's very important. I think personally that you shouldn't be allowed to have the test done unless you agree to have any contacts notified – and your GP and dentist – if you have a positive test...' His views were supported by a staff nurse in a small clinic: 'I think contact tracing has to be done with everything you see in a GU clinic. You only need one missing link and you've wasted all the work you've done...'

Most of those who considered partner notification essential said they would try to persuade patients to inform the contacts or partners themselves, but, if all else failed, they would regard partner notification by the clinic as necessary.

Around one fifth of doctors and nurses and over 40 per cent of health advisers said they would encourage patients to take the responsibility themselves to inform partners or contacts, but that it should be done purely on a voluntary basis. A junior doctor reflected the views of a number of younger doctors: 'I feel quite

Table 9.3 Views on partner notification/contact tracing in connection with all STDs

		column percentages	
	Doctors	Nurses	Health Advisers
Should be activePN/has to be done	67	66	55
Would encourage patients to take responsibility/voluntary basis	16	11	9
Active PN only with patients' consent	15	13	23
PN entirely up to patient	1	5	23
Should not be a legal requirement	1	0	0
Difficult in practical terms	0	2	0
Opposed to it	0	1	0
Mixed feelings/complex question	0	1	0
Base: all respondents	*89*	*98*	*22*

strongly that it's done with the full cooperation of the patient concerned. I wouldn't want to approach people whose name had been given to me as a possible partner. It's a breach of civil liberties of the person you're notifying...'

The question of the legality of partner notification with regard to HIV/AIDS was raised by a number of doctors and health advisers, and there appeared to be some confusion on the actual legal position. Some thought it would be a breach of confidentiality. One clinical assistant spoke of a colleague who had taken advice from the Medical Defence Union who had apparently said that there had been no precedent and they were unsure of the potential outcome if a patient brought a case against a doctor.

There was certainly a feeling among a further fifth (18 per cent) of the doctors that active partner notification should only take place with the patients' consent, but, again, health advisers were much less likely to agree. Their main aim, if they agreed with HIV/AIDS partner notification at all, was that the patient should be supported and encouraged to do it themselves.

Some health advisers described in detail how they went about ensuring the voluntary cooperation of the patients. Health advisers from the larger clinics usually had far more experience of the practicalities than those from the smaller clinics: 'It's the responsibility of the patients, but it's the responsibility of the health professionals to bring the subject up. When you pre-test counsel, you can find out about previous partners – who, how, when, where – and armed with that knowledge, when you give the result you can say, "Any thoughts about telling your partner?" It's mainly done by the individual. Most do – not those from years ago – but they're aware of recent, regular or current partners...'

Another health adviser from a large clinic pointed to the problems involved: 'I sit on the fence on that one. On the one hand, if you're talking about active partner notification, I'm not in favour. It's an infringement of human rights. However, we undertake informal and agreed partner notification. If a patient is positive and they have a regular partner, we will discuss the issue of partner notification. It will be discussed at pre-test and later. We discuss, "Will you tell him and how?" We will facilitate it. That's being undertaken. But actively, like syphilis and gonorrhoea, it's not on, even with the patient's permission, and definitely not without...'

Some nurses were also concerned about the lack of clarity of the legal position, and a staff nurse in a large clinic was worried about the spread of infection: 'I'm very disappointed with the way it's done here. Even if a patient walks in and is HIV positive or has AIDS and has all the information on their partners and says, "Can you tell them for me?" the patient is actually told it's against the law. Those people then suffer and the patient can't do it because they're sick...'

The importance of discussing partner notification at pre-test counselling was stressed by a number of health advisers and consultants. One consultant said that agreement that patients would notify partners was sought before testing, and that in some circumstances, if no agreement was given, the clinic would not do the test.

There was often disagreement within clinics, with consultants and other medical staff taking a different line from each other, and nursing staff and health advisers holding different views again. It was quite clear that there had been no exchange of views in some clinics. A staff nurse in a clinic where the consultant was strongly in favour of active partner notification in connection with HIV/AIDS was quite oblivious of his views, and explained her own: 'You can only appeal to people. The confidentiality bit comes into it. It's a two-edged sword, You must be fair to the partner, but what about the confidentiality you owe to your patient here? They're adults. We live in a democracy. You can't go around with a big whip...' Another nurse in a small clinic endorsed her view: 'You can't play God, unless children are involved...You try to do it in a nice way – try and bring pressure to bear on the patient to allow us to do it. But you can't march in and grab someone and say, "Your husband's got it". These people on the whole are very responsible...'

Around one in ten of the doctors and health advisers and one in six of the nurses thought that partner notification in connection with HIV/AIDS was entirely up to the patient. Interestingly this view was held by junior doctors more than by other medical staff. A registrar spoke for a number of his colleagues in other clinics: 'I don't think it's terribly important. It's not like people are totally uneducated. They know about the risks. My inclination is not to contact trace because of the issue of patient confidentiality...'

Around 10 per cent of the doctors, and a rather higher proportion of nurses and health advisers, held firm views that partner notification or contact tracing in connection with HIV/AIDS was simply impracticable, mainly because patients would not tell the truth or would not give all their contacts for a variety of reasons.

Others were concerned about not being able to cope with the potential influx of people requiring testing and counselling, as this health adviser in a large clinic explained: 'We haven't got enough resources to deal with the people involved if partner notification was introduced. I think the resources would be better spent on safer sex education. We couldn't deal with the increase in people with anxiety. While there is the stigma of HIV testing, problems with insurance and limited resources, it's not practical...'

There was a strong fear among health advisers in particular that partner notification would drive patients away and would reduce the number of tests, although this view was held by far fewer doctors and nurses: 'Ultimately it shouldn't be forced by law on people or health professionals. It wouldn't work and would drive it underground...' A consultant in another clinic agreed: 'I would presume it's unworkable. It would push people underground and make things more difficult...'

The question of guaranteed confidentiality for patients was uppermost in the minds of many health advisers, and a number of them were opposed to any idea of partner notification other than on a purely voluntary basis by the patient. Some expressed the view that while no cure for AIDS was possible at present, partner notification was not appropriate, although some doctors thought that advances in drug treatment had made it more important for contacts to be approached. An HIV counsellor disagreed: 'There shouldn't be any partner notification. People prefer not to know. We can't offer treatment or cure. It increases stress and anxiety. We should leave well alone. We would be breaking confidences. We can't *treat* or *control* infection. Therefore the 1974 Act does not allow contact tracing of HIV...'

There was a strong indication that many staff would welcome more discussion and clearer guidelines on partner notification in connection with HIV/AIDS, although there were fears that too much public discussion, fuelled by ill-informed views of the necessity of partner notification, might be counter-productive. (Since the present report was prepared, the Department of Health has issued guidance on partner notification for HIV infection (Department of Health, 1992)).

An experienced health adviser from a large clinic reflected the views of others faced with a changing scene: 'There are lots of issues which need to be discussed in more detail. My views have changed in the last year. It's an extremely sensitive area and it needs a lot more discussion before guidelines are produced and rushed into. It depends on the total cooperation of the patient. If that's not given, you can't do *any* partner notification. So it has to be handled very carefully. It already happens informally, through the patient...'

The need for more guidelines on partner notification in connection with HIV/AIDS was also noted in a recent study on the attitudes of 105 consultant physicians and 141 health advisers working in GUM clinics to tracing and notifying contacts of people with HIV infection (Keenlyside et al, 1992). It was found that 63 per cent of all respondents had available written guidelines for counselling HIV infected patients, usually drawn up by the clinic staff, only 24 per cent of which contained recommendations for notifying partners.

That study also noted the reluctance of both health advisers and physicians to become closely involved themselves in partner notification in connection with HIV/AIDS. Health advisers were particularly likely to think that informing contacts was of no value in controlling the epidemic, and would deter clinic attendance, threaten confidentiality, undermine the professional-client relationship and make informed contacts unnecessarily anxious. It was interesting that the health advisers in the Thames regions, which had the highest incidence of HIV/AIDS, were the most sceptical of the desirability of partner notification programmes. This finding was confirmed in the present study, in which we found that the health advisers in the clinics with a large number of HIV/AIDS patients were the most reluctant to become involved in 'active' partner notification in connection with HIV/AIDS.

Partner notification/contact tracing with other STDs

It was clear that the GUM clinic staff held very mixed views about partner notification with regard to HIV/AIDS. As Table 9.3 shows, staff were much more united as far as contact tracing in general was concerned, but, even so, there were many provisos concerning different types of STDs. Although the majority of all types of staff thought that active contact tracing was necessary to ensure infection control, there was strong support among all professionals for patients to take the responsibility for informing contacts and partners, and for contact tracing to take place only with the patients' full cooperation.

Health advisers went further, and a quarter of those interviewed thought that partner notification for all STDs should be entirely the responsibility of the patient. Health advisers interviewed for this study had certainly moved a long way from the contact tracers of the traditional STD clinic.

There was no doubt that many staff held quite different views about partner notification or contact tracing for traditional STDs from those they held about HIV/AIDS, summarised by a consultant: 'With STDs it has worked reasonably well. It's a treatable condition. People with the condition know it's treatable and do not mind the contact tracing. It's different from HIV...'

The traditional aim of infection control was adhered to strongly by some of the older doctors – 'For syphilis, gonorrhoea and chlamydia it's routine. We trace those religiously. We existed for this originally...'

But some younger doctors were much less directive, as this junior doctor explained: 'The day of knocking on doors and anonymous letters has gone. That shouldn't be our job. You explain to the patient the nature of the infection, the risk of reinfection and work through that. You can apply strong persuasion...'

Clinical assistants often agreed that 'knocking on doors' should be the 'last resort', and these views were endorsed by nurses from many clinics, like this enrolled nurse: 'The clinics shouldn't be actively involved in writing people letters and so on. It must be awful to receive letters or be called on...'

Health advisers, as we have seen, were often reluctant to become involved in 'active' contact tracing, but tried to involve the patient as much as possible, like this health adviser in a large busy clinic: 'It's obviously very important. I worry about how we go about doing it. We've got our priorities wrong. I don't like being seen as medical police – knocking on doors. It's got to be up to the index case to take it on with health education. We're educational, not punitive...'

The move towards education and helping the patient to take and feel responsibility for informing contacts was marked among the health advisers interviewed and, perhaps to a lesser extent, among the doctors and nursing staff. There were certainly strong indications that, although infection control was seen as an important function of contact tracing, the days of active contact tracing appeared to be over.

In-patient care of HIV/AIDS patients

We collected a great deal of information about the care of patients with HIV/AIDS. We have already noted that the majority of the clinics had very few patients with HIV/AIDS, and that only the large, full-time clinics had much experience of working with these patients.

We were particularly interested in examining the care and treatment of HIV/AIDS patients admitted to hospital. But where did they go? There was a wide variety of practice:

- 9 clinics reported that their HIV/AIDS patients were admitted to the *same* hospital in which the GUM clinic was located. This should have allowed easy liaison between the GUM clinic staff and the in-patient team but, as we shall see, this did not always happen.
- 6 clinics reported that HIV/AIDS patients were admitted to a *different* hospital from the one in which the GUM clinic was based
- patients attending the 2 clinics based in the community were admitted to a local hospital
- 3 clinics reported that the hospital to which their HIV/AIDS patients were admitted varied: sometimes the same hospital as the one in which the clinic was based and sometimes a different hospital.

The wards to which the HIV/AIDS patients were admitted varied even more:

- patients from 7 clinics were admitted to a general medicine ward
- patients from 5 clinics were admitted to the infectious diseases ward
- patients from 2 clinics were admitted to the respiratory/chest ward
- patients from 1 clinic were admitted to the haematology ward
- patients from 2 clinics were admitted to wards with mixed use: one to a general medicine and infectious diseases ward, and one to a ward that was used for haematology, oncology and respiratory patients
- in 2 clinics, the ward to which HIV/AIDS patients were admitted varied depending on what the patient's symptoms were: they might be admitted to the respiratory, neurology or infectious diseases ward

- patients from the last clinic were admitted either to the infectious diseases ward or to the HIV/AIDS and infectious diseases ward. This was the only hospital which had a designated ward for HIV/AIDS patients (albeit combined with infectious diseases).

But if most hospitals did not have a designated ward for HIV/AIDS patients, did they have designated beds? Only three of the clinics reported that the hospital to which HIV/AIDS patients were admitted had designated beds for these patients. One hospital had two designated beds and one had six. The other was the hospital which had a designated HIV/AIDS ward with 24 designated HIV/AIDS beds.

Five of the 20 clinics reported that at least one of their HIV/AIDS patients was an in-patient at the time of our study: three clinics had one in-patient and one clinic had two HIV/AIDS in-patients. The fifth clinic was the large, full-time clinic with the designated HIV/AIDS ward, and, at the time of our study, there were 16 in-patients with HIV/AIDS who were registered with the GUM clinic. There were seven additional HIV/AIDS in-patients in the hospital but these were registered with the infectious diseases team.

The specialty of the consultant(s) responsible for in-patient care of HIV/AIDS patients varied almost as much as the type of ward to which they were admitted:

- 6 clinics reported that chest/respiratory physicians managed the in-patient care of their HIV/AIDS patients
- in 3 hospitals it was managed by a consultant in infectious diseases
- in 3 hospitals it was managed by a consultant haematologist
- in 1 hospital it was managed by a consultant general physician
- in 6 hospitals responsibility for HIV/AIDS in-patients varied, depending on the ward to which the patient was admitted and the patient's symptoms. In these hospitals, general physicians, chest physicians and infectious diseases consultants were often involved, though mentions were also made of gastroenterologists, neurologists, nephrologists and micro-biologists
- in the last clinic, patients were managed either by the GUM team or by the infectious diseases (immunology) team. This was the only clinic where the GUM clinic staff were responsible for managing the in-patient care of their HIV/AIDS patients

Given that only one clinic was responsible for the in-patient care of its HIV/AIDS patients, we were interested in exploring whether GUM staff generally had any input into the in-patient care of HIV/AIDS patients, what the nature of this input was, and which staff were involved. We put these questions to the medical staff and the health advisers.

The out-patient GUM team had an input into the in-patient care of HIV/AIDS patients in 13 of the 20 clinics. The staff of four clinics had no input, and three clinics had no HIV/AIDS patients and so the situation had not arisen.

Medical staff were the most likely staff to have an input into the in-patient care. Consultants were more often involved, although the doctors in training grades were often involved as well. Clinical assistants did not have a role to play in in-patient care.

Health advisers were quite likely to have an input into the in-patient care of HIV/AIDS patients and 14 of the 22 health advisers interviewed said they were involved in in-patient care to a greater or lesser extent. This represented staff from 8 of the 14 clinics which had a health adviser.

The GUM nursing staff were less likely to play a part in the in-patient care of HIV/AIDS patients; the sister/charge nurse from five clinics had some involvement, while one clinic had an HIV nurse who was involved.

The medical staff were usually involved in visiting patients on the ward, attending ward rounds and offering medical advice on the care of these patients. The health advisers also visited patients on the ward, where they offered on-going support and counselling to patients. Where nursing staff were involved, they offered nursing advice on the care of HIV/AIDS patients.

In the GUM clinic which had *full* responsibility for the in-patient care of their HIV/AIDS patients, medical staff and health advisers, as well as the HIV nurse, were actively involved in the care of HIV/AIDS patients admitted to hospital.

We were interested in examining whether there were any problems in liaising or working with the in-patient team. In many cases, patients were admitted to the hospital in which the GUM clinic was located, so there should not have been problems of access and geographic location.

In clinics where GUM staff had an input into the in-patient care, one third of the medical staff, and almost half of the health advisers, said there were problems in liaising with the in-patient team. (This represented around one fifth of all the medical staff interviewed and a quarter of all the health advisers.)

Medical staff were most likely to complain about the lack of liaison and communication between the consultant(s) responsible for in-patient care and themselves. One registrar said: 'We don't have any set rules about when to refer our patients to them, at what stage of the disease. And there are no rules about when they should be referred back to us when they have recovered from their bout of illness...'

Some, however, complained of the lack of coordination between medical staff and other professionals involved. One consultant said: 'There are different teams and they're all still jockeying for position. It's early days. The problem of a multidisciplinary approach is that you need a strong leader who consults widely and it's quite hard to pull that off...'

The doctors in one GUM clinic said that they had difficulty gaining access to beds for HIV/AIDS patients, even though there were designated HIV/AIDS beds. And the doctors in another clinic complained that patients were admitted to a hospital some distance away, so that access to patients and liaison with the in-patient team was difficult. Others said the involvement of the GUM team in the in-patient care of HIV/AIDS patients was too limited.

The health advisers also complained of a lack of communication and liaison between the in-patient team and the GUM team. A couple, however, reported problems of access because of the geographic locations of the GUM clinic and the ward or hospital to which patients were admitted.

But even though at least some of the staff in 13 of the 20 GUM clinics were involved in the in-patient care of HIV/AIDS patients, it is clear that this kind of involvement was by no means standard. What about the other clinics? We have already seen that the staff of three clinics were not involved because there had been no HIV/AIDS in-patients. But the staff of four other clinics had not had any input, even though there had been in-patients with HIV/AIDS.

There were mixed views among the staff of these clinics on whether they should have been involved in the in-patient care of HIV/AIDS patients. The medical staff often said that their lack of input was appropriate, as they had neither the time nor the resources to become involved in caring for HIV/AIDS patients admitted to hospital.

But the health advisers, as well as a minority of the doctors, thought the GUM team should be involved. One senior registrar said: 'I find that very lacking. I'd like to change that soon so we're more involved in the in-patient care. We have no involvement, there is no management. When patients are discharged, the infectious diseases consultant continues with them which is not very good. At my previous hospital, GUM clinic staff could do ward rounds and patients returned to the GUM clinic when they were discharged...'

There was certainly a wide variation in the extent to which GUM clinic staff were involved in the in-patient care of HIV/AIDS patients. Much appeared to depend on personal contact and good relations between the relevant consultants, as well as the extent to which the GUM consultants took a particular interest in HIV/AIDS. There was evidence that a multidisciplinary approach was hard to achieve, particularly where there were few patients. The question of 'ownership' in such cases sometimes led to patients with HIV/AIDS being lost to the GUM clinic which had originally diagnosed and treated them.

10 Counselling

The extent to which the staff provided counselling, and their interpretation of what counselling meant, varied greatly among the different types of staff. We distinguished between counselling in connection with HIV/AIDS and counselling patients with other conditions, and asked clinic staff whether they were involved in either type of counselling.

All the health advisers, all but five of the doctors (a staff physician and four clinical assistants), and two-thirds of the nursing staff said they provided counselling in the clinic. However, not all these staff provided counselling in connection with HIV/AIDS and not all provided counselling to patients with other conditions.

Definition of counselling

We asked all the medical, nursing and health advising staff how they would describe what they meant by counselling. We were aware that the word counselling means different things to different people, and that it certainly carries different connotations for different types of professionals. This came through very clearly in a study of counselling in connection with termination of pregnancy, sterilisation and vasectomy (Allen, 1985), in which medical staff had very different views from social workers or from lay counsellors, and all three groups had different views from nursing staff. Training in counselling was an important factor in modifying definitions of counselling, but, even so, there appeared to be something inherent in the original training of professional workers, as well as in the role they saw themselves undertaking in a consultative or counselling setting, which affected the way different professionals interpreted counselling.

Table 10.1 summarises the definitions the GUM clinic staff gave to counselling. Clearly some staff used a number of different categories, but the reader can see at a glance the relative proportions of each type of staff describing counselling in different ways. These are arrived at by an analysis of their answers to an open-ended question.

The table is constructed by giving first the order of 'definitions' given by the health advisers, who were the staff most involved in counselling. It can be seen that the most frequent comment made by health advisers was that counselling meant listening to patients. This was mentioned by 50 per cent of the health

Table 10.1 How respondents described what they meant by counselling

column percentages

	Health advisers	Doctors	Nurses
Listening to patients	50	21	61
Information giving	41	54	33
Support/reassurance	32	24	13
Sympathy/empathyacceptance	27	6	10
Helping patient solve/ come to terms with problems	23	21	15
Enabling patient to make informed decision	23	21	15
Education	23	16	8
Advising patient	18	21	20
Discussion	14	17	6
Not directive	14	9	7
Base: all respondents	*22*	*89*	*98*

advisers, and was by far the most frequent definition given by nurses (61 per cent), but, interestingly, by only one fifth of the doctors.

Medical staff, on the other hand, were much more likely to define counselling as information giving. Over half the doctors, compared with 41 per cent of the health advisers and only one third of the nurses, thought that counselling was primarily a matter of giving practical information.

The difference between the three types of staff was clearly shown in the next category, with one third of the health advisers saying that counselling involved giving support and reassurance, compared with a quarter of the medical staff and only just over one in ten of the nurses. There was an even greater gap in the next category, with over a quarter of the health advisers thinking that counselling involved sympathy and acceptance, compared with only 6 per cent of the doctors and 10 per cent of the nurses.

The differences between professionals demonstrated in these first four categories were striking. Essentially, health advisers were much more likely to define counselling as listening to patients with sympathy and offering reassurance than the doctors were. Counselling, in the view of medical staff, was much more a matter of giving the patient practical information and advice. Nurses, on the other hand, were more likely to stress the need to listen to the patients, to hear what they were saying, and then to proceed from there. What was interesting, of course, was the extent to which health advisers were more likely than medical and nursing staff to talk about counselling in terms of sympathy or acceptance and being non-judgmental. The emotional side of counselling was not something with which doctors and nurses appeared particularly familiar – or comfortable.

However, there were obviously doctors and nurses who had thought deeply about counselling and stressed its emotional and non-judgmental elements. Some doctors were keen to establish that they saw counselling as a two-way process. A clinical assistant defined it as 'a dialogue with the client or patient aimed primarily at helping them to understand what they perceive to be the problem, and acting upon those feelings that they themselves see appropriate for the problem. It's partly information and partly helping the patient make the right decision for themselves – an *informed* decision...'

A consultant went into detail about his understanding of the term 'counselling' and described his practice: 'Counselling is an open discussion with a patient about a condition and their lifestyle. It's a two-way thing. It's not a question of you giving advice. The patient should be talking as much as you do. You should allow them every opportunity to question you as they feel the need. Every patient I see, man or woman, there's routinely a discussion of HIV irrespective of what condition they have. You need no special skills. You must be sympathetic and compassionate. The knowledge can be picked up quite easily...'

Another consultant emphasised the need to show empathy with the patient, but underlined the information and advice-giving role of doctors: 'Very simply, counselling is giving advice in a humane, compassionate and professional way. I'd put *humane* first. I've been counselling for twenty years now. Humane, non-judgmental and expert advice – a very important job...'

Nurses used the word 'listening' far more than any other professional, like this nurse in a large clinic: 'I think it's listening to everything they've got to say, and then gently asking questions to find what's underlying what they say. It's very intuitive. Sometimes you could offer practical advice and discuss it. It gives them a chance to open up. Once they have, and they understand what you say, you can try to help them resolve it...' Her view was supported by a nurse in a much smaller clinic: 'Someone can offload a problem without you necessarily giving advice. It's a listening role – a supporting role. It's not critical in any way...'

Just over one fifth of all types of staff thought that counselling involved helping patients solve or come to terms with their problems, and a similar proportion of health advisers and doctors thought it meant enabling patients to make an informed decision, a view less frequently held by nursing staff.

The importance attached by health advisers to their educational role was indicated by the fact that nearly a quarter of them stressed education as part of their definition of counselling, something which was much less frequently mentioned by doctors, and even less often by nurses. Advising patients was mentioned in connection with counselling by around one fifth of all types of staff.

Discussion was mentioned again more by health advisers and doctors. The idea that counselling should be non-directive was mentioned rather more by health advisers than other staff, perhaps reflecting the fact that more of them had been on counselling courses, where the non-directive nature of counselling is often stressed.

Some health advisers distinguished between different types of counselling for different conditions. This health adviser in a busy clinic with relatively few HIV positive patients explained: 'I separate HIV and other counselling. STD counselling is really interviewing, not counselling. I'm giving them information about the disease and how it's spread and they give me information about contacts. But I don't count that as counselling. With HIV – it's listening initially and helping them to talk through their worries. I get their understanding of HIV and if they can't explain or tell me, I explain it to them. I then go back to letting them tell me their story. It's mainly listening, but prompting them and helping them go through it...'

Another health adviser thought that counselling in a GUM clinic was probably rather different from 'pure' counselling: 'Pure counselling is somehow working with someone in an equal capacity to facilitate change that is appropriate. In this job it involves advice, education and information – which isn't counselling. This job contains a lot of advice and information-giving which is sometimes called counselling, but I don't think it is...'

Other components of counselling included eliciting information from the patient, referral to other staff or agencies, counselling about relationships and 'persuasion'.

The difference between the groups of staff was striking and undoubtedly influenced their answers to the questions we asked them subsequently about counselling. It helps to put into perspective the responses of doctors who said that *all* their work involved counselling when they defined counselling as giving information and advice. It shows how difficult it is for a nurse to say that she counsels or does not counsel if she defines counselling as listening to patients. It shows how superficial the concept of 'HIV counselling' is when GUM clinic staff have so many different definitions of what counselling means.

The following chapter gives a factual background to what staff said they were doing in GUM clinics in terms of counselling patients. But in reading this account, it must always be borne in mind that much depended on their definition of counselling, and that there was a very wide spread of counselling techniques, let alone practice, within these clinics. If the 'counselling' offered by voluntary agencies and other professionals is added to this mixture, it can be seen that there was a clear recipe for confusion and potential bad practice in the delivery of counselling services to very vulnerable groups of people.

Staff involved in HIV/AIDS counselling

All the health advisers, and almost all the medical staff (89 per cent), said they provided counselling for patients attending the clinic with, or in relation to, HIV/AIDS.

The consultants and doctors in training grades were all involved in HIV/AIDS counselling, and so were more than three-quarters of the clinical assistants, but only one of the three doctors in non-consultant career grades provided counselling in relation to HIV/AIDS.

The nursing staff were less likely to be involved in HIV/AIDS counselling, although one third of them (33 per cent) said they were. More than half of the sisters/charge nurses/clinical nurse specialists provided HIV/AIDS counselling, compared with 24 per cent of the enrolled nurses.

Staff involved in counselling for other conditions

All the health advisers, and almost all the medical staff (91 per cent), also provided counselling for patients attending the clinic with other conditions. Only eight doctors, (one consultant, one registrar, one staff physician and five clinical assistants), said they were not involved in counselling for other conditions.

Nursing staff were twice as likely to provide counselling for patients with other conditions as they were to provide HIV/AIDS counselling (66 per cent compared with 33 per cent). But they were less involved in counselling than the medical staff and health advisers.

Extent of counselling role

We were interested to know what proportion of their time these staff spent on counselling and the extent to which it was a major part of their job. We also wanted to establish how much of this time was spent on HIV/AIDS counselling and how much on counselling patients with other conditions.

Health advisers

All the health advisers were involved in counselling and, as might have been expected, they spent a higher proportion of their time counselling patients than other clinic staff did. There were, however, wide variations in the time spent by different health advisers, ranging from one who said she spent around 15 per cent of her time counselling, to one who said she spent *all* her time counselling. On average, however, the health advisers said they spent around *half* their time counselling patients.

There were also wide variations among health advisers in the balance of their counselling work between counselling patients about HIV/AIDS and counselling patients about other conditions. Three of the 22 health advisers said that around a quarter of the counselling they did related to HIV/AIDS, while, at the other end of the spectrum, one said that *all* the counselling she did related to HIV/AIDS. On average, health advisers spent 60 per cent of their counselling time on HIV/AIDS-related issues and 40 per cent on *other* conditions or problems.

Medical staff

Although almost all the doctors were involved in counselling, they spent less time on it than the health advisers. On average, doctors of all grades spent around a quarter of their time counselling patients attending the clinic.

A small proportion of the doctors, however, were unable to indicate how much of their time was spent counselling. This was because they felt their counselling role was bound up with other aspects of their job, and they felt unable to separate it from these other activities. One consultant said: 'I don't separate counselling from consultation. Every consultation in my position has a large element of counselling. It's a very large proportion. Even taking a history is counselling in my view...'

Unlike the health advisers, the doctors usually spent more time counselling patients with *other* conditions, rather than about HIV/AIDS: around two-thirds of the time they spent counselling related to *other* conditions, while one third related to HIV/AIDS. Again, however, there were wide variations between the different clinics, some of which were related to the different interpretations given by doctors to the meaning of counselling. Five doctors said they did no counselling in relation to HIV/AIDS, while three said that *all* the time they spent counselling related to HIV/AIDS, in that they discussed this condition with *all* their patients. Similarly, a small number of the doctors were unable to split the time they spent counselling between HIV/AIDS counselling and counselling other patients because the two were so closely intertwined, as one consultant explained: 'Most people with other conditions want to talk about HIV as well, so the HIV-related counselling includes STD queries about HIV...'

Nursing staff

Around two-thirds of the nursing staff said they provided counselling to patients. While there were variations between the clinics, the nurses who were involved in counselling spent around a quarter of their time counselling in the clinic. Like the doctors, however, a small proportion of the nurses felt unable to say how much of their time was spent counselling. One staff nurse explained why: 'That's impossible to say. I spend an awful lot of time when I'm painting people's warts chatting to them about all sorts of things. I know they look on me as a counsellor...'

The nurses were most likely to provide counselling to patients about *other* conditions, rather than counselling in relation to HIV/AIDS. Half the nurses who were involved in counselling did no HIV/AIDS counselling. And even those who provided HIV/AIDS counselling spent a much greater proportion of their time counselling patients about other conditions than in relation to HIV/AIDS.

Training in counselling

Given that all the health advisers, all but five of the doctors and two-thirds of the nurses were involved in counselling patients attending the clinic, we were interested in examining how much training in counselling they had received.

Health advisers

All but one of the 22 health advisers had attended a training course in counselling. The 'health adviser' who had *not* attended a course was, in fact, the HIV/AIDS support nurse/infection control who assisted the specialist health visitor to the GUM/AIDS coordinator. While these two respondents were not 'true' health advisers, they were fulfilling the health advising role in the clinic in which they worked. The HIV/AIDS support nurse was relatively new in her job and had not received any training in counselling at the time we interviewed her, although she wanted to attend a general counselling course.

Six of the 21 health advisers had attended just one counselling course, seven had attended two courses and six had attended three or four courses. Two health advisers said they had attended 'numerous' counselling courses.

Half of the health advisers (11) had attended a general counselling course, while three had taken a diploma in counselling. One of these respondents had attended a general counselling course as well as taking a counselling diploma. Overall, therefore, 13 of the health advisers had had a general counselling training course. These had been organised by a variety of organisations including district and regional health authorities, the Central School of Counselling and Therapy/the Centre for the Advancement of Counselling (CSCT/CAC), and various educational institutions.

Fifteen of the health advisers had attended a course on HIV/AIDS counselling. In most cases, this was a specific HIV/AIDS counselling course, although sometimes it formed part of a general HIV/AIDS course. Nine of them had been on a course organised by the National AIDS Counselling Training Unit (NACTU), but others had attended courses organised by St Mary's or St Stephen's Hospitals in London, or the Terrence Higgins Trust.

Three health advisers had received training associated with a voluntary organisation: bereavement counselling (CRUSE), relationship counselling (Relate) and counselling for drug users. Two had attended a course on motivation therapy, two had attended a course on dealing with aggression, anxiety or depression and one had attended a course on psychosexual counselling.

The length of the counselling courses ranged from a two year full-time course to a one day course. The majority, however, had attended courses that lasted between one and five days.

The health advisers were generally positive about the courses they had attended. But it was notable that many of the courses did not result in a certificate or qualification. Eighteen of the 21 health advisers had attended one or more courses which were not certificated, while one had received only a letter of attendance following a course.

Less than half the health advisers (9) had attended a certificated course, while three had attended a course which had resulted in a diploma. However, nine had attended counselling courses but had received neither a diploma nor certificate for any of them.

Medical staff

While almost all the doctors were involved in counselling patients in the clinic, only just over one third said they had had any training in counselling (36 per cent). Training in counselling had been received by:

- 52 per cent of the consultants and two of the three non-consultant career grades
- 27 per cent of the clinical assistants
- 19 per cent of the doctors in training grades

Nearly three-quarters of the doctors who had received training in counselling had attended only one course (23 of the 32 doctors), but seven had attended two courses, one consultant had attended three courses and one clinical assistant had attended four courses.

Two-thirds of the doctors who had had training had attended a course on HIV/AIDS counselling (representing around a quarter of *all* the doctors interviewed). These doctors had most commonly received their training from St Mary's Hospital, Paddington, but two had received it from St Stephen's Hospital, two from Westminster Hospital and one had attended a NACTU course.

One doctor, a clinical assistant, who had attended two HIV/AIDS counselling courses, had also attended training courses on vasectomy counselling and counselling in relation to termination of pregnancy, all organised by the Family Planning Association.

Seven doctors had received training in psychosexual counselling, while one had taken a diploma in psychological medicine. This training was most commonly organised by the Institute of Psychosexual Medicine. Five of the doctors had received training in counselling generally.

The doctors had generally attended one, two or three-day courses, though four had attended a one week course and five had received part-time training over a one to two year period. They were generally positive about the training they had received, but 29 of the 32 doctors had not gained a qualification of any kind from the courses. Only two had received a diploma and one had attained Membership of the Institute of Psychosexual Medicine.

However, around two-thirds of the medical staff had not received any training in counselling. These doctors were divided equally between those who said they would like training in counselling and those who did not want any, mainly because they thought they did not need training of this sort, or they were too experienced to need it or they did not have time to attend training courses.

Around a third of all the doctors interviewed, therefore, had not had any training in counselling but wanted some. The most common request was for a basic course in counselling generally, but a third of these doctors wanted training in HIV/AIDS counselling. Two requested training in psychosexual counselling.

Nursing staff

The nurses were less likely to say they provided counselling in the clinic than the health advisers or doctors; two-thirds of them said they were involved in counselling. But they were rather more likely than the doctors to have received training in counselling: 40 per cent of the nursing staff who were engaged in counselling said they had had some training in it. Nearly three-quarters of the sisters/charge nurses/clinical nurse specialists involved in counselling had had training in counselling, compared with 42 per cent of the staff nurses and 19 per cent of the enrolled nurses. Two-thirds of the nurses who had had training had attended only one course, but seven nurses had attended two courses and three had attended three courses.

Half of the nurses who had received training in counselling had attended general counselling courses, usually organised by the hospital or by the district health authority, although some had attended an educational institution and a small number had attended a CSCT/CAC course.

A further four nurses had received training in counselling as part of a course for health advisers, while two had received it during their training to become a registered mental nurse.

Around two-fifths of the nurses who had received training had attended a course specifically on HIV/AIDS counselling. (This represented just under one fifth of all the nurses interviewed.) These courses were organised by a variety of organisations including the district health authority, St. Mary's Hospital, Paddington, a voluntary organisation or an educational institution.

Three nurses had received training in bereavement counselling, one had had training in psychosexual counselling and one had had training to counsel women about breast cancer.

Most of the courses attended were one, two or three day courses, though four nurses had been on a one week course and four had been on longer full-time courses, lasting two months, six months, one year and 18 months respectively. Similarly, four nurses had been on part-time courses over a 12-18 month period.

Like the doctors and health advisers, the nurses were generally positive about the courses they had attended, but almost three-quarters of them had not received either a diploma, certificate or even a letter of attendance following the course. Only five had received a letter of attendance and only six had received a certificate.

Of the 60 per cent of the nursing staff who had not received any training in counselling, as many as three-quarters said they would like some. (This represented 47 per cent of all the nurses interviewed.) More than two-thirds of them simply wanted a basic course in counselling generally, while a quarter wanted training in HIV/AIDS counselling specifically.

Support and supervision in counselling role

The question of support and supervision in counselling was an important part of this study. There was a clear distinction drawn in the interview between support in the counselling role and supervision in the counselling role. This distinction was not always clearly understood by the staff, however.

Support and supervision for the health advisers

The health advisers, who were the staff most involved in counselling patients attending the clinic, were the most likely to receive *support* in their counselling role; three-quarters of them said they received support, usually from another health adviser or a senior health adviser in the clinic.

Where there was only one health adviser in the clinic, support was usually received from the consultant or from a professional outside the clinic, such as a clinical psychologist or an HIV/AIDS coordinator, or from colleagues outside the clinic. Some health advisers received no support at all.

The support was most commonly informal, involving discussion about patients or mutual support between health advisers. But some received more formal types of support. The health advisers in two of the large, full-time clinics with a high proportion of HIV/AIDS related work all attended a support group. One of these groups was for the health advisers only and was run by a professional facilitator. The other was for key HIV/AIDS workers in the hospital and was attended by other health care workers, as well as the health advisers. This group was also run by an independent facilitator. Four health advisers had access to a clinical psychologist for emotional support.

However, some health advisers received much better support than others, particularly in the larger clinics. Some of these had the support of other health advisers in the clinic as well as a clinical psychologist and a support group. Others relied solely on other staff in the clinic: another health adviser where possible, but if not, then the consultant or perhaps the sister. Some sought support from colleagues or professionals outside the clinic.

Most of the health advisers were quite happy with the support that they received. But three said they would have liked more regular support and two, both of whom attended support groups, said they would prefer one-to-one support for themselves. There was little doubt that health advisers who were engaged in a lot of HIV/AIDS counselling were in considerable need of support, particularly on a personal basis.

A quarter of the health advisers, however, said they did not have any support at all. Most of them would have liked some, generally in the form of one-to-one personal emotional support from a professional counsellor.

The health advisers were less likely to receive *supervision* in their counselling role than they were to receive support. Only 7 of the 22 health advisers interviewed received supervision (32 per cent), usually from another health adviser or a senior health adviser, although two were supervised by the consultant. The supervision usually took the form of informal discussions about patients and particular problems. Most were happy with the supervision, though one felt it should be more regular and one thought it should be formalised.

Of the two-thirds of health advisers who did not receive any supervision in their counselling role, all but three said that they would like to have supervision. They wanted regular, one-to-one contact to discuss cases and to provide help with their counselling skills. However, they were divided as to who should provide this supervision; professionals mentioned included the senior health adviser, the consultant, a clinical psychologist, a psychiatrist, a professional counsellor or a colleague outside the clinic.

Support and supervision for medical staff

Almost all the doctors were involved in counselling patients in the clinic, but less than two-thirds of them (61 per cent) said they received *support* in their counselling role. The consultants were the least likely and the clinical assistants the most likely to feel they were supported.

The definition of 'support' by the medical staff was different from that given by the health advisers. The notion of support in their counselling role was clearly rather foreign to many of the doctors interviewed. Most of them interpreted it as being able to call on help in discussing cases or asking for advice if necessary, or, more often, as being able to refer cases to someone else.

The clinical assistants said that they were supported in this way by the consultant, the health adviser, the sister/charge nurse or other staff in the clinic. Some said they shared the responsibility for counselling and did not contradict each other. Most of these clinical assistants were happy with this 'support'.

The doctors in training grades generally received support from the health adviser(s) or other medical staff in the clinic. Again, they largely thought of support as referring a patient to their colleagues where necessary, or asking for advice.

The consultants were less likely than other medical staff to say they were supported in their counselling role, but where they were, they said they were supported by the health adviser(s) as well as other clinic staff. Two cited a clinical psychologist, one a psychiatrist and one was supported by colleagues outside the clinic. Like the other medical staff, the consultants most commonly felt they were supported by being able to refer patients to others if they needed to do so.

Virtually all the medical staff who received support, therefore, were supported informally, which usually meant informal discussion of cases and problems, and referral where necessary.

Only one doctor attended a support group. Nevertheless, at least these doctors felt they were receiving some support, and most of them were happy with the support they had. However, one third of the doctors who were counselling were not receiving any support at all.

The majority of the doctors with no support in their counselling role said that they did not want, or need, any. However, a small number of doctors (8) did want support. These doctors generally worked in the large clinics with a high proportion of HIV/AIDS work. Their requirements varied, however. Three wanted to be able to discuss difficult cases with another professional, three wanted to attend a support group and two wanted personal emotional one-to-one support.

Only around 10 per cent of the doctors received *supervision* in their counselling role, and these were most likely to be clinical assistants receiving supervision from the consultant. Again, supervision was thought of as informal case discussion, seeking advice and referring patients where necessary. But medical staff were happy with the 'supervision' they received.

The vast majority of those who did not receive supervision in their counselling role did not want any, but 12 doctors said they would like supervision. They included five consultants, three doctors in training grades and four clinical assistants. Half of them wanted the opportunity to discuss difficult cases or problems, most commonly with colleagues or professionals outside the clinic. The others wanted help with their counselling skills, usually in the form of a training course with a trained counsellor.

Support and supervision for nursing staff

Two-thirds of the nurses were involved in counselling patients in the clinic, and around two-thirds of these said that they received *support* in their counselling role. The staff nurses were more likely to report that they received support than the enrolled nurses or the sisters/charge nurses.

Nurses received support from other staff in the clinic: the consultant and other medical staff, from the sister and other nursing staff, from the health advisers and sometimes from the administrative and clerical staff. None mentioned support from professionals or colleagues outside the clinic. Support as far as the nursing staff were concerned generally meant informal discussions and asking for advice or information, or referring a patient when necessary.

Most were happy with the support they received, although a minority, eight nurses, were dissatisfied. They would have preferred more regular or more formal sessions, and three said they would have preferred support from a professional outside the clinic.

A third of the nurses who were counselling in the clinic, however, said they did not receive any support in their counselling role. Half of them said they did not want, or need, any, but the other half, twelve nurses, said they would like support from the health adviser or from a trained counsellor, and they wanted training or help with their counselling skills.

Only nine nurses who were counselling (14 per cent) received any *supervision* in their counselling role, usually from the sister/charge nurse, the consultant or from other doctors, in the form of informal discussion of cases and patient referral. These nurses were happy with this supervision.

The majority of the nurses who were counselling, therefore, received no supervision. Two-thirds of them said they did not want, or need, any, but around one third, 16 nurses, said they would like supervision in their counselling role. These nurses wanted supervision from the sister/charge nurse, from the health adviser or from a professional outside the clinic. They wanted help with their counselling skills, some said it would help if they could sit in with the health adviser while she was counselling, and some said they would like to attend a training course in counselling.

HIV/AIDS counselling

We found that the blanket term 'HIV counselling' was much too simplistic. Our pilot work had made it clear that we should distinguish between pre-test counselling, the giving of test results, either negative or positive, post-test counselling when the test was negative and post-test counselling when the result was positive. There was also on-going support and counselling for patients with HIV/AIDS. We explored HIV counselling in some detail and established that staff had very different views on who should give what counselling and at what stages.

We have seen that all the health advisers, most of the doctors (89 per cent) and one third of the nurses were involved in counselling patients with HIV/AIDS or in relation to HIV/AIDS. Before exploring in detail at what stage they were involved, we first asked them whether, in their view, counselling for HIV/AIDS patients was different *in kind* from other counselling they carried out in the clinic.

HIV/AIDS counselling and other counselling

More than three-quarters of the medical staff, nursing staff and health advisers who were involved in HIV/AIDS counselling (77 per cent, 72 per cent and 82 per cent respectively) thought that counselling for HIV/AIDS patients was different in kind from other counselling they carried out in the clinic .

The respondents usually said it differed because HIV/AIDS was a terminal illness and a positive test result had serious and complex implications. One doctor said: 'The patient is aware that it is their final sentence, whereas when you're counselling in other conditions, that's the last thing it is. That's why experience and competence is so important. At my age, you know, life is sweet. And at 30, it is even sweeter and there you are, you're told it's the end. It's tough...' A sister agreed: 'You're not going to be able to offer any treatment. Patients are ashamed and feel dirty and unclean if they have got gonorrhoea, but we can offer the reassurance of treatment. With HIV, you can't...'

Because of this, patients were said to be more acutely anxious and to need more reassurance during counselling. One of the health advisers said: 'Counselling for someone who's just been found positive is different. The anxiety is heightened for the patient who's just got their result. It's more crisis counselling. But pre-test counselling differs as well – the anxiety levels are high. If you're counselling someone with gonorrhoea or herpes, you give more information and advice...'

Counselling for HIV/AIDS also had more of a practical content than other counselling and involved more information-giving; and the information given tended to be more detailed and more complex. One health adviser said: 'There's a whole lot of information that the clients ought to know. How much they know about HIV, information on insurance and mortgages and the implications, information on safer sex. There's loads...'

Patients with HIV/AIDS might also need other services or benefits, and there was a need to discuss these and to discuss the patient's housing. Staff might also be involved in helping to gain access to services or benefits.

The fact that HIV/AIDS was usually a terminal illness meant that counselling these patients was more emotionally demanding, for both the patient and the counsellor. It usually involved discussion of the patient's relationships or lifestyles and it might also involve counselling the partner or family of a patient. And because it was a chronic illness, counselling was more long-term since continuing support and counselling were required. One senior registrar said: 'With STD patients, the need is for short-term, immediate counselling. With HIV, there's no end to it until they die. You're opening up an on-going thing...'

It was thought that the need for more information, more reassurance, and more discussion of the implications meant that counselling for HIV/AIDS patients was more time-consuming than other counselling in the clinic. One health adviser summed up the differences:

> A lot of the counselling for other conditions is very practical. It's also practical for people who are positive but it's also more emotional. There are a lot of issues to discuss. It makes a lot of difference how people cope with a positive result. We discuss who will be told. If we spend a lot of time before, they will ask for their result. We find out who is supportive. It takes much longer. We ask who they have told. And we ensure they are not going to damage themselves and how they are going to protect themselves from stigma. Where are they going to get support from? It's information, but it's counselling as well. You spend longer with a positive result...

The majority of the respondents, therefore, thought HIV/AIDS counselling, both pre-test counselling and counselling of patients with HIV/AIDS, was different in kind from other counselling in the clinic. But not all the staff interviewed agreed with this. Some said the principles were the same and that other conditions could be just as devastating to patients. One health adviser said: 'The issues are different but the basics are the same. You're helping people solve their problems. It is different but parts overlap. You flit from one to the other, you might not be conscious you're doing it. The issues are different, it's more serious, but it's not different. A woman with gonorrhoea, her world might collapse. It's no less important...'

In any event, many staff commented that HIV/AIDS counselling was no different from counselling patients with other terminal illnesses. One consultant said: 'It's a lot of hocus-pocus. People have made a lot of fuss about it because it's telling patients about death. You had to make counselling more and more important because people were looking after themselves. A surgeon tells you how difficult his work is. What's the difference between telling someone they have HIV and telling them they have breast cancer...'

Another consultant agreed: 'I think patients who are HIV positive are a favoured species. I don't think that as much time is allowed for, say, women with carcinoma of the breast, which causes just as much anxiety and great deal more morbidity...'

Pre-test counselling

All the health advisers provided pre-test counselling, and so did virtually all the doctors who were involved in HIV counselling. (This represented 84 per cent of all the doctors interviewed, including all the doctors in training grades, and all but two of the consultants.)

One third of the nurses were involved in HIV counselling, but only a third of these (11 nurses) provided pre-test counselling, representing 11 per cent of all the nurses interviewed. Seven of them were sisters/charge nurses, three were staff nurses and one was an enrolled nurse. These nurses generally worked in clinics without a health adviser.

Table 10.2   HIV pre-test counselling

			column percentages
	Medical staff	Nursing staff	Health advisers
Pre-test counsel in clinic	95	34	100
Do not pre-test counsel in clinic	5	66	-
Base: all staff involved in HIV counselling	*(79)*	*(32)*	*(22)*

We also asked the respondents who (else) provided pre-test counselling in the clinic, so that we could build up a profile of who was involved in pre-test counselling in GUM clinics. In 13 of the 14 clinics with a health adviser, the pre-test counselling was carried out by the medical staff and the health advisers. In the remaining clinic, pre-test counselling was carried out by the medical staff, the health adviser, the HIV counsellor or the sister. In the large, full-time clinics with a higher proportion of HIV work, health advisers carried out the majority of the pre-test counselling. Not every member of the medical staff was involved in pre-test counselling and this task was generally carried out by the consultant or by experienced or designated doctors. Clinical assistants were less likely to provide pre-test counselling.

In the 6 clinics without a health adviser:

- in 3 clinics, the doctors or the sister gave pre-test counselling. (The sisters were taking on most of the health advising tasks in these clinics)
- in 1 clinic, pre-test counselling was carried out by the doctors alone
- in 1 clinic the clinical nurse specialist gave all the pre-test counselling

- in 1 clinic counselling was shared between the doctors and HIV counsellors

We asked the respondents who they thought *should* carry out the pre-test counselling in the clinic. As far as the doctors were concerned, half of them (49 per cent) thought medical staff should give pre-test counselling and more than half (58 per cent) thought health advisers should give pre-test counselling. It was usual for medical staff to say that pre-test counselling should be carried out *either* by a doctor or by a health adviser (39 per cent). But the doctors in five clinics laid the responsibility firmly in the hands of the health advisers.

In the clinics without a health adviser, the doctors generally thought that they themselves should give the pre-test counselling. But the doctors in one clinic felt the sister/health adviser should do it, and the doctors in another clinic said it should be done by the doctors or the HIV counsellors.

The medical staff who thought doctors should be involved commented that the procedure required input from a medically qualified professional. But it was widely recognised that health advisers had more time to spend with patients, they had generally had more training and were often more experienced in pre-test counselling. A clinical assistant said: 'In general, a well-trained health adviser is the person to do it. They have the time and often doctors are not that ambidextrous. There are some awful doctors, terrible ones...'

A fifth of the doctors, however, considered that *anyone* who was trained or experienced could give the pre-test counselling, as long as they were competent and felt confident of carrying out this task. A consultant said: 'Whoever's trained and feels they can do it comfortably. It's not necessarily the exclusive pre-requisite of health advisers. Doctors and nurses could if trained and they want to. And often, it's appropriate. For example, if a doctor is treating a patient for other conditions or if it is likely that the result will be positive...'

The health advisers, on the other hand, usually thought that health advisers alone should be responsible for pre-test counselling. 19 of the 22 health advisers said health advisers should do it, for reasons similar to those cited by the doctors; health advisers had more time, they tended to have more experience and they were often trained in counselling. Three of the health advisers thought that counselling required the input of a non-medically qualified, less authoritarian figure, and health advisers fitted this bill. One health adviser said: 'I should do it. I'll spend an hour telling them about every type of implication. The consultant doesn't have the time, so people are not informed to make a decision. But if people don't want counselling, the consultant will test them anyway...'

Only two health advisers said that medical staff should be involved as well as health advisers and only one referred to the involvement of an HIV counsellor. Three of the health advisers, however, said *anyone* could give pre-test counselling, as long as they were trained or experienced.

The nursing staff also thought that health advisers should give pre-test counselling; two-thirds of the nurses involved in HIV counselling thought health advisers should be involved because they had the time, the training and the experience. But it was interesting that nurses often felt that nursing staff were as well-equipped to pre-test counsel as medical staff: 11 nurses said nursing staff should pre-test counsel, while 10 said medical staff should. The nurses felt that there was a place in pre-test counselling for a less authoritarian person than a doctor, such as a nurse and it was said that patients talked more freely to a non-medical person. Four nurses, however, thought that anyone could counsel with the appropriate training and experience.

HIV test results

We asked the health advisers and the medical and nursing staff who were involved in HIV counselling if they gave any HIV test results in the clinic, either positive or negative.

Table 10.3 HIV test results

| | | *column percentages* | |
	Medical staff	Nursing staff	Health advisers
Positive HIV test results only	-	-	-
Negative HIV test results only	29	47	23
Both positive and negative HIV test results	61	-	64
Do not give HIV test results	10	53	14
Base: all staff involved in HIV counselling	(79)	(32)	(22)

90 per cent of the doctors involved in HIV counselling in the clinic gave HIV test results. (This represented 80 per cent of all the doctors interviewed.)

One third of the doctors who gave HIV test results, however, only gave *negative* test results. These doctors were usually clinical assistants; half of the clinical assistants who were involved in HIV counselling (48 per cent) only gave negative test results, compared with 25 per cent of the doctors in training grades and 15 per cent of the consultants.

Two-thirds of the doctors who were involved in HIV counselling, therefore, gave *both positive and negative* test results. (This represented 54 per cent of all the doctors interviewed, including three quarters of the consultants, two-thirds of the junior doctors and just over one third of the clinical assistants.)

Ten per cent of the medical staff involved in HIV counselling did *not* give any HIV test results. This included four consultants, two clinical assistants and two junior doctors.

19 of the 22 health advisers gave HIV test results in the clinic, while three did not (two from one clinic and one from another clinic). Of the 19 health advisers:

- 14 gave both positive and negative test results
- 5 (from four clinics) only gave *negative* test results

Around half of the 32 nurses involved in HIV counselling did not give *any* HIV test results; the other half only gave negative results. None of the nurses, therefore, gave positive HIV test results. Where (negative) results were given, these were usually given by a senior nurse, such as a sister, charge nurse or clinical nurse specialist. This was most likely to occur in clinics without a health adviser.

To sum up the picture, the medical staff were involved in giving positive test results in all 20 GUM clinics, although not all medical staff were involved. It was usually the consultant, doctors who were designated to HIV work or experienced doctors who gave positive results, and clinical assistants rarely did so.

The health advisers were often, but not always, involved in giving positive HIV test results. 14 of the 20 clinics had health adviser(s) in post:

- in 6 clinics health advisers did *not* give positive HIV test results:
  - in 2 of these clinics, the health advisers did *not* give *any* HIV test results
  - in 4 clinics, the health advisers only gave *negative* HIV test results

- in 8 clinics health advisers were involved, with the medical staff, in giving positive test results

In the 6 clinics with no health adviser the medical staff gave positive test results (rather than a sister or an HIV counsellor).

Since practice in most clinics was clearly geared towards medical staff giving positive HIV test results, we were interested in exploring the GUM staff's attitudes towards the question of who should give such results.

Three-quarters of the medical staff said that doctors should give positive HIV test results, mainly because HIV was a serious diagnosis which needed a medical input. They felt that doctors were responsible for their patients, and would also be responsible for the future care and management of the patient. It was appropriate, therefore, that they should be responsible for passing on test results to the patient. One clinical assistant said: 'The doctor – he has the ultimate responsibility in the decision-making and in the welfare of the patient...', while a consultant said: 'The consultant should give the results because the patients come to see the doctor and the total responsibility for the patient lies with the doctor. If you've got a serious thing like telling a patient they've got HIV, the ultimate responsibility lies with the doctor...'

One third of the doctors believed that health advisers should be involved in giving positive HIV test results. In most of these cases, the doctors thought it was important to have an input from both the doctor *and* a health adviser, since although the doctor had overall responsibility for the patient, the health adviser had more time and more experience of counselling. But occasionally, the doctors thought the health adviser alone could give positive HIV test results; this was most likely to happen in two of the large, full-time clinics.

Nine of the doctors considered that whoever had given the pre-test counselling should give the test result, whether this was a doctor, a health adviser, or some other member of staff. This individual would already have built up a relationship with the patient during pre-test counselling, and giving the test result would provide continuity for the patient.

Eight of the 22 health advisers, all of whom were currently involved in giving HIV test results, thought that health advisers alone should give the positive HIV test results in the clinic. They said that they would already have formed a bond with the patient during pre-test counselling and their giving the test result would provide continuity for the patient. One said: 'I think I should. I've formed a relationship with them. It takes an hour to an hour and a half, the first session. Sometimes you see a person five times before they have a test. It's inconsistent if they see others when they're devastated...'

Four of the health advisers, on the other hand, who were not involved in giving positive HIV test results, thought the medical staff alone should give HIV test results. They felt that the medical staff were responsible for the care and management of the patient and it was their responsibility to give the test result.

A further two health advisers said that positive test results should be given either by a doctor or a health adviser, while another one said they should be given by a doctor *and* a health adviser together.

Overall, half of the health advisers (11) thought health advisers should be involved in giving test results and seven thought medical staff should be involved, most usually the consultant specifically, rather than medical staff generally.

Seven of the health advisers, however, commented that whoever had given the pre-test counselling should give the positive test result, whether this was a doctor, a health adviser or another professional, mainly because of the relationship which had been built up with the patient and the need for continuity.

The nursing staff, like the doctors, usually thought that medical staff should give positive HIV test results (60 per cent). But many of them recognised that the health advisers had an important role to play; 44 per cent of the nurses involved in HIV counselling said health advisers should give positive test results. Few thought other professionals should be involved: two said nursing staff should give positive test results and one said the HIV counsellor should give test results. But three said *whoever* did the pre-test counselling should give the test result.

Immediate post-test counselling

Finally, we asked the GUM staff if they personally provided any immediate post-test counselling in the clinic.

More than 80 per cent of the doctors involved in HIV counselling provided immediate post-test counselling. This might have been expected given that the

Table 10.4 Immediate post-test counselling

column percentages

	Medical staff	Nursing staff	Health advisers
Post-test counselling after positive results only	8	-	5
Post-test counselling after negative results only	25	19	18
Post-test counselling after positive and negative results	51	13	68
Do not give immediate post-test counselling	16	69	9
Base: all staff involved in HIV counselling	*(79)*	*(32)*	*(22)*

medical staff were the most likely to give HIV test results. But not all of these doctors were involved in giving post-test counselling after a positive result.

Half of the doctors who gave post-test counselling did so after both positive and negative test results. A further 8 per cent provided post-test counselling after positive results only. But a quarter of the doctors only gave immediate post-test counselling after negative test results. These doctors were most likely to be clinical assistants; 41 per cent of the clinical assistants gave post-test counselling after negative results only, compared with 25 per cent of the doctors in training grades and 12 per cent of the consultants. This reflects the fact that clinical assistants were much less likely to give positive HIV test results.

All but two of the health advisers gave immediate post-test counselling in the clinic (91 per cent). Most of these gave post-test counselling after both positive and negative test results; but one provided counselling after positive tests only and four provided counselling after negative tests only. The health advisers who did not give post-test counselling after a positive result also did not give positive test results in the clinic.

The majority (69 per cent) of the nurses involved in HIV counselling did not give any of the immediate post-test counselling in the clinic. If they did they usually provided counselling after negative results only (19 per cent). But four nurses, three of them sisters and three of them from clinics without a health adviser, said that they provided immediate post-test counselling whether the test result was positive or negative.

To sum up the overall picture in the clinics, medical staff were involved in giving immediate post-test counselling after positive HIV test results in *all* the clinics. Once again, these were usually the consultant(s), designated doctors or experienced doctors who gave the positive test results and then went on to give immediate post-test counselling.

Health advisers in 10 of the 14 clinics with health advisers provided immediate post-test counselling. In one of these clinics, one of the two health advisers gave post-test counselling after both positive and negative test results but the other did not provide *any* post-test counselling.

The health advisers in three clinics did not give post-test counselling after positive results (though they gave it after negative results); and the health adviser in another clinic did not give any post-test counselling at all.

In the six clinics without a health adviser, the medical staff usually gave positive HIV test results and provided post-test counselling. But in three of these clinics, the sister/charge nurse was also involved in post-test counselling after a positive result and in one clinic, HIV counsellors provided this counselling.

Who did the GUM staff think should give post-test counselling? Around two-thirds of the doctors said medical staff should give post-test counselling and half said health advisers should give it. The doctors usually considered that a serious medical diagnosis like HIV required medical input and that it was necessary for them to be involved in post-test counselling for the same reasons that they should give positive test results, since they would be responsible for the future care and management of the patient. But they thought the health advisers usually had more time, training and experience and usually provided a more appropriate setting in which to talk to patients. Most of the doctors, therefore, were satisfied with the situation as it stood, with doctors and health advisers providing counselling where there was a health adviser, and doctors giving counselling in clinics without a health adviser (sometimes with the help of an HIV counsellor or a sister). Four doctors said post-test counselling should be provided by doctors and health advisers *together*. And some said whoever gave the pre-test counselling should give the post-test counselling (as well as giving them the test result), thus providing continuity for the patient.

The health advisers, on the other hand, usually said that health advisers themselves should provide the post-test counselling after a positive test result (86 per cent), mainly because they had the time and the setting to talk to distressed patients, they had the experience and they had been trained. Few of the health advisers felt that the medical staff should be involved in post-test counselling, but almost a quarter said that whoever did the pre-test counselling should give the post-test counselling.

The nursing staff were divided in their views of who should give post-test counselling. It could be given by the health adviser; by a member of the medical staff; or it could be given by the HIV counsellor or the sister/charge nurse.

The general picture of HIV/AIDS counselling

It can be seen that health advisers play an important part in pre-test counselling, particularly in the large, full-time clinics with a relatively high proportion of HIV/AIDS related work. In some of these clinics, the health advisers were spending the vast majority of their time pre-test counselling, to the exclusion of counselling other patients and to the exclusion of contact tracing. Where there were no health advisers, doctors were the most likely staff to provide pre-test counselling, helped by the sister or an HIV counsellor.

Medical staff generally played the key role in giving positive HIV test results. Health advisers were often, but not always, involved. Some consultants considered it was a medical duty to give results of this sort, and confined health advisers to giving negative test results. But, once again, the health advisers in the large clinics played a full and active part in giving positive test results. Health advisers also played an important role in post-test counselling.

It was not usual for other professionals to give positive test results; where there was no health adviser, the consultant would normally give positive HIV test results. The nursing staff usually had a very limited role in formal HIV counselling. They were more involved in clinics without a health adviser, but the involvement was usually confined to a sister who was taking on the health advising duties. 'Counselling' provided by other nursing staff usually consisted of informal support during tests or treatment.

The health advisers, and many of the doctors, generally felt that the health advisers were the best professionals to provide counselling because they had more time, they had a non-medical setting, and they generally had more training and more experience. But the medical staff, and a substantial minority of the health advisers, felt that doctors should give positive HIV test results. There was also agreed to be a case, however, for maintaining continuity, and for the professional who gave pre-test counselling, whatever their background, to give the test results and post-test counselling.

Counselling provided by a variety of professionals

Our pre-pilot and pilot work had indicated that there were many different types of people working with HIV/AIDS patients, both inside and outside GUM clinics. A patient might receive information or counselling from different members of staff working in the GUM clinic; from a doctor, a health adviser and possibly a nurse. But the patient might also receive information and counselling from professionals working outside the clinic, for example, a social worker, a GP or from a voluntary organisation. It sometimes seemed that everybody was trying to get in on the act and take their share of work in this field.

Given the number of professionals who might have an involvement with patients, we sought the views of clinic staff on the potential impact. More than 80 per cent of the doctors and health advisers considered there was a danger of HIV/AIDS patients being given conflicting or confusing advice, information and counselling, a view shared by the majority of the nursing staff (59 per cent).

Around a quarter of the respondents felt there was a danger, but had no personal experience of patients being given conflicting information. But many of the staff were able to cite problems. There appeared to be three key areas of conflicting advice: advice on testing; advice on transmission; and advice on treatment.

Advice and information about transmission of HIV/AIDS were said to be most commonly conflicting or confusing. One senior registrar said: 'THT think using condoms for anal sex is safe. But I've seen five seroconversions in those cases. It depends on who is counselling and what their prejudices are. Voluntary organisations are staffed by people who are patients themselves. They do the counselling. My worry is they lack the objectivity...' while a sister in another clinic said: 'There are conflicts with voluntary helplines. I can't agree with some of the things they say. Patients have been told that oral sex is safe. We've designed our own booklet and we update all our information...'

Some respondents thought the media could be misleading. One doctor said: 'The obvious thing is the media. It highlights low risk patients. It brings in whole groups who have a guilty conscience but aren't high risk, and seem to do nothing for the ones who are at risk...' Others commented that not all those who were involved in counselling were qualified counsellors.

But some staff thought it was inevitable that there was conflicting advice and information, because HIV/AIDS was a new and developing area and there was bound to be confusion. Certainly some respondents felt that there were too many people or agencies involved in working with HIV/AIDS patients and that care and management should be left to the GUM clinic.

Following on from this, we asked the staff specifically whether they thought anything should be done about rationalising the provision of counselling to HIV/AIDS patients. Almost two-thirds of the doctors (61 per cent), more than half of the health advisers (55 per cent), and just under half of the nurses (45 per cent) considered something *should* be done about rationalising the provision of counselling to HIV/AIDS patients.

It was thought that there were three main ways in which HIV/AIDS counselling could be rationalised: by improving liaison between different professionals and services; by standardising policies, information and training; and by reducing the number of professionals involved in HIV/AIDS work.

Communication and coordination between different professionals could be improved by holding joint meetings. Some thought a coordinator of HIV/AIDS services could be appointed, while some felt that GUM clinics should oversee other services and groups, particularly the work of voluntary bodies.

Staff were keen on introducing agreed standards and policies for counselling HIV/AIDS patients. It was thought that standardised policies should operate together with improvements in training and that standardised information should be provided to improve the quality of counselling.

Finally, some staff thought that the number of services and people working with HIV/AIDS patients could be reduced. Some were of the opinion that GUM clinics should do all the counselling and some said no-one untrained should be allowed to counsel at all.

11 Extending the boundaries

Many of the GUM clinics in which we conducted our research were characterised by their isolation from the mainstream of the hospital, community or district in which they were located. This was evident in a number of important ways, not least of which was the lack of contact with staff at all levels in other specialties and disciplines, both within the hospital and in the community.

The problem was not necessarily related to physical proximity to other services, although we have seen that some of the clinics were geographically and physically isolated from other clinics and other parts of the hospital. We have also seen that clinic staff often referred to the stigma and negative image which they felt was associated with the specialty and with this type of clinic. There was evidence among some GUM clinic staff of perceived lack of resources and status in comparison with other departments and specialties. These factors, together with the fact that GUM clinics operated a policy of patient confidentiality, meant that the clinics often operated quite independently of other hospital staff and clearly led to some clinic staff feeling isolated from other professionals.

This isolation had important implications for the morale of staff within individual GUM clinics as well as for the perceived status of GUM clinics in general. We were therefore particularly interested in examining the extent to which the GUM clinic staff liaised with other professionals, both within the hospital and outside the hospital, the nature of their liaison and any problems which might occur. These are explored in the first part of this chapter.

In the second part we examine the role of GUM clinics in giving family planning and contraceptive advice. The potentially important liaison between family planning clinics and GUM clinics was only one aspect of our interest. We also considered it important to establish to what extent GUM clinic staff thought they had a role to play in giving family planning and contraceptive advice.

Liaison with other hospital staff

More than 80 per cent of the doctors and health advisers said that they liaised with other hospital departments. It was perhaps indicative that the medical staff most commonly liaised with other departments less than once a week, even in GUM clinics which were held more frequently. However, contact between the health advisers and other hospital departments was more frequent, with health advisers generally liaising with other staff at least once a week.

Two-thirds of the nurses and half the administrative and clerical staff reported that they liaised with other hospital staff. Contact was, however, fairly infrequent, generally occurring less often than once a week.

Around one third of the doctors sometimes attended a ward round, and rather more (42 per cent) said they sometimes admitted a patient to a ward. But apart from the large, full-time clinic with a very high proportion of HIV/AIDS related work, ward rounds and admission of patients were relatively infrequent occurrences.

Around one third of the health advisers also said they sometimes attended ward rounds. These health advisers generally worked in the large, full-time clinics with more HIV/AIDS patients. Few of the nursing staff attended ward rounds.

Problems in liaising with other hospital staff

We asked the medical, nursing and health advising staff if there were ever any problems in liaising or working with other medical or nursing staff in the hospital in relation to GUM clinic patients. Just over one third of the doctors and nurses (36 per cent and 35 per cent respectively) and two-fifths of the health advisers (9 of the 22 interviewed) said there *were* such problems.

The health advisers were most likely to mention problems and misunderstandings about patient confidentiality. They said hospital staff did not always understand why they could not receive information from the GUM clinic about a patient, mainly because they did not appreciate the fact that the GUM clinic operated a confidential service.

Sometimes problems arose because health advisers had to counsel patients on the wards. In these cases, they had to make notes on general hospital notes which were not subject the VD Act and which could therefore be disclosed to GPs.

Some health advisers had concerns about HIV counselling and HIV testing practices in the hospital. Some said that other clinics insisted on testing any patients referred to them by the GUM clinic, while others referred some of their own patients to the GUM clinic for HIV testing.

Health advisers were particularly concerned that patients were being tested in other departments without proper counselling. This health adviser worked in a large clinic and described the problems encountered in the hospital: 'The dental department send individuals to us for pre-test counselling when the request has not come from the patient. Other departments test without proper counselling. They're not sending them to us but they contact us when the results are positive so we've not been able to build up a relationship with the patient. They're being selective about who they're testing...'

Another health adviser in the same clinic told a similar story and gave more details of the 'selective' treatment of patients: 'Some wards test patients without referral to the GU clinic. When they're found to be positive, then they are referred to us to pick up the pieces and it's much more difficult then. The problems occur mainly with surgeons and dentists. They are referring patients to be tested because of the professionals' own fear of being infected. It's particularly bad in the dental department. There is blatant discrimination. If a patient is from Africa or if they're gay, they are sent to us...'

The nursing staff, on the other hand, considered the main problem in liaising with other departments related to the stigma associated with GUM clinics. The sister of one clinic told us: 'The outpatient nurses and receptionists have a good look at the patients and laugh and they see if they know anybody. I had to talk to them about it. I put the ball in their court and said, "It could be you, or your friend, or your husband". I put the onus on them...'

Some staff in the hospital seemed to view the work of GUM clinics as low status work, as this enrolled nurse described: 'Almost everybody resents the mention of it and think we're a different category of nurses working in this field. They think we're the "permissive" ones. They don't class it as a field of nursing...'

Related to the stigma associated with GUM clinics, some nurses commented that hospital staff were sometimes unpleasant to GUM clinic patients: 'In casualty, they won't do anything for a patient who comes in with an STD. Their attitude is, "This is *your* department". Out of clinic hours, they haven't got the right attitude. They're not nice – they could be nicer to them. They pick them up by the scruff of the neck and throw them through to us...'

The attitudes of hospital staff towards GUM clinic patients sometimes affected other patients, as one staff nurse described: 'You get some silly situations. There are still some fairly bigoted ideas. For example, a rather scruffy young man turned up at the path. lab. and they sent him here and said he must be "one of ours". In fact his GP had sent him to the path. lab. for routine tests that were nothing to do with GU. But they presumed from his appearance that he belonged here...'

The nursing staff also referred to the problems mentioned by health advisers of non-GUM clinic staff not understanding the need for confidentiality: 'Because we are confidential, we use a number system and not names. If someone goes for an X-ray or for a scan, it can be a problem because they want names and addresses. In one case they went directly to the patient and it caused a problem. They don't understand why and how important confidentiality is...'

Other problems occurred when hospital staff referred patients to the GUM clinic without an appointment.

The medical staff cited a wide range of problems associated with their liaison with other medical and nursing staff in the hospital. These included those mentioned by the health advisers and nurses, such as a lack of understanding of confidentiality, the stigma associated with GUM clinics and the poor treatment of GUM clinic patients, and the practices of other clinics and departments in relation to HIV counselling and testing. But medical staff also referred to a range of other problems, including difficulties in referring patients and difficulties getting treatment for HIV positive patients, lack of liaison or poor liaison with other medical staff, and referral of inappropriate patients to the GUM clinic.

Liaison with GPs

More than 80 per cent of the doctors and health advisers said they liaised with GPs. Contact between these professionals was most likely to occur less often than once a week, although around a quarter said they liaised with GPs at least once a week and some doctors said they liaised with GPs every day they worked in the clinic.

Less than half the nursing staff (44 per cent) liaised with GPs and even then it was generally less often than once a week. However, around half of the administrative and clerical staff said they liaised with GPs, divided more or less equally between contact on a weekly basis and less often than once a week.

As many as half the doctors said that there were problems in liaising with GPs. Just under half the health advisers and around one third of the nurses also reported problems working with GPs. The main problem related to patient confidentiality. Staff commented that GPs did not understand the basis on which the clinic worked and that they were bound by the VD Act to ensure patient confidentiality. Subsequently, GPs frequently rang up for results and some became annoyed that GUM clinic staff would not give them details about their patients.

The medical staff and health advisers were particularly likely to mention problems relating to confidentiality. One associate specialist explained: 'The problem is confidentiality. A lot of GPs either don't understand or resent the degree of confidentiality we observe. They think it's old-fashioned. More recently, they've got a bit angry that they're not given patients' smear results because it affects their pockets. It causes aggression...'

Other doctors also referred to particular problems relating to the results of smear tests, mainly as result of the new GP contracts and the payments related to targets for cervical cytology: 'Some GPs insist we send cervical smear results. If the patient doesn't want the GP to know they have been here, we can't do it. Some doctors don't like that but I'm of the opinion that if I haven't referred a patient to a clinic, then I don't get a reply from the hospital. It should be left to the patient to decide...' And this was the basis on which many of the doctors operated. If the GP made the referral, then they would write with results, but otherwise they would inform the GP only at the patient's request or with the patient's permission.

The medical staff, and to a lesser extent the nurses, also complained that GPs started treating patients, often inappropriately, before they referred them to the GUM clinic. This sometimes caused problems, as an SHO explained: 'Sometimes patients see their GP before they come to see us. The GPs carry out a meagre investigation and start treatment and then send them to us. It makes diagnosis and treatment from our point of view more difficult...'

179

The nursing staff were particularly likely to say that GPs sent patients to the clinic at the wrong time and without an appointment. Nursing staff are likely to bear the brunt of anxious or disgruntled patients because receptionists usually refer patients without an appointment to a member of the nursing staff to assess the urgency of the case. One staff nurse said patients sometimes turned up 'all ready, with their bottles in their hand', but had to be sent away as the clinic was fully booked. One enrolled nurse said that the GPs in his area 'had got the attitude that VD clinics should be open at all hours'.

The staff mentioned a range of other problems which they encountered when liaising or working with GPs. These included referral of patients with inappropriate conditions (for example, thrush), lack of communication, GPs testing patients for HIV infection without proper pre-test counselling, as well as the stigma which some GPs associated with GUM clinics.

Liaison with social services departments

Health advisers were the most likely GUM clinic staff to liaise with social services departments. All but two of the health advisers said they liaised with social services, a third of them on a weekly basis and two-thirds of them less often.

More than two-fifths of the medical staff reported that they liaised with social services departments but only around one fifth of the nurses and administrative and clerical staff did so. Contact between these staff and the social services department was relatively infrequent, usually less often than once a week.

Liaison with social workers

We asked the doctors, nurses and health advisers if there were any problems in liaising or working with social workers, both in the community and those based in the hospital.

Very few of the staff reported problems in liaising with hospital social workers. However, this was mainly because few medical and nursing staff had any personal contact with hospital social workers. Most health advisers said that there were no problems in their dealings with hospital social workers.

Only 6 doctors, 5 nurses and 3 health advisers reported such problems, the main one being simply getting hold of a social worker. This was a particular problem in one hospital, as this health adviser explained: 'We can't get them, it's really difficult to get one. A few years ago, we had a designated social worker for the clinic. Now the medical social workers work on a life and limb policy... We're doing it, we've taken the social work on...'

Other problems mentioned in connection with hospital social workers included, on the one hand, their reluctance to see GUM clinic patients and, on the other hand, the desire of hospital social workers to take on HIV counselling.

There were rather more problems relating to community based social workers. As many as a quarter of the health advisers (6 of the 22 interviewed) said there were problems when liaising with social workers based in the community. Nurses were unlikely to have contact with community social workers, as were many of the medical staff. But nine doctors and three nurses also referred to problems associated with social workers.

As far as the health advisers were concerned, the problem related to the social workers' lack of understanding of HIV/AIDS, their wanting to become involved in HIV counselling and HIV-related work, and problems with confidentiality. The medical and nursing staff also referred to worries about maintaining confidentiality, as well as poor communication with social workers. Some doctors felt strongly that social workers had an inappropriate attitude or approach to patients, while others reported problems in getting hold of social workers.

Liaison with social security offices
The health advisers were also the most likely of the GUM clinic staff to liaise with social security offices, although contact was less widespread than with social services. Almost half the health advisers said that they liaised with social security offices. This compared with one fifth of the medical staff. Contact between GUM clinic staff and social security offices was relatively infrequent, usually less often than once a week. Hardly any of the nursing staff or administrative and clerical staff liaised with social security offices.

Liaison with housing departments
Half the health advisers interviewed said they sometimes made contact with housing officers though this generally happened only on an occasional basis. More than one fifth of doctors liaised with housing departments, but again contact was less frequent than once a week. Few of the other staff liaised with housing departments.

Liaison with voluntary organisations
More than 80 per cent of the health advisers said they liaised with voluntary organisations. Such contact was quite common; around half the health advisers made contact at least once a week. Half the doctors and a third of the nurses also said that they liaised with voluntary organisations, but these staff were most likely to do so less often than once a week. Just over ten per cent of the administrative and clerical staff also liaised with voluntary organisations.

Liaison with private organisations
Half the health advisers said that they liaised with private organisations. This compared with just over a quarter of the doctors and just under a fifth of the nursing staff, but few of the administrative and clerical staff. Contact with private organisations was relatively infrequent.

Liaison with prisons
There has been much debate about the incidence of HIV infection in prisons. Professionals in the medical and prison services have discussed the pros and cons

of testing prisoners for HIV and the ways in which the incidence of HIV infection can be controlled.

We were interested in the extent to which staff working in GUM clinics worked with prisons. We asked the medical and nursing staff and the health advisers if they ever liaised or worked with prisons, remand centres or young offenders' institutions. Around a quarter of the medical staff (28 per cent) said that they sometimes liaised with prisons or other penal institutions. The consultants were more likely than other doctors to work with these institutions (39 per cent). The main work was with prisons, but some said they worked with remand centres and some worked with young offenders' institutions (8 doctors in each case).

The frequency with which the doctors worked with the penal establishments varied widely. Of the 25 doctors involved, a fifth of them said they worked with the prison service at least once a week. Others, however, had rather less contact, liaising with the service only once a month (4) or every 2-3 months (2 doctors). Around one third of them said they worked with the prison service as and when required.

Most commonly, the medical staff were involved in seeing prisoners in the GUM clinic, alongside other clinic patients. But 11 of the 25 doctors, 9 of them consultants, said they visited, examined and treated prisoners in the prison. Two of the doctors were Home Office Medical Officers.

The health advisers were more likely than the doctors to liaise with prison establishments; more than half of them were involved in this type of work (12 of the 22 health advisers). Seven of them worked with prisons and five of them with remand centres. Two of them also worked with a young offenders' institution. A third of these health advisers worked with these establishments once a month, while a further quarter made contact once every 2-3 months, and the rest less frequently.

While the medical staff were most likely to have contact with prisoners in the GUM clinic, the health advisers were just as likely to visit the prison in person as they were to see prisoners in the clinic. Three of the health advisers, however, said they did not see prisoners at all, but worked with prison staff.

The health advisers were involved in HIV counselling of prisoners, as well as contact tracing partners of prisoners and counselling the families or partners of prisoners. Some liaised with prison staff or contact traced prisoners through the prison staff, and one was involved in training prison staff.

The nursing staff, however, were much less likely than either the health advisers or the medical staff to work with the prison service. Less than one fifth of them said they had contact with either prisons, remand centres or young offenders' institutions. The sisters/charge nurses were more likely than other nurses to have contact of this sort. In the majority of cases, the nurses saw prisoners in the GUM clinic, where they were examined and treated like other patients (though nurses commented that they often had a police escort and that they were usually seen at the beginning or at the end of a clinic). But two of the sisters said they visited the prison and were involved in examining prisoners and training staff, and two others said they liaised with prison staff, usually about prisoners' test results.

Role of GUM clinics in giving family planning advice

Traditionally, the GUM clinic appears to have played little or no role in encouraging the use of contraception as such. This seems odd in many ways, considering that barrier methods of contraception, such as condoms, help to prevent the spread of sexually transmitted infections. Although most clinics have suggested the use of condoms to prevent infection, it has really only been with the advent of HIV/AIDS that stress on condom use has been incorporated in educational material to the general public.

A rather curious distinction has arisen between condom use to prevent HIV/AIDS, which has been regarded as something to be encouraged and suitable for widespread public campaigns, and condom use to prevent pregnancy, which has hardly been mentioned in the same context. The dual purpose of condoms, which might be considered an important educational message, rarely appears to be mentioned in campaigns, and it was interesting in this research to see how many of the GUM staff also skirted round the subject.

We asked the GUM clinic staff what they considered to be the role of GUM clinics in giving family planning and contraceptive advice. Again we found a wide range of opinion among staff of the same and different disciplines, both across clinics and in the same clinic. Table 11.1 presents the results of this open-ended question in tabular form for ease of reference, and it can be seen that respondents often mentioned more than one aspect of the role.

One third of doctors thought that GUM clinics should refer people requesting or needing contraception to family planning clinics or GPs, a view shared by 40 per cent of nurses and nearly 60 per cent of health advisers. However, consultants were more likely than clinical assistants and junior doctors to want to refer patients on. Similarly, a quarter of GUM clinic doctors thought that contraceptive advice or help was not part of their role at all, again a view held more frequently by consultants than other doctors – 'We'd grind to a halt – it's not our remit and we'd be clashing with the family planning clinics and GPs...'

Some consultants thought that if GUM clinics started giving contraceptive advice, family planning clinics might start expanding their own role – 'We don't want family planning clinics dealing with GU problems...' Others felt that there were enough family planning clinics and GPs offering contraceptive services and that GUM clinics should concentrate on their main role. A few doctors were concerned that offering family planning or contraceptive advice would detract from the specialised nature of GUM and 'dilute' the specialty, which they felt was under attack from other specialties in any case.

Some clinical assistants were worried about having to develop another area of expertise in addition to 'in-depth urology, in-depth medicine, in-depth gynaecology – you have to spend a lot of time getting on top of it. We don't

Table 11.1 Role of GUM clinics in family planning

column percentages

	Doctors	Nurses	Health Advisers
Refer to FPC/GP	33	40	59
Part of consultation/ advice	30	28	45
No role/inappropriate place	26	19	14
Some role but not primary purpose	18	17	23
Important – 'at risk' population	18	21	23
Encourage use of condoms	13	23	32
Give out condoms	13	17	9
Should be integrated services	12	9	5
Should be concurrent clinics	8	0	0
Would detract from/dilute GUM specialty	7	0	0
Should answer patients' questions	7	13	5
Encourage use of (other) barrier methods	6	1	5
Should give PC contraception	4	4	5
Base: all respondents	*89*	*98*	*22*

have the expertise to do family planning as well...' However, some GP clinical assistants also thought they could not offer the GUM clinic patient the time they considered was needed for a proper examination and history in connection with family planning as well as the follow-up needed – 'All we actually do is to recommend condoms...'

One consultant pointed up the distinction between condom use for disease prevention and condom use for contraception: 'I think GUM clinics should give this advice, but I'm not going to give it. It's different for HIV patients – but that's safer sex, not family planning...' His view was endorsed by several nurses, like this staff nurse: 'We see condoms as preventing diseases rather than as family planning advice. I don't think there is a role. It's not part of our primary reason for being here...'

However, one third of doctors considered that family planning advice was a normal part of the GUM clinic consultation, a view endorsed by over a quarter of the nurses and nearly half the health advisers. Clinical assistants, particularly women who also worked in general practice, often stressed this point: 'I ask *everyone* – male or female – about contraception. I think all GU doctors should have their family planning certificate. We get people who don't use the family planning services well. We should be allowed, within budget, to hand out condoms. There is no budget for them...'

An associate specialist agreed: 'It's an absolutely essential part of the role and one that is probably ignored. My view is that we have a unique opportunity to find young women who are not contracepting. I think it would be negligent of the GU doctor not to pick this up. It's part of counselling. Contraception is still very difficult to get hold of, particularly for the under-16s. I point them very firmly towards a family planning clinic. Nursing staff should all be family planning trained...'

Just under one fifth of the doctor and nurses and quarter of health advisers thought GUM clinics had some role in family planning advice but should recognise that it was not their primary purpose. On the other hand, similar proportions of staff thought that it was an important role because the population attending clinics were demonstrably 'at risk'. An enrolled nurse in a small clinic summarised the views of several nurses, while underlining the rather complicated logic behind her argument: 'I think it's an ideal place to do family planning because we get a lot of young girls that have sexual intercourse. It would be an opportunity to talk to them about contraception and to prevent unwanted pregnancies. You get a few where it's too late...'

The question of encouraging condom use was mentioned by around 10 per cent of doctors but rather more nurses and health advisers, while a similar proportion of doctors and nurses said GUM clinics should give out condoms - something mentioned by less than one in ten of the health advisers, who were often thinking of their own role in the matter. They did not all agree with one health adviser who advocated 'giving out condoms like sweeties' because it was embarrassing for women to get them.

It was, however, a matter of great concern to some staff that they were not able routinely to give out condoms, and there were allusions to budgets for condoms 'running out'. Different clinics clearly had different practices, as a sister in one clinic illustrated: 'We get lots of requests for contraceptive help. I think it would be rather interesting. We don't really do anything in that regard. We tell them where to go, advise on safer sex, but we don't provide condoms or anything like that...'

A consultant in another clinic said: 'Condoms are available in this clinic for a very few, selected patients at the present time...We've been wondering whether we should have free condoms available for all patients, but we're not sure how to give these out and how to maintain stocks. We've always felt that as a clinic we do not want to charge for any of our facilities...'

A health adviser pointed up the problem of encouraging safer sex without giving people help in achieving it: 'We don't have a budget for condoms. The consultants aren't keen. We're asking people not to have sex while they have an infection. You have to be realistic about what people can manage. I think we should give them out...'

Just over 10 per cent of doctors and nurses, but only one health adviser thought there should be integrated GUM and contraception services. However, around one third of the junior doctors held this view, and, again, the forward-looking opinions of doctors in training grades often contrasted sharply with those of some consultants. There were also differences among clinics, with staff in the larger clinics more likely to favour integrated or concurrent clinics than those in smaller clinics. Sometimes, their views were affected by the conditions operating in the clinics, as this consultant noted: 'I feel it's a shame that a woman comes here and waits three hours and gets GU treatment and then has to go elsewhere for her pills. You must have trained staff. We've talked about getting a person to run a session in a clinic. Family planning clinics don't give treatment, and we're getting patients toing and froing between the two clinics. It would be fairly well-subscribed here as well, because patients want this service...'

Staff clearly referred patients to family planning clinics and to GPs for contraceptive advice and help, but essentially there was little evidence of liaison between the GUM clinic and these contraceptive services. There were few indications that most staff were really aware of what was going on in family planning clinics, and it was interesting to note the discussion and differing practice on the question of GUM clinics giving out condoms. The fact that issuing condoms is common practice in family planning clinics appeared to have passed most of them by, and there seemed to be an urgent need for some information exchange, if nothing else, on the respective practices of the two types of clinic. There were also few references to the role of family planning clinics in offering advice or help on sexually transmitted diseases, except in rather disparaging terms. There appeared to be little contact between the two types of clinic and little attempt to encourage referrals from family planning clinics to GUM clinics.

On balance, GUM clinic staff were more likely to favour a continuation of a specialised role for GUM clinics rather than extending it to giving contraceptive advice and help. Even on the question of condoms, as we have seen, they often felt themselves constrained either by a lack of budget or by consultant attitudes. Some staff, on the other hand, were clearly very keen to see an extension of the traditional role of GUM clinics into giving advice and help on a whole range of matters connected with sexual health. However, there would be a need for staff to have some family planning training, to complement the GUM training that so many of them wanted and needed.

The division between the treatment and prevention of sexually transmitted disease and the provision of contraceptive advice and relationship counselling often appeared to be completely artificial, and to be perpetuated for reasons which had rarely been examined and did not always appear to be in the best interests of the patients. It is probable that people seeking contraceptive advice and supplies might not necessarily relish the thought of attending a GUM clinic for them, but there is absolutely no reason to believe that the converse is true. There is plenty of evidence to suggest that young people in particular are anxious about using health services, particularly in relation to contraception, and that they welcome the provision of help for their problems under one roof (Allen, 1991). The opportunity of providing sexual health education in one consultation should always be grasped.

12 Overlap and duplication between staff in GUM clinics

One of the aims of this study was to identify any areas of overlap or duplication of the work carried out in GUM clinics. We asked all the staff interviewed if there was any overlap or duplication between their job and that of each of the other types of staff in the clinic.

Overlap between medical and nursing staff

Just over half the doctors and nurses thought there *was* overlap or duplication between the medical and nursing roles (54 per cent of doctors, 56 per cent of nurses). Overlap was most likely to occur in clinics where the nurses had a more extended role.

The main area of overlap was in the examination and testing of patients. Around a fifth of all the doctors and a quarter of all the nurses said that both doctors and nurses in the clinic examined or took tests from new patients, and around one fifth of the doctors and nurses said that both doctors and nurses took tests from follow-up patients.

The other main area of overlap was in the treatment of warts; 16 per cent of both doctors and nurses said that sometimes doctors treated warts and sometimes nurses did. In two clinics, both doctors and nurses were carrying out cryotherapy.

A wide range of other activities were carried out by both doctors and nurses, including patient information and counselling patients, microscopy, venepuncture and dispensing drugs. Around one in ten of the doctors said that there was general overlap between the medical and the nursing role.

The majority of the medical and nursing staff thought the overlap had a positive effect. If duties such as examination or taking tests could be carried out by either doctors or nurses, the work flow of the clinic was maintained by saving time and providing cover if necessary. One enrolled nurse said: 'It ensures that patients are seen quicker. They're not waiting around to see a doctor. It allows the doctor to see more difficult cases while we see ordinary, routine cases...' And a consultant said: 'It keeps the clinic moving. It's part of the overall service. They're not just a pair of hands out there, which is what I find so difficult to get over to our manager sometimes. He thinks any nurse can help me...'

Overlap between nurses and doctors in terms of patient information and counselling was thought to reinforce the information given and to help reassure patients. A staff nurse said: 'We don't always hear what the consultant says, so we go through it again with the patient – the condition, treatment, prevention. We sometimes repeat to patients what the doctor has already said. But there is no harm in repeating it. Patients are nervous with him and sometimes they haven't understood. It can only be a good thing. Patients take in very little to start with...' And a consultant said: 'Sometimes the patients tell the doctor something and sometimes they tell the nurse something else and so we talk to the patient again. We get more information. At first patients are apprehensive and they muddle up what we say. They talk to the nurses and they get more information...'

Overlap between roles was also said to improve accuracy, promote good staff relations and give variety in staff roles. Many of the respondents talked about 'working together' and 'assisting each other' and 'working as a team'. One consultant said: 'We work as a team. The doctor shouldn't be regarded as a boss or a manager. Junior nurses will learn a lot from experienced nurses, and nurses will learn from doctors...'

The 'overlap', therefore, was most commonly seen as beneficial. Only a handful of doctors and nurses felt that the overlap between them was inappropriate and resulted in reduced efficiency and patients confused over staff roles.

Overlap between medical and health advising staff

Around one fifth of the doctors interviewed worked in the six clinics with no health adviser in post at the time of fieldwork. We asked the 73 doctors and the health advisers in the remaining 14 clinics whether there was any overlap or duplication between their roles. Three-quarters of the health advisers, and 89 per cent of the doctors said there was.

The main area of overlap was in counselling, mentioned by two-thirds of all the doctors in clinics with a health adviser, and more than half of all the health advisers. Almost all these health advisers said it occurred mostly in relation to HIV infection, but the doctors thought there was overlap when counselling patients generally, as well as in HIV counselling.

Around one fifth of both doctors and health advisers though that there was overlap in giving patients information about conditions or treatment, and a further fifth of both groups thought there was overlap in contact tracing. A third of the health advisers also said their roles overlapped with the doctors in terms of patient education, although this was mentioned by only one in ten of the doctors.

The vast majority of the doctors saw the overlap as beneficial. They considered the fact that both they and the health adviser counselled the patient or gave them information or education provided reinforcement and reassurance to the patient. They also said that the overlap between them saved time and helped the flow of the clinic. If they were busy, they could refer a patient to the health adviser for counselling or information or contact tracing, which freed them to perform duties, such as taking a medical history or examination, which were strictly in the domain of medical staff.

The medical staff cited other positive effects of the overlap between the doctors' and the health advisers' roles such as improving the accuracy of procedures, providing cover for a member of staff if they were busy or away from the clinic, as well as promoting good staff relations. One consultant explained: 'Overlap is always a good thing. It's a form of internal audit. There's a better chance of the job being done well rather than being done badly...'

Few of the doctors cited negative effects of the overlap between medical staff and health advisers; those that did were generally puzzled about when they should refer a patient to the health adviser. One said: 'I'm still finding the balance of how much to say to the patient before handing them over. Sometimes I feel you've gone so far, you might as well carry on and finish it. I'm not as systematic as I would be if I knew from the start that I was doing it and not her...' And another said: 'With the education, I'm not quite sure exactly what her role is in that, and when to refer patients and when I'm wasting her time. It's the same with contact tracing. If I see someone with warts who's got one regular partner and no other STDs, it seems sensible enough for me to give them the slip. Whether I should refer them all to the health adviser, I don't know...'

The health advisers also saw the overlap between their role and the doctors' role as a good thing in general, especially in reinforcing information and education, and offering reassurance for patients. They also said it improved accuracy in the clinic and provided cover for staff if necessary. One said: 'The consultant gives health advice routinely. I pick up where she stops and reinforce and go on. She does a hell of a lot of health education. I reinforce what she has said and build on it...'

Some of the health advisers thought the overlap had no effect, either good or bad. But the health advisers were rather more likely than the doctors to cite disadvantages, mainly in reducing efficiency and the danger of confusing patients if they were given conflicting information or advice. One health adviser said: 'There's quite a lot of crossover between us in pre-test counselling. We book patients in for an HIV test. The doctors do the pre-test counselling when they are getting the history. And when they see us, we churn it all out again. We both do it and the patients think they've already been through it all. There's a lot of duplication there. But it's both good and bad. It can be positive, it reaffirms things. But you might get one of the doctors saying, "You don't need a test" or "You ought to have a test". When the patient comes to you, they ask you what *you* think. It can be difficult...'

Overlap between nursing and health advising staff

Around a quarter of the nurses interviewed worked in the six clinics with no health adviser in post at the time of fieldwork. More than half (59 per cent) of the 75 nurses in the 14 clinics with a health adviser said there was overlap or duplication between their job and that of the health adviser. But only a third (36 per cent) of the health advisers thought there was such overlap.

Around a quarter of the nurses said that there was an overlap with the health advisers in giving patients information about STDs and their treatment, and a further quarter said there was an overlap in terms of counselling patients in the clinic. Other areas of overlap cited by the nurses included patient education and contact tracing (12 per cent in each case), as well as giving support to patients and giving results (around 5 per cent in each case).

One staff nurse said: 'We overlap in quite a few fields. If a patient has gonorrhoea, I'm basic with them. I say, "No sex for one week". I explain to them. The health adviser will then go through it again. And with contact tracing, if the health adviser is not in, then I will give out contact slips. Some patients here are thick. They think they can have sex when they've got an STD. They don't have enough education, the right information is not given to them. If a patient has been to the health adviser for pre-test counselling, when they come to me for a test, I ask them if there are any questions they'd like to ask. They might not have taken everything in. I make sure they understand. I ask them if they re happy, if they've got any more questions...'

Only eight health advisers thought their roles overlapped with the nurses, mainly in giving patient information and patient education (three health advisers each) and counselling (two health advisers). These health advisers all thought the overlap was a good thing in helping the flow of the clinic, providing cover for staff, reinforcing information, providing additional reassurance for patients, and promoting good staff relations.

The majority of the nurses also thought the overlap between the nursing and health advisers' roles was an advantage, with the greatest benefit coming from the reinforcement of patient information, counselling and reassurance. A staff nurse said: 'It increases the patient's awareness, knowledge and understanding of his condition. We build on what our colleague has said. No-one here is vying for a position of responsibility. We're doing what's best for the patient...' The nurses also said that they could cover for the health adviser if she was out of the clinic, and that the overlap meant that the clinic ran more smoothly.

But a small proportion of the nurses did not think the overlap in the two roles was a good thing. They said it could mean that the nurses neglected their own duties and that it could result in patients becoming confused about staff roles, as this staff nurse explained: 'I feel very sorry for the patients. They look confused a lot of the time. They have several trips through all the staff...'

Overlap between medical and administrative and clerical staff

One clinic (with two doctors) had no receptionists. In the 19 other clinics, one third of the doctors and a quarter of the receptionists said there was overlap or duplication between their respective roles.

As might be expected, the overlap was confined to medical staff carrying out activities which would normally be carried out by the receptionists, rather than the receptionists carrying out medical duties. There was most overlap in the large, full-time clinics, especially those based in London.

The doctors were most likely to say that they 'pulled' and filed patient notes (14 per cent of all doctors) and answered the clinic telephone (11 per cent). But a wide range of other activities were mentioned by both doctors and receptionists, including booking-in patients, making appointments for patients, giving patients information, looking for and giving out results, processing laboratory results, allocating codes for the KC 60 return, and other clinic paperwork. None of these activities was mentioned by more than 10 per cent of the doctors or receptionists.

Around two-thirds of both the doctors and the receptionists who said there was overlap in their jobs thought it was beneficial. They said it helped the work flow of the clinic by saving time and providing cover for the receptionists if necessary. The doctors also said that working on reception kept them in touch with what was going on at the front-line and promoted good staff relations. The overlap could also act as a check to improve the accuracy of procedures, such as collecting and collating the statistics.

But around a third of these doctors and receptionists considered that the overlap was inappropriate and reduced the efficiency of the clinic and the staff. They thought it could result in doctors neglecting their other duties, while receptionists sometimes complained that the doctors did not always file notes correctly and 'meddled with their appointment books'. The doctors in one large, full-time clinic were particularly critical of the way in which they had to carry out reception duties.

Only nine clinics had administrative staff other than receptionists and we asked the 57 doctors, six medical secretaries and five managers/supervisors in these clinics about overlap between their respective jobs.

Six of the ten doctors who said there was overlap between their job and that of the administrative staff, came from one large, full-time clinic. All the overlap was with medical secretaries, covering such activities as word-processing, sending letters to patients (recall letters or follow-up appointments), allocating codes for the KC 60, and making appointments. Five of the doctors thought the overlap was beneficial. But the other five, all from the one large clinic, said it meant they neglected their other duties, and resulted in their working longer hours.

Two of the six secretaries and two of the five managers/ supervisors said there was overlap between their jobs and those of the doctors. The secretaries cited processing of results and filing notes, while the two managers referred to the clinic statistics. But there was no consensus among them on whether the overlap was a good or a bad thing.

Overlap between nursing and administrative and clerical staff

One clinic (with three nurses) did not have any receptionists. In the other clinics, more than two-thirds of the nurses and half the receptionists said there was overlap in their respective jobs. As with the medical staff, the overlap was in reception duties, rather than in nursing duties. The most common tasks carried out by nurses were answering the clinic telephone and dealing with clinic enquiries (33 per cent of all nurses), booking in patients at reception (23 per cent), making appointments for patients (13 per cent) and 'pulling' and filing patient notes (21 per cent).

Just under one fifth of the nurses and a quarter of the receptionists said that the nursing staff covered for the receptionist when necessary, carrying out all reception duties. The receptionists also said the nurses answered the clinic telephone and made appointments, as well as helping them with processing the test results and other paperwork.

Around two-thirds of the nursing staff and receptionists who said there was an overlap felt it was beneficial for the familiar reasons of helping the clinic work flow, providing cover if necessary, and promoting good staff relations.

But around a third of these nursing staff and receptionists considered the overlap to be detrimental to their own work and the running of the clinic. The nurses most commonly said that carrying out reception duties meant that they neglected their own nursing duties. Some said it meant that they were busier and had to work longer hours. The receptionists agreed that it was not very efficient, and some also complained that the nurses did not always carry out the reception tasks properly. One said: 'Sometimes the nurses help on reception. I say help but they can be a hindrance. They will help if I'm on the phone or at the other window. But they can do it wrong, especially if they haven't been here very long. They've made a few boobs. And it's a very small office; we fall over one another...'

We found very little overlap between the nurses and the other administrative and clerical staff in the nine clinics with medical secretaries and managers/supervisors. Only three of the 44 nurses and two of the 11 administrative staff referred to overlap in their respective roles. The nurses said that there was some overlap in terms of processing laboratory results and filing notes, which they thought was not a very effective use of their time. The two administrative staff, one secretary and one manager, both referred to the help given by nursing staff in processing laboratory results and were both grateful for the help they received.

Overlap between health advisers and administrative and clerical staff

We asked the 22 health advisers and 32 receptionists in the 14 clinics with a health adviser if there was any overlap between their jobs. Three-quarters of the health advisers (16), but only one third of the receptionists, said there was such an overlap.

The health advisers said they answered the clinic telephone and dealt with telephone enquiries (10), pulled and filed notes (5) and covered for the reception staff (4). But two or three also said they looked for laboratory results or patient notes, gave patients their results and collected the clinic statistics.

Just under half (7) of the health advisers who mentioned overlap with the reception staff thought it was a good thing in helping clinic flow and promoting good staff relations. But just over half (9) thought the overlap was inefficient and inappropriate by causing health advisers to neglect their own duties, risking conflicting advice or information to patients, and sometimes resulting in health advisers having to work longer hours to catch up on their own work.

The receptionists agreed on the areas of overlap: patient information, answering the clinic telephone and working on reception. All but one of them said the overlap had a beneficial effect in promoting good staff relations, providing reassurance for the patients and providing cover for the reception staff.

In the eight clinics with both health advisers *and* other administrative and clerical staff there were 14 health advisers and 11 administrative and clerical staff. Eight of the health advisers mentioned overlap of roles: five with the medical secretaries and three with the health advisers' clerk/assistant. The overlap was generally in secretarial type work such as sending out (recall) letters, answering telephone enquiries and processing laboratory results, as well as other paperwork such as filling in forms and collating the statistics.

Although two health advisers thought the overlap helped the work flow of the clinic, the majority said it resulted in their having to work longer hours.

Two of the secretaries and two of the managers said their jobs overlapped with those of the health advisers. The secretaries said that both they and the health advisers listened and gave support to the patients. One manager said that both she and the health adviser were involved in the management of the clinic, while the other manager said they both gave patients information. All of them thought the overlap had a good effect in that it provided cover where necessary and reinforced patient information.

Overlap between receptionists and other administrative and clerical staff

In the nine clinics with other administrative staff only six of the 25 receptionists said they overlapped with the medical secretaries in that they both answered telephone enquiries, updated the clinic records and sent out follow-up appointments and the medical secretaries covered on reception when necessary. Similarly, four of the secretaries and three of the managers said they helped out on reception when necessary. This overlap was said to help the work flow of the clinic and was all part of working as members of the GUM team.

Implications of overlap between GUM clinic staff

It could be argued that a certain amount of overlap of functions is inevitable in most organisations, and that GUM clinics are no different from most out-patient clinics. There is, however, a fine line to be drawn between overlap and duplication, particularly when no-one is really sure what everyone else is doing. There are also a number of important questions about the most appropriate use of the time and expertise of different types of staff.

The overlap between professionals and the receptionists, administrative and clerical staff mainly involved the doctors, nurses and health advisers in carrying out reception and clerical duties. The professionals were more likely to refer to overlap than the administrative staff, perhaps indicating that they were taking on more administrative and clerical tasks than the others realised.

While it was recognised that this overlap had advantages, such as helping the work flow, promoting good staff relations and providing cover for staff where necessary, a substantial proportion of the professionals felt it was inefficient and inappropriate. The overlap was often a result of busy reception staff or an insufficient number of reception staff. We have already noted that the majority of the professionals considered that the receptionists could not take on any more responsibilities because they were already too busy, and a substantial number of them thought there were not enough staff working on reception. This was a recurring problem in many clinics, but was most pronounced in the larger, busy clinics.

There can be little doubt that professional time was inappropriately used in mundane clerical or administrative tasks in most of the clinics in which we carried out our fieldwork. Although this was most noticeable in the larger clinics, it was clearly prevalent, to a greater or lesser extent, in most clinics. It is obviously difficult to measure, and was not recorded on the activity sheets filled in by staff to the same extent as they reported in interview or, for that matter, to the extent observed by the researchers. In some cases, it was worse at certain times than at others, for example, during a very busy clinic or when staff were off or unavailable.

Some of the most wasteful overlap and duplication was between the health advisers and clerical staff. Perhaps duplication was a misnomer, since the main problem appeared to be that health advisers were carrying out duties which could have been done more appropriately by clerical or administrative staff.

However, as we have noted in earlier chapters, the overlap or duplication was not only observed in professional staff carrying out administrative tasks. We have seen that clerical or reception staff were involved in allotting diagnostic codes, that reception staff gave advice and results on the telephone, and that some were keen to counsel patients.

The most difficult overlap and duplication to measure and assess was probably that between medical and nursing staff. We have seen that around half the medical and nursing staff thought that there was duplication of roles, but that most of these regarded it as beneficial. The main duties performed by both doctors and nurses were tests, examinations, and treatment of warts, but there were a number of other functions carried out by both medical and nursing staff. Not surprisingly, there was little or no overlap between medical and nursing staff in clinics staffed by out-patient nurses, but more in clinics staffed by dedicated GUM nurses.

It could be argued that the sharing of tasks, for example, examination or treatment, with doctors and nurses being virtually interchangeable, improves the work flow of the clinic and makes the patients happier because they are not having to wait around. However, the question then arises of whether the staffing is correctly balanced, if nurses can substitute for doctors to such an extent that it does not matter who sees whom.

Another area for concern which covered all the professional staff was undoubtedly in counselling. Not only were definitions of counselling different among different groups, but there was also a risk of conflicting or confusing messages getting through to patients. There was little doubt that within most clinics there was insufficient recognition of the extent to which there was duplication of effort. The situation could well have benefited from supervision and rationalisation in this most important area.

The question of the appropriate use of doctor and nurse time and expertise in GUM clinics has arisen throughout this report. The skill mix in general is clearly something which needs to be assessed at a local level, but it also raises many issues which could be addressed at a national level.

13 Discussion of findings

The purpose of this study was to identify the roles and responsibilities of all staff in Genitourinary Medicine (GUM) clinics, to identify areas of overlap or duplication and to make recommendations, in the light of the need for efficiency and cost-effectiveness, for changes in existing roles. It was recognised that work roles and responsibilities varied widely in GUM clinics, and it was hoped that the research would not only provide a detailed account of the varying roles of staff in the clinics, but would also furnish evidence of how best these roles could be refined and, if necessary, rationalised so that the optimum use could be made of existing staff resources.

This report has given details of the great variety of work roles and responsibilities in the 20 GUM clinics selected for this in-depth study. We selected clinics at random from each health region in England, having stratified our sampling in such a way as to ensure representation of both large and small clinics. The resulting study of around one in ten of the GUM clinics in the country should therefore give a representative account of what was going on in GUM clinics in 1990-91.

Chapters 1 and 2 described our difficulties in establishing 'typologies' of clinics according to such criteria as size, location, workload, type of work or mix of staffing. Every attempt to impose some kind of a pattern of response across the clinics ran into the problem noted throughout the report that each clinic had several unique features which inhibited comparison across clinics. This was particularly true of the skill mix.

This led us to analyse and present our data largely in terms of the material collected from the different disciplines working in the clinics, rather than as a series of case-studies. Although this approach has meant that the presentation of data in the report is largely descriptive, this discussion of findings will give an analytical interpretation of the descriptive data presented.

We begin by drawing together the main topics covered in the report – the actual work roles and responsibilities of the different types of staff – and then look in some detail at the skill mix, the extent of overlap and duplication of function, and the management of the clinics. We continue by returning to the problem of defining different types of GUM clinic, since this is clearly of crucial importance in determining future policy towards the provision of services in connection with HIV/AIDS and sexually transmitted diseases. We then examine some of the implications of other factors which undoubtedly had a major influence on how the work roles and responsibilities had evolved. It is impossible to understand the distribution of work within the GUM clinics studied without understanding the background and culture within which they are operating. Many of these factors have been touched on in the course of this report, but the discussion will attempt to show the importance of these factors and will point towards recommendations for action.

The medical staff

The structure and composition of the medical staffing played a key role in determining the rest of the staffing of the clinic as well as the responsibilities carried out by these staff. The medical staffing was by no means as standardised as might have been expected. This was most clearly seen in the varied number and use of clinical assistants by clinics of similar size and location, but there were also marked differences among the consultants, not only in terms of such measurable characteristics as sex, age, country of medical qualification, length of experience and so on, but also in terms of their interest in the specialty, in administration, in research, in HIV/AIDS, in statistics and in diagnoses.

There were similarities among consultants in that for many, although GU medicine was not the specialty of their first choice, most found it one which suited their temperament and interests. Many of them stressed the pleasure of working in a specialty with young, healthy people who could be easily cured and helped. The advent of HIV/AIDS had had a major impact on some consultants who found difficulties in adapting to the changing profile and needs of patients.

The consultants divided equally into three groups – UK-qualified men, overseas-qualified men and UK-qualified women. There were clear differences between some of the older and some of the younger consultants, and between many of the overseas qualified consultants and the UK-qualified men and women. There were also differences between men and women in terms of motivation and dynamism. Many of the women brought a high level of professional expertise and interest into the clinics which was not always matched by their male counterparts.

There was little doubt that the extent to which consultants worked part-time or full-time in the clinic also affected their roles in the clinic. There was, however, another factor which affected not only their own roles in the clinic, but also the standing of the clinic itself, and this was the perceived status of the consultants within the hospital or locality. This was a factor which was difficult to measure but was hinted at time and again within interviews with all staff in the clinics. There can be no doubt that it was an important factor in the extent to which the GUM clinic suffered from the isolation which was such a marked feature of most clinics in this study.

The larger clinics usually had junior doctors in training grades. This should have led to increased status for the clinics, but there were some doubts about whether this was always so. It clearly led to some tensions within the medical staffing, particularly when doctors in training grades, not unnaturally, wanted to

197

gain experience in HIV work, which, as we have seen, was not evenly spread across the clinics, but the consultants preferred to do it themselves. In some cases, however, the tensions arose when the consultants handed over all or most of the HIV work to the junior doctors because they themselves did not like this work, or found themselves inadequately equipped to do it. There was thought to be a danger that in neither case would the junior doctors receive a sufficiently broadly-based training in GU medicine. There were also some indications that not all doctors in training grades felt that they were receiving a sufficiently rigorous training in general in the clinics in which they were working.

Clinical assistants were used in a variety of ways, much depending on the way in which the consultants operated. In some cases there were good and easy relationships, with shared responsibilities in almost every aspect of the medical work. In other cases, clinical assistants were used as another pair of hands, engaged in repetitive routine work, and there were some doubts about whether much of the work they were doing could not have been done as competently by a senior nurse. There were also marked differences in the qualifications, as well as the motivation and reliability, of the clinical assistants. However, on the whole, most clinical assistants wanted more recognition for the work they were doing in the clinic, many wanted more training, both in GU medicine and in counselling, and it appeared that they were often an under-exploited resource.

Clinical assistants can bring a much-needed breath of the outside world into GUM clinics. Many of them were GPs who were in touch with patients in a rather more holistic way than was the case with most of the other staff in GUM clinics. They themselves may have benefited by taking their expertise back into their practices, but they could also bring qualities to the GUM clinics which were sometimes notably absent, particularly among the medical staff.

Clinical assistants could also increase the number of women staff or even bring women doctors into an all-male medical establishment. There were nine clinics where there were no women medical staff at all, and the use of women clinical assistants would undoubtedly have given a much-needed choice to patients. However, where women doctors were not available or were thin on the ground, it appeared that there was an opportunity for the nurses' role to be enhanced. This did not necessarily happen, and many more factors appeared to be affecting the relative use of female staff than the mere presence or absence of women doctors on any grade.

The mix of medical staffing was difficult to assess, but it was clear that the role of the consultants was key, in terms of leadership, policy, use of staff, teaching and training. On the whole, the presence of training grades, which should have enhanced the status and quality of the clinics, did not always lead to happy relationships, and there were some doubts about whether the optimum use was being made of their talents, or whether they were receiving a broad enough training. The use of clinical assistants was mixed, but there were certainly indications that the policy in some clinics of using clinical assistants with little or no commitment to GU medicine for one session a week did not bring about the cohesion or continuity which many staff thought GUM clinics needed.

The work of some of the consultants themselves was often said to be routine and repetitive, and, although there was general agreement that their level of skill and knowledge was essential in GUM clinics, there were muted rumblings among staff that a close look at the responsibilities of medical staff alone, leaving aside the question of how these mixed with the responsibilities of other staff, might be appropriate.

The nursing staff

The varied roles and responsibilities of nursing staff in the GUM clinics were one of the most striking features of this study. Although both Rogers and Adler (1987) and the Monks Report (Department of Health, 1988) had drawn attention to the diversity of work and responsibilities of nurses in GUM clinics, we found that the situation in individual clinics was even more complicated than suggested. Not only did nurses have different roles in different types of clinics, but it was also clear that nurses, often of the same grade, had different responsibilities within clinics. The rationale for the way in which different nurses were used within clinics was often difficult to establish and, in our view, did not always stand up to close scrutiny.

It was quite clear that tradition, and the policies of consultants, some of whom might have been less than up-to-date with current nurse practice, often dictated the roles of nursing staff in GUM clinics. As a general rule, the larger the clinic, the more likely they were to be staffed by dedicated GUM nurses, at least some of whom had training in GU medicine, and who tended to have greater responsibilities and an extended role. Small to medium-sized clinics were rather more likely to be staffed by general out-patient nurses, but, as we have seen, this was not always the case, and in some of the smallest clinics, the nurses had a role which extended far beyond that of nurses of comparable grades in larger clinics, and included health advising responsibilities as well.

Although consultant, or sometimes hospital, policy usually dictated what the nurses did, there were other constraints on the extent to which nurses were able to take on the full range of responsibilities. One of these was simply the question of space and facilities. If there was no room for the nurses to do microscopy, or the microscopes were in the consultant's room, it was difficult in practical terms for the nurses to do microscopy. But there was also a substantial minority of both doctors and nurses who thought that nurses should not do microscopy, but should leave it to trained technicians or medical staff. In some cases there was a curious sex bias, with male nurses being thought capable of microscopy while female nurses were not.

A main constraint was, of course, the question of training. General out-patient nurses were rarely capable of carrying out microscopy, and in one clinic they did not carry out *any* of the potential functions of GUM nurses, including venepuncture. It must be asked whether using nurses as chaperones and tray-carriers was really the best way of maximising the skills of professional staff in GUM clinics.

We were surprised to find that it was often difficult to establish exactly what nurses did in the clinic because there was a discrepancy between what the medical and nursing staff reported. We sometimes felt a certain unease that the right hand did not always appear to know what the left hand was doing. There were certainly disagreements in some clinics about whether or which nurses did microscopy, cryotherapy and female examinations. There was also a general problem in the clinics where the nurses had a more extended role about the definition of what constituted an examination of a female patient.

Although the majority of all types of staff thought that nurses could take on more responsibilities, there was no doubt that nurses were more keen to extend their role in general than the doctors were for them to do so. The main problems lay in the extent to which consultants were willing for nurses to have a more extended role, the extent to which nurses were sufficiently well-trained to carry out more duties, and, not least, the layout and physical characteristics of the clinic. Some nurses, of course, had what was termed at the time of the fieldwork as an extended role in any case, although this did not necessarily mean that they did not want to do more.

There was certainly evidence that in a substantial minority of clinics nurses were not fulfilling functions which nurses were undertaking as a matter of course in others. We came to the conclusion that serious consideration should be given to the roles of nurses in these clinics, with a view to implementing a more extended role with considerably enhanced responsibilities for nurses in all GUM clinics as a matter of policy.

The main need in general was for a more systematic approach to training, not only in terms of initial courses in GU medicine, GU-related subjects, HIV/AIDS and counselling, but also reinforced by continuing education. An English National Board working party has been addressing these issues, and its report and recommendations are to be welcomed (ENB, 1992a). A new modular ENB Course 276 with two levels of training is to be introduced (ENB, 1992b).

Two-thirds of the nurses had not received any specific training to work in GUM clinics, and the strong desire among many nurses, whether they had received training or not, for training of all kinds was one of the striking features of this research. The age distribution of nurses and their career histories indicated that GUM clinic nurses were often embarking on a second career as their domestic responsibilities were diminishing. Many brought a maturity and dedication to their work which was reflected time and again in interviews. They were on the whole a highly motivated group of professional staff, and we were convinced that the potential contribution of nursing staff within GUM clinics was not being fully exploited, even in clinics where they had an extended role.

We also thought that serious consideration should be given to the extension or introduction of nurse-run clinics or sessions, which were, in fact supported by a majority of both nursing and medical staff, particularly by younger doctors in training grades. There are clearly important economic factors to be taken into account when examining the future distribution of roles in GUM clinics, and the use of highly skilled and trained nurses for some of the functions at present carried out by medical staff must be high on the agenda.

Health advisers

The role of health advisers was one of the most interesting aspects of the study. In six of the twenty clinics there were no health advisers in post at the time of the fieldwork, with the health advising being undertaken by a variety of staff, some of whom were clearly fulfilling the role adequately. The arrangements in other clinics were perhaps less than satisfactory, if only because of overload on staff whose main function lay elsewhere. The Monks Report specifically recommended that every GUM clinic should have at least one health adviser (see recommendation 16, Department of Health, 1988).

The main factor affecting the role of health advisers in the GUM clinics was, not surprisingly, the extent to which HIV/AIDS work played a major role. In the few clinics with a high proportion of work with HIV-positive patients, the health advisers did little or nothing else. This did not appear to be either acceptable to the health advisers themselves or to be in the interest of the clinics, since the emotional stress and potential burn-out of dealing day in and day out with counselling and advising HIV positive patients clearly put a great strain on the health advisers concerned and provided little variety or relief. It was not only consultants who derived satisfaction from being able to offer speedy curative treatment to young, healthy patients.

However, even in the majority of clinics where there were few HIV positive patients, HIV testing was widespread, as we have seen, and many health advisers were heavily involved in pre-test and post-test counselling, again, it appeared, often at the expense of other work in which they were interested or which was part of their job description.

In both cases, health advisers were often concerned that their work was too heavily biased towards HIV, and that they had too little time to develop other aspects of their work, such as patient education, community involvement and the preventative side of their work in which many of them were particularly interested. Health advisers were clearly often in a unique position to offer counselling and sex education at a time when young people in particular were likely to be receptive, but the existing balance of the work, with the domination of HIV-related work in so many instances, often militated against the development of this role. Although health advisers often said that they used the opportunity of pre-test counselling to stress the general benefits of safe sex and the dangers and risks of other infections, there was an impression that fears of HIV could sometimes get in the way of the general educational message, and, if the test proved negative, the message could be forgotten altogether.

There were certain aspects of the health advisers' role which we thought should be examined, and many of these centred around the fact that the health advisers were mainly working alone in a clinic environment which was characterised by patients being passed in quick succession from one member of staff to another at different stages of their consultation. There were indications that single-handed health advisers tended to be better integrated within the clinic than others. This is perhaps not surprising in organisational terms. Where there was more than one health adviser, they tended to seek support from each other and to reinforce each other's role. It did appear that other members of staff regarded *one* health adviser as part of the GUM team to a greater extent than two or more. There were indications that much of the work of health advisers was thought to go on 'behind closed doors', and that where more than one was working behind closed doors, the 'mystery' deepened.

Part of the problem undoubtedly related to HIV counselling, which had more mystery attached to it than other work of the health advisers. It also took longer, which meant that sessions with the health adviser could be seen to hold up the clinic. It also meant, literally, more isolation for the health adviser, and added to the 'exclusive' nature of the health adviser's role. Certainly, where nurses also saw themselves as counsellors – and as we have seen, this was a role which many nurses wanted to develop – there did appear to be some room for misunderstanding.

All this underlines the need for health advisers to maintain a mixed role within the clinic, and certainly points away from the employment of HIV counsellors within clinics. It does not make for a happy team if some members are seen to be doing 'the interesting bits' – even if the 'interesting bits' may lead to burn-out and emotional stress. But, in any case, there was a feeling among a substantial minority of health advisers themselves that their roles and responsibilities were not recognised or appreciated within the clinic. In some instances, they were concerned about lack of support from the consultant or hospital management, but in other cases there was clearly a sense of lack of acceptance from the other members of the GUM clinic team. The health advisers usually had better academic qualifications than the nursing staff, and had often had a more broadly-based career than any other members of clinic staff, but there were clear indications that neither the medical nor the nursing staff always understood the potential contribution of health advisers in terms of patient education, counselling and prevention of infection.

There was no doubt that health advisers themselves usually felt under pressure, with not enough time to devote to individual patients and too little time to develop the educational, preventative and outreach activities mentioned above. In addition, most of them thought they were having to do too much routine clerical, administrative or reception work which they considered could and should have been done by other staff within the clinic, giving them more time to carry out the duties for which they had been employed and to develop the functions which they felt they were neglecting. There were also concerns about unfilled health adviser vacancies, which were said to lead to overload on existing staff.

And, of course, there were repeated complaints about the physical conditions in some clinics which were said to inhibit a suitable atmosphere for counselling or for any kind of confidential discussion. Some health advisers had no counselling rooms at all. We firmly agreed with health advisers who thought that the canteen, the corridor or the car park were not the most suitable sites for counselling.

Health advisers, like nurses, often expressed anxiety at their lack of training, and the fact that more than 50 per cent of the health advisers interviewed had had no specific training to work in GU medicine, and a similar proportion had had no training in GU-related topics, must be a cause for concern. They were much more likely to have had some kind of counselling training, but, even so, they had attended a variety of courses, and we concluded that there was an urgent need for a more coordinated and rational approach to the training of health advisers, both in GU medicine and GU-related areas, and in counselling. One of the recurring themes in the interviews with health advisers was the desire for a recognised, accredited, certificated health advisers' course which led to a qualification, preferably including skills which were transferable to work in other areas. This again was one of the recommendations of the Monks Report (see recommendation 16, Department of Health, 1988).

Before this study began, we were involved in a number of discussions on the relative merits of health advisers having a nursing training. In the event, few respondents considered that it was a matter of great importance, and, although it was felt that it might be useful, it was by no means thought to be necessary.

The health advisers themselves were crying out both for greater professionalism and for recognition of their roles and potential contribution within the clinics. There was general agreement among them that the main roles of health advisers were patient education and information, counselling, and contact tracing or partner notification. But the emphasis placed by individual health advisers on these different roles varied considerably, with some health advisers virtually ignoring partner notification altogether, either because they were too busy with HIV/AIDS work or because they did not think it important.

There was undoubtedly a strong desire on the part of many health advisers to be more closely involved in education and outreach work within the community. We certainly thought there was scope for health advisers to work more closely with GPs, for example, and we also considered that if health advisers could play a wider role in the community and in educational or work establishments, it would help to demystify, and perhaps destigmatise, the work of GUM clinics. It would be ironic if the emphasis placed on sexual health in *Health of the Nation* (Department of Health, 1992) were to be inhibited by concerns by purchasers of health services about paying for the development of health advisers' functions outside GUM clinics.

In general, we saw a need for a more clearly delineated and agreed role for health advisers, not only in order that some of the misunderstanding about their work which was fairly widespread among other members of staff could be ironed out, but also so that they could develop the professional qualities which many of them brought to the clinics. We considered them to offer an important resource which was not always being used to the best advantage of either GUM clinic patients or the wider community.

Administrative and clerical staff

Concerns about the calibre and contribution of administrative and clerical staff in GUM clinics had been expressed in the Monks Report (Department of Health, 1988) and informally in our pilot study, with particular concern attaching to the variable quality of reception staff.

We found that the main problems with administrative and clerical staff were found predominantly in the larger, full-time clinics, which were usually very busy, with a high turnover of patients and more than one clinic session operating at a time. They were also often characterised by poor physical lay-out or reception facilities which made the jobs of some of the receptionists almost unbearable by any standards. It was not surprising that there was a relatively high turnover of staff in some clinics, and, indeed, we were surprised that so many reception staff carried out their duties with such patience and good humour. These staff were in the front-line for patient abuse, and, if the medical staff thought patients were becoming more demanding and abusive, the receptionists were usually in a less powerful position to deal with increasing aggression among patients.

There was no doubt that administrative and clerical staff in the smaller peripheral clinics were usually more satisfied with their jobs than those in the larger, busier clinics. They also tended to feel more part of the 'team', and it was interesting how often administrative staff stressed the satisfaction they found in working as part of a team in a non-hierarchical staff setting. Again, the closely-knit, rather isolated nature of the GUM clinic could be observed. If the team got on well together, the staff were happy and were prepared to put up with poor conditions. If the team was larger and more diffuse, and particularly if there was a high staff turnover, morale was lower, and there was more evidence of tension.

Reception staff in smaller clinics were more likely than those in larger clinics to say how much they enjoyed the contact with patients and the satisfaction they got out of being able to reassure people and put them at their ease. It was clear that some went beyond their roles and became more involved in cases than perhaps some of the medical and nursing staff were aware. It was indicative that more than ten per cent of the reception staff said they would like to start counselling patients and a similar proportion wanted to give test results and information about diseases and treatments. In some clinics, receptionists routinely gave test results over the telephone, and there was clear evidence that some gave advice over the telephone as well. There was surprisingly little supervision of what the receptionists took upon themselves, and it often appeared that medical and nursing staff were too busy to note what was going on, although health advisers were often more concerned about the situation.

But it was also clear that some clerical and administrative staff had too much responsibility placed upon them, and we found it particularly worrying that in more than one clinic receptionists were responsible for allocating the diagnostic codes. We did not think that untrained receptionists should be responsible for looking through medical notes and trying to 'figure out a diagnosis'. One receptionist said she would not mind doing the diagnoses if she felt sure she knew what she was doing. We found it alarming that she had the responsibility in the first place, and even more alarming that no-one had recognised that she did not feel at all secure in her function and that no-one had felt it necessary to give any training or support. The problem was, of course, compounded when two receptionists allotted diagnostic codes in different ways.

Although the administrative and reception staff were said to be very busy, there was evidence that their time was not always used to the best advantage. Sometimes the lay-out or conditions in the clinics were such that there was no room for them to work more systematically. But in other clinics there was a general consensus that there were not enough staff on reception and that doctors or nurses or health advisers were doing reception work, or pulling notes or doing other clerical work, simply in order to keep pace with the throughput of patients. Medical staff in particular thought that there were not enough staff on reception, and this view was shared by the researchers, particularly in some of the large clinics where it was not uncommon for patients to be packed into waiting rooms or to be queuing in corridors.

There was a marked contrast, however, between clinics, and, indeed, one of the larger clinics in this study had only one receptionist who managed a busy clinic with calm and friendly single-handed efficiency. The stability of staff was clearly a key element in the smooth running of a clinic, and the use of temporary reception staff was not welcomed and was thought to disrupt the clinic. However, in some of the larger clinics, the problem appeared to be circular, in that permanent reception staff were difficult to find and keep because of the conditions, which were not improved by the use of temporary staff who often had no training, interest, aptitude or loyalty.

It was perhaps surprising that more attention was not paid to making the clinics more welcoming and friendly. We have noted in the report that staff were often working under poor physical conditions, but the waiting areas of some of the clinics we visited were very unattractive, with little or no effort made to improve the furnishings or atmosphere. It was perhaps little wonder that reception staff sometimes appeared to take on the grimness of their surroundings.

There were very few clinic managers or supervisors in the GUM clinics covered in this survey, and most of these did not have a real clinic management role. There certainly appeared to be a real need for a clinic manager function, particularly in the larger clinics. The historical function of the consultant running the clinic and all its administration had certainly been overtaken by events in most of the clinics in this survey, and there was clear evidence that many of the clinics would have benefited from a close analysis of the administrative and clerical functions carried out by *all* members of staff.

Overlap and duplication of roles and responsibilities

One of the main characteristics of GUM clinics is the nature of the patient flow, which is rather different from that found in most out-patient clinics. Most patients arrive and are booked in, and then see a doctor who takes a history; they are examined and have tests, some of which are looked at under a microscope; they are given the results, treatment by a doctor or nurse, and then may or may not see a health adviser who discusses contacts, gives advice and education and possibly counselling; after which they check out and are given a follow-up appointment.

Patients will usually pass through the hands of a number of different types of clinic staff, and at a first visit with a new condition or conditions will often see at least one doctor, nurse, health adviser and receptionist. They will sometimes see more than one of each. In most clinics, they will probably be unaware of the relative status of the staff they see within each discipline, and, indeed, there may be no pattern in the deployment of different members of staff for them to discern.

The question of overlap and duplication of staff roles in GUM clinics was an area of crucial importance in this study. It was, however, difficult to describe in detail exactly how much overlap and duplication existed for a number of reasons, all of which have been described in the report.

One of the most important factors which tended to obscure the extent of overlap was the fact that so many of the medical and nursing staff either had no job description or had one which was out-of-date, irregularly reviewed or irrelevant. If so few people had jobs which were actually described, it was perhaps not surprising that they took on other bits of work or did not actually always know exactly what was expected of them. But job descriptions alone were not enough, since, although all the health advisers had job descriptions, there was considerable dissatisfaction among them about their relevance and current applicability.

Another important factor which inhibited an accurate assessment of overlap and duplication among GUM clinic staff was the absence of clearly delineated duties among different types of staff on the same grade. This was found not only across clinics but within clinics. It was most marked among nursing staff, but was also found among medical staff, health advisers and administrative and clerical staff. For example, as noted in the report, there often appeared to be no logical reason why some nursing staff did microscopy and others did not. But these differences were relatively easily recognisable. It was more difficult to measure the extent to which some medical and nursing staff took on roles as educators or counsellors while others did not. And it was particularly difficult to establish to what extent doctors, nurses and health advisers all gave patients advice or information about the same condition. The staff concerned were often unaware of what others were doing. Without a survey of patients' views and experience, it was impossible to measure with any degree of accuracy the overlap and duplication among staff in the care and treatment of patients as they proceeded through the clinic.

Essentially, there was no general consensus in GUM clinics on what the respective roles of medical staff, nursing staff, health advisers and clerical and administrative staff *should* be. Therefore, it was not surprising that a multiplicity of combinations of functions had arisen in different clinics. All this might not have mattered – or been noticed – when GUM clinics were coping with the workload, or were regarded as a peripheral activity to the mainstream of medicine. But as the workload has increased, and as HIV/AIDS has tended to give GUM clinics a higher profile, the lack of clarity about work roles and responsibilities has become more apparent and the extent of overlap and duplication of roles has been questioned.

In many instances, staff of all types thought that overlap of roles and function was a good thing in that it helped to reinforce information and advice to the patients, offered continuing reassurance and helped the flow of the clinic. Perhaps most important in some clinics, it was thought to create a team spirit among the staff. The question of whether or not the duplication was appreciated by the patients and the extent to which different members of staff were in fact giving the same messages did not appear to have been examined.

Why was the overlap thought to be so good? It was not at all unusual for staff of all kinds to stress the benefits to the 'team' of 'helping each other out'. But was it really beneficial for everyone to 'do whatever job they can'? What was the point of having different functions if everybody could do everybody else's job? And who was managing the various functions? Who decided who did what? The answer in many cases appeared to be that nobody was actively managing the functions and nobody was taking a fresh look at who did what. The system had evolved over time and had continued and nobody had queried it until the workload became too great.

It should be stressed that not all the staff thought that overlap of staff roles was a good thing, and there were certainly concerns about duplication, particularly with regard to counselling. However, the main problems cited by staff arose when doctors, nurses or health advisers were involved in administrative, reception or clerical duties. There was certainly evidence in some clinics of an inappropriate use of medical, nursing and health advising skills, simply to keep the clinic running. On the other hand, we have noted the inappropriate use of clerical staff for duties like diagnostic coding which was beyond their competence. But in many cases, staff did not think it unsuitable for a doctor to pull notes or book in a patient, while the constant stress on 'team- working' in many clinics helped to disguise the fact that team members, in carrying out routine administrative tasks, were not really functioning at optimum efficiency, let alone in a cost-effective manner.

It was relatively unusual for medical, nursing or health adviser staff to express real concern about the overlap between their respective roles. Most thought the overlap reinforced information and advice to the patients, and few picked up the possible effect of confusion of roles and messages from a bewildering variety of staff. Again, there was little evidence that staff had considered the possibility that some of the overlap might be unnecessary, and could have been avoided if they had had a clearer idea of what the rest of the team were actually doing. Few staff shared the concerns of the health adviser who was worried about the fact that she 'churned it all out again' after a patient had seen a doctor. Most staff thought it safer to duplicate or reinforce just in case the message had not been taken in first time. Perhaps the extended use of written information might help to avoid this possibility.

But, of course, the problem was much more fundamental than one which could be solved by stop-gap measures. Staff in many clinics complained about the increasing workload and the burdens this imposed upon them. Throughout this report there has been evidence of staff taking on duties which might more properly be the responsibility of others. The absurdity of doctors, nurses and health advisers carrying out reception or clerical duties at the expense of their own responsibilities could often have been solved by a more systematic use of reception and clerical staff, and, in some instances by an increase in numbers of such staff. There were surely better ways of improving the clinic flow and fostering good staff relations than by professional staff performing clerical duties. The Monks Report made a clear recommendation that 'clerical staffing levels should be such as to ensure that other health care professionals do not have to undertake clerical work and that clerical staff are not exploited' (see recommendation 21, Department of Health, 1988). Our evidence strongly supported this recommendation.

Overlap and duplication between professional staff was often condoned or even approved because of the reinforcement of information it offered. Again, a proper audit should be made of the nature and content of the work carried out by the different members of staff. We conducted an activity analysis, which showed clearly that different types of staff were carrying out the same functions. What is needed is more detailed analysis within individual clinics of who does what, to whom and with what result. Without such an analysis, there is a danger that clinics will continue to be increasingly busy, staff will continue to do each other's jobs, and there will be no guarantee that the best possible service is being provided for patients.

Health gain to patients is seen to be of increasing importance at a national level, but there was little or no indication in any of the clinics covered in this study that 'patient outcomes' were being seriously considered. Much greater emphasis often appeared to be given to whether the staff got on well together than to what the patients thought of it all. Patients who complained about the lengthy waiting-times were thought to be difficult, if not aggressive, and lacking in understanding of the constraints under which the staff were undoubtedly operating. On the other hand, there were indications that, particularly in HIV counselling, the length of sessions could be completely dictated by patient demand. A well-conducted audit of the clinics appeared to be a top priority. At the time we conducted our research, clinical audit was in its infancy. It is to be hoped that improved audit mechanisms have enabled clinics to make more informed decisions about work roles.

Management of GUM clinics

This study was not primarily about the management of GUM clinics, but a number of questions on work roles and responsibilities were interrelated and centred around the management of the clinic. The main questions were: what should the roles and responsibilities of the different types of staff be? Who should be deciding the staffing numbers and levels of the four types of staff? To whom should the different types of staff be professionally and managerially accountable? Who should give additional support and supervision to the staff in carrying out various aspects of their roles, like counselling, which might not necessarily sit easily on the shoulders of a manager or even the person to whom the staff were professionally accountable?

The managerial questions were, of course, related to the larger question of what the function of the GUM clinic was and what it should be. The balance of work in GUM clinics has been changing, not only with the increase in HIV/AIDS-related work, but also with the relative increase in viral conditions. In some clinics there was interest in extending the functions further into other areas, with particular interest in colposcopy. There were few examples of working partnerships with other departments, such as obstetrics and gynaecology, but there were indications that some of the younger consultants were aware of the advantages of collaboration with other specialties. On the other hand, there was a clear fear on the part of some consultants that opening up the GUM clinic might encourage predators, not only as far as the HIV/AIDS work was concerned, but also in other areas of work. There was undoubtedly an interest among some consultants in maintaining the isolation of GUM clinics, in spite of the fact that many of them felt they suffered from it.

The managerial questions were also related to the actual location of GUM clinics, although, of course, it should be stressed that running a GUM clinic in an out-patient department by no means guaranteed that it was integrated into the department or that it lost its traditionally insular qualities.

The traditional manager of the GUM clinic has been the consultant, who has established the policy and practice of the clinic and has decided on the staff needed for the clinic to function and on their roles and responsibilities within the clinic. GUM clinics have been traditionally more autonomous than other out-patient clinics, partly because they have often been physically isolated from the out-patients department, partly because of the 'special' nature of their function, partly because of confidentiality factors, and partly because the consultants, having no in-patient beds, have naturally concentrated their activities within the clinic. GUM consultants have therefore established managerial roles which other consultants may have had neither the time nor the inclination to develop. However, GUM consultants, like other consultants, have usually not had management training and may well not have the management skills for the increasingly complex task of running an out-patient clinic.

But it is not only a question of management of resources and administration, it is also a question of managing staff. The days of the nurse as the 'handmaiden' of the consultant have long been numbered, but there was evidence in this study that, in spite of the 'team spirit' of so many GUM clinics, not all consultants were aware of this. There were some grey areas surrounding the professional accountability of the nursing staff which needed to be sorted out. The fact that so many nurses were vague or ill-informed about the people to whom they were professionally accountable, let alone to whom they were managerially accountable, was indicative of the need to establish clear lines of management and accountability.

The problem was even worse among health advisers, who were professionally and managerially accountable to a wide variety of people, both inside and outside the clinic, and often seemed to be swimming around in a sea where nobody really wanted them. It was perhaps not surprising that they clung together if they could.

The medical, nursing and health adviser staff who complained about insufficient management support often directed their criticism at managers outside the clinic. It was surprising that more of them did not complain about the management arrangements within the clinic. But, in many ways, this was typical of the insulated and isolated nature of the GUM clinics. It was probably easier to grumble about the perceived low status of the clinic in the eyes of outside managers, particularly when the staff worked so well together and the team spirit was so important. It was more difficult to attribute managerial blame within a clinic, especially when the team was very small, and willingness to help each other out was more highly regarded than what was perceived as a hierarchical adherence to managerial efficiency.

Much of this analysis underlined the need for the development of clinic managers within GUM clinics, particularly the large and medium-sized clinics. It also underlined the need for business plans. There was little doubt that many consultants were still attempting to run all aspects of the clinic, a task for which most of them were ill-equipped, and which, in any case, was usually a waste of their time and talents. As this report has shown time and again there was a case for rationalising the reception, clerical and administrative support of most clinics, leaving the consultant to be concerned with managing the change in direction and emphasis which was facing all GUM clinics.

Since this research was carried out, there have been considerable changes in the management of provider services within the health service. The management structure of many of the clinics described in this report will have undergone change in the period since the fieldwork took place. It is likely that some of the recommendations for more focused management of different aspects of the clinics have been tackled and implemented.

The clinics and HIV/AIDS

We return to the problem of defining different types of GUM clinics, since this was clearly of crucial importance in determining future policy towards the provision of services in connection with HIV/AIDS and sexually transmitted diseases. Probably the most important distinguishing factor in the clinics was the extent to which they were involved in work related to HIV/AIDS.

One of the main reasons for the increasing workload of GUM clinics in recent years has been said to be the increasing amount of work connected with HIV infection and AIDS. This has undoubtedly been true of the large clinics in the main centres of population, most especially in London, and most especially in particular hospitals in London. There is, however, a danger that the tremendous increase in work associated with HIV and AIDS in a very small number of large clinics has distorted the overall picture of what is happening in GUM clinics in the country in general. The four clinics described in Chapter 2 as Type 1 clinics were really the only clinics in this study which had any substantial experience of treating patients who were HIV positive or with AIDS.

There can be little doubt that work with HIV positive or AIDS patients is found by staff of all types to be much more time-consuming and emotionally draining than work with patients with traditional sexually transmitted diseases. However, of the GUM clinics in this study, two-thirds had registered fewer than 20 patients with HIV infection since the beginning of the AIDS epidemic and the majority of these clinics had registered fewer than 10 such patients. Two of the clinics had never had an HIV-positive patient. Only two of the clinics had ever had more than 10 patients with AIDS, and, indeed, six clinics of the twenty had never had a patient with AIDS.

It was the larger full-time clinics, particularly those in the south, which had had a greater number of patients with HIV infection, but, as our figures show, only one third of all the clinics in the sample had ever registered more than twenty HIV positive patients, and only two clinics had had more than 100.

These figures have a number of important implications, which are central not only to the analysis of work roles and responsibilities in GUM clinics, but also to the way in which these roles and responsibilities should be developed in the future. They are also important in putting into perspective the distribution of services which are capable of delivering the best possible service not only to people who have developed HIV or AIDS but also to those who are at risk of doing so.

Although the current number of HIV/AIDS patients was very low in most of the clinics we studied, work in connection with HIV took up quite a lot of the time of the staff in many clinics. There were two main reasons for this: one was the fact that HIV positive or AIDS patients were said to take up more time than patients with other sexually transmitted diseases, for a variety of reasons; and the second reason was that HIV testing, and pre-test and post-test counselling was also said to take up a great deal of time.

The second of these two reasons was undoubtedly the more important in determining the workload of most of the GUM clinics in this research. We were only able to collect with any degree of accuracy the actual number of HIV/AIDS patients *ever registered* in the clinics, and even then we had doubts about the reliability of some of these figures. It was freely admitted in most clinics that no accurate figures were available on the *current* number of HIV/AIDS patients attending the clinics. However, it was quite clear that the vast majority of the clinics had very few current patients who were HIV positive and even fewer who had AIDS. It was doubtful whether more than four of the twenty clinics were currently supporting more than ten HIV-positive patients, and we had serious doubts about the extent to which more than two clinics were supporting more than a handful of AIDS patients.

It was for this reason that a close look needed to be taken at the amount of HIV related work that was being undertaken in GUM clinics. There was no doubt that much of the reported increase in HIV/AIDS work was due to testing and counselling people who did not have the virus. This did not mean that they were not at risk of acquiring it, since it could be argued that anyone attending a GUM clinic had probably run the risk of becoming HIV positive. However, the crucial questions to be asked in assessing the time spent in GUM clinics on work associated with HIV/AIDS must be how good the work is, how necessary it is, who is doing it and what are the results.

It should be stressed that it was very difficult to find out exactly how much time was really being spent in the clinics on HIV/AIDS related work. The report has discussed the problems we encountered in determining the real extent of this work, not least because of the way the statistics are designed and collected. We strongly recommend that more accurate measures of HIV/AIDS related work should be instituted and that a high priority is given to removing inconsistencies in the way the work is recorded.

There is clearly a danger that the extent of work in connection with HIV/AIDS might well be misrepresented by some clinics for a variety of reasons. In some cases, it might be over-represented, while in others it might be under-represented. In certain cases, some of the intense and lengthy counselling which was undoubtedly being undertaken might well have been misplaced, while in other cases, necessary counselling might have been overlooked. It was almost impossible to establish what was going in the clinics in relation to the real demand and the real need for such work. It was also difficult to assess the real nature of the work.

There were few obvious indicators of a mismatch between need and services, since the statistics were so unclear. However, it must be queried whether a clinic which had only ever had six HIV-positive patients registered should be running an HIV session once a week, and, similarly, it should be asked whether another clinic which had only ever had 19 HIV-positive patients should employ two HIV counsellors and also run a weekly HIV session. It should also be asked whether there should be a waiting-time of over a month before people could get an appointment for pre-test counselling, as was happening in one of the clinics in which we carried out the research.

There was clear evidence in some clinics of duplication between the roles of doctors, nurses and health advisers in connection with HIV counselling, in spite of the assertions by most staff that overlap in roles was not a problem and served to reinforce information and support. This might have been true in connection with some conditions, but there were many indications that HIV/AIDS was a completely different type of condition which needed a much more rationalised and structured approach.

The stress in so many clinics on HIV testing and counselling clearly led to a bias in the work of health advisers towards HIV-connected work, potentially at the expense of STD-related work and contact tracing/partner notification. But this again was difficult to quantify because of the nature of the statistics, or even to assess qualitatively, since so much of the work of health advisers remained hidden. There can be little doubt that in some, but not all, of the largest clinics, counselling in connection with HIV dominated the work of the health advisers, simply because of the numbers, but there were also indications that HIV-related work took up what might have been a disproportionate amount of time of health advisers in smaller clinics, some of them very small.

Workload, diagnostic coding, collection and collation of statistics
In terms of numbers of consultations and diagnoses, the statistics collected in the clinics did not actually indicate an increased overall workload in most clinics over the period immediately preceding the survey, although there were fluctuations and a general upward trend in some clinics in particular conditions, such as warts or non specific urethritis (NSU). But as noted throughout the report, the statistics were not as reliable as they ought to be for a number of reasons, and it was argued forcibly in some clinics that they did not reflect the true workload connected with HIV infection, particularly in pre-test counselling.

We were concerned about the extent to which standards and methods of collection, diagnostic coding and collation of statistics varied from clinic to clinic. There was evidence that each of these tasks was performed by a wide variety of staff with a wide variety of skills and motivation, often without noticeable supervision, leaving them considerable scope for interpretation. Medical staff themselves interpreted the requirements in different ways, and this raises the question of whether aggregation of the data both on attendances and diagnoses presents a valid picture of what is going on in GUM clinics. There appeared to be a need for clear, up-dated guidelines from a central source to ensure standardisation.

Counselling
In spite of the fact that the overall workload had not usually increased to any extent, one of the most interesting aspects of the research was the perception by

a majority of staff that the clinic workload had, in fact, increased overall. It was particularly notable that this view was held by three-quarters of the health advisers. When the differing components were analysed, the main reason for the increase in workload was said to be an increased need, and demand, for counselling. The counselling was generally related to HIV infection and usually took up more time than an ordinary consultation. In addition, the patient requiring counselling often had more tests and generated more paperwork and telephone calls than other patients. The knock-on effect of the increase in counselling could be seen in most clinics, since many staff said they had to spend less time with some patients in order to accommodate the counselling needs of others.

The study has clearly shown that the demand for HIV testing has increased in many, if not all, clinics. However, the numbers of HIV positive patients remain very low in most clinics, so that the demand for supportive continuing counselling will be limited except in the well-known large clinics, mainly in London, which will continue to serve the majority of HIV positive patients.

There were problems connected with HIV testing and counselling. The policy of the GUM clinics regarding testing varied widely. Some clinics were prepared to test anybody and everybody who asked for a test, often with the minimum of counselling, while others imposed a rigorous screening process before anybody could be tested, followed by extensive counselling. In other cases, HIV testing of all patients attending the GUM clinic was actively encouraged as part of a preventative policy.

There was, in our view, an urgent need in most clinics to review the counselling that was being given. It is probable that too many staff were giving too much 'counselling' in too many clinics, while, on the other hand, in two or three of the large clinics, the health advisers were overwhelmed by an unremitting workload of counselling HIV positive patients to the exclusion of virtually anything else. They usually had a much clearer understanding of what counselling was, but there was plenty of evidence that their jobs were barely related to the conventional role of health advisers.

It was expected that there would be a wide variety of interpretations of 'counselling', but the study has shown that the spectrum was even wider than expected. Practice varied widely between clinics and within clinics. There was no doubt that much of the work described as counselling by doctors and nurses in particular would not have been described as such by many health advisers or professional counsellors. But 'counselling', particularly HIV counselling, had a mystique attached to it which was not necessarily healthy for the development of GUM clinics. Few staff had had any training in counselling, and even the health advisers appeared to have had very limited training, with most courses lasting between one and five days and only a minority attending a certificated course.

There was evidence that counselling in connection with HIV took up a disproportionate amount of the time of GUM clinic staff, while counselling in connection with other conditions might not always have been recognised as necessary. It sometimes appeared that the balance was wrong, and this was undoubtedly exacerbated in the clinics which employed HIV counsellors who did no other work.

There was a danger that everyone wanted to do more counselling without any real assessment of the need for such counselling, the nature of what it involved, the implications of overlap and duplication, and the effect both on the patients and on the role and function of the GUM clinic. There were many indications that 'unofficial' counselling was already going on. It seems to be time not only for a review of practice in individual clinics but also for guidelines on the proper role of counselling in connection both with HIV and with other conditions in GUM clinics.

Indeed, there were many indications throughout this report that there was an urgent need for guidelines on counselling in connection with HIV infection in general. If less than half of the health advisers working in the GUM clinics in this survey had attended a course organised by the National AIDS Counselling Training Unit (NACTU), there must be serious doubts about the qualifications of many of those involved in HIV counselling, both professionally and for voluntary organisations. The dangers of conflicting or confusing advice and information given to vulnerable people may pale into insignificance in comparison with the results of well-meant but misdirected 'counselling' given by people who have no training or skills in helping those faced with the threat or reality of life-threatening illnesses.

Education

The crucial importance of GUM clinics in providing patient education was often under-exploited. This was particularly noticeable in two types of clinics: those in which there was a traditional approach to treatment and contact tracing, and, conversely, those with a heavy workload in relation to HIV/AIDS, in which education of patients with other STDs was limited, mainly, as we have seen, because the work of health advisers was so dominated by HIV/AIDS.

We found the relative lack of emphasis on patient education disappointing, particularly since there was evidence of considerable interest among a variety of staff in expanding and developing their educational roles. Clinic policy and practice did not always facilitate this, but the potential role of the GUM clinic, not only in controlling the spread of infection but also in creating and maintaining 'sexual health' in the population cannot be underestimated.

We develop this theme in the next section, but we feel it important to underline the need to assess and develop the roles of GUM clinic staff in providing education to patients. In our view, the present balance of work in GUM clinics should be shifted away from 'counselling' towards education, and a concerted drive to this end is strongly recommended. Although patient education is not a simple matter, an educational programme is considerably easier to implement and monitor than a counselling programme. It is also probable that many of the patients at present receiving counselling of varied quality from a

215

variety of sources might benefit more from well-focused education at an individual level.

It has become increasingly clear that large-scale campaigns may not be the best way of getting across the important messages about sexual health. A clear focus on education in sexual health and personal relationships delivered by GUM clinic staff, both within GUM clinics and in the hospital and the community, with targeted groups of people potentially at risk might well prove to be particularly beneficial.

Extending the boundaries

There are, in our view, compelling arguments for GUM clinics to throw off their 'special' and isolated image. There are many indications in this report that their traditional role is out-dated and in urgent need of refurbishment. Clinic staff, particularly medical staff, thought that part of the problem lay in their legal obligations for confidentiality, a fact which was little understood by outsiders, including many GPs and other hospital departments. However, we suspected that the isolation of so many clinics was more complicated than this, and that in some instances, consultants and other staff were not playing an active role in opening up the clinics to new relationships and collaborative ventures.

There was evidence of considerable variation in the extent to which GUM clinics were extending the boundaries of their traditional roles. This was by no means related only to the impact of HIV/AIDS work, although this had extended their potential activities into in-patient care and social work related tasks, as well as liaison and collaboration with voluntary bodies. Some clinics were expanding their work into gynaecological-related areas, such as colposcopy, cytology and laser treatment, or into family planning and psychosexual counselling, or into other counselling and health education, both within the clinic and in the community, although, as we have noted above, this could well have been more actively pursued.

The expansion of activities often appeared to be ad hoc, and did not always lead to harmonious relationships with other departments, although there was evidence of some forging of imaginative and innovative partnerships, which could only benefit patients. Questions of territory and responsibility were clearly issues of great importance for future collaboration and it did not always appear that all the implications had been fully considered. On the other hand, some respondents were determined not to stray too far from the traditional responsibilities of GUM clinics, and it sometimes appeared that patient care and education might be unnecessarily limited because of this.

But extending the boundaries does not only imply greater collaboration with other hospital departments. There is ample evidence in this report of poor or non-existent relationships between GUM clinics and GPs, other members of primary health care teams, hospital social workers, community social workers, local authority and health authority HIV/AIDS coordinators or officers, health education officers and, of course, with notable exceptions, the wide variety of voluntary bodies concerned with HIV and AIDS.

The lack of liaison with other professionals and agencies had implications in both directions. On the one hand, GUM clinic staff were often unaware of the work which was going on in the hospital or the community, some of which was both imaginative and well-directed. On the other hand, however outside staff and agencies were often completely oblivious of the first-class work going on within GUM clinics. The undoubted expertise of GUM clinic staff was not being exploited and there were obviously instances in which inappropriate treatment or counselling was being given by outside professionals and agencies to people who could have benefited from referral to GUM clinics.

Less than 50 per cent of HIV tests are conducted in GUM clinics, with a much lower proportion going through clinics outside London than in London itself. The implications of this have not been examined in this report since it was outside our terms of reference, but it is easy to see the relevance of it to the future role of GU medicine. What is happening to the people who are tested by GPs and other agencies? Would they benefit from attendance at GUM clinics? And why are they not being referred?

The incidence of HIV testing outside GUM clinics is perhaps only a measurable example of the work in connection with sexually transmitted diseases which is going on outside GUM clinics. GPs have traditionally treated STDs and will continue to do so. But this only underlines the need for GUM clinics to open up to the outside world and to spread their influence and expertise as widely as possible.

The future

There can be no doubt that the winds of change were blowing through and around GUM clinics at the time of the study, but there are many indications in this report that isolated and insulated GUM clinic staff from all disciplines were not really aware of what was happening. This report can be read simply as a snapshot of what was going on in GUM clinics in 1990 and 1991, but in fact it should be read as a description and analysis of a specialty and a service undergoing a process of change.

Failure to grapple with the larger issues of change could only lead to GUM clinics becoming increasingly marginalised rather than taking the lead in developing services for which they are particularly well-suited. There were indications in this report of staff pursuing policies and practices which were no longer suitable in a climate of increasing rationalisation and accountability. There were indications that clinics found great difficulty in coming to terms with the changing balance of conditions which were being presented in the clinics, particularly the shift towards work connected with HIV infection. Most important, perhaps, there were indications of GUM clinic staff seeking to find new roles but being frustrated in implementing their imaginative ideas. This report demonstrates the need for leadership and vision in ensuring that a rational development of staff roles in GUM clinics will lead to continuing development of the role of GUM clinics.

14 Policy implications of key findings

The study examined in detail the work roles and responsibilities of staff in 20 Genitourinary Medicine (GUM) clinics in England, with the purpose of identifying areas of overlap and duplication and of making recommendations, in the light of the need for efficiency and cost-effectiveness, for changes in existing roles. The research looked at the work of medical staff, nursing staff, health advisers and administrative, reception and clerical staff within the clinics.

The report is a description and analysis of a service and a specialty undergoing a process of change. It has identified wide variations in the work roles and responsibilities of GUM clinic staff and has documented the wide diversity in size, structure, location and organisation found in the clinics selected at random for intensive study.

The policy implications of the key findings are outlined below. They include recommendations, and are presented in this form to allow further discussion at a national, regional and local level.

There can be little doubt that urgent action is required on some of the key findings in order that GUM clinics can deliver the best possible service to the public they seek to serve. In other instances, a review of existing policy and practice appears to be crucial, not only in the interests of the clients but also in the interests of the staff, whose personal and professional development cannot be overlooked in delivering the most efficient and cost-effective service for the public. The responsibility for implementing action and review rests with the Department of Health, with Regional Health Authorities, with District Health Authorities, with provider units and Trusts, and with the GUM clinics themselves.

In assessing the work roles and responsibilities of staff in GUM clinics, it is essential to know what the clinics are doing, how much they are doing, who is doing what to whom, what the lines of managerial and professional accountability are, and what the outcomes are. In looking to the future, it is necessary to identify areas which should be developed and activities which might be reviewed.

Clarification of the role of GUM clinics
One of the main characteristics of the GUM clinics studied was a lack of clarity about work roles and responsibilities and a lack of appreciation of the extent and nature of the overlap and duplication between individuals and types of staff. This was closely related to a lack of clarity about the role of GUM clinics themselves.

There was evidence of difficulty in developing the optimum balance between the treatment of individuals and the public health role of prevention and education. The advent of HIV/AIDS has exacerbated the existing problem of lack of clarity by introducing an illness which lacks the curative element of most other sexually transmitted diseases. There was evidence of isolation of GUM clinics from other agencies, professionals and services, both within the community and the hospital.

1. In developing GUM clinic services, there should be a fundamental review of the aims and objectives of the clinics themselves and of their place within the wider health service.
2. There should also be a review of the most appropriate skill mix within GUM clinics to meet the aims and objectives, with recognition that GUM clinics are by no means homogeneous in terms of the populations they serve, the conditions they see, the staff they can attract, the physical conditions in which they are housed and the areas of the country in which they are situated.
3. There is a need for a review at a national, regional and local level of the balance of work in the GUM clinics between HIV/AIDS and other sexually transmitted diseases. The nature of the work should be assessed and measures taken to ensure that the appropriate staff time is spent equitably.

Workload

There was little concrete evidence on which to base the assertion of staff in all or most clinics studied in this research that the workload of clinics had increased recently. Most of the reported increase related to work in connection with HIV infection, but most HIV work, in all but a tiny proportion of clinics, was concerned with pre-test counselling, the giving of negative test results, and counselling of the 'worried well' which might not result in testing. Much of this work was said to be under-reported in the official statistics, partly because of the limitations of the forms intended to measure workload and partly because of the present lack of recognition of the time taken in these procedures. There was evidence of differences in recording and assessing workload both across clinics and even within clinics. It is impossible to make meaningful comparisons across clinics under these circumstances.

4. It is essential to institute a reliable statistical basis by which the workload of GUM clinics can be measured so that accurate forecasting and strategic planning can be developed.
5. There is a need for a clearer understanding and assessment of what constitutes workload in GUM clinics.
6. There is an urgent need for a review of workload measurements. This should cover both sets of Korner returns – the KH09 and the KC60.
7. The KH09 review should aim for a clearer definition of clinic sessions, cancelled clinic sessions, attendances, non-attendances, telephone consultations, etc. There is a need to be able to measure (a) the number of individuals attending the clinic in any one year, (b) the number of occasions

on which each individual attends the clinic and (c) the number of 'threshold crossings' in any one year. There is also a need to be able to make proper distinctions between 'new' and 'old' patients.

8. The KC60 review should determine the nature of the information currently required, and should recognise the present wide anomalies and inconsistencies in allocating codes in GUM clinics.

9. Both reviews should examine the process by which data are collected and collated, with special attention to how diagnostic coding of conditions is recorded, supervised and checked in GUM clinics. There is a need for guidance and agreement on the level and type of staff who should be responsible for the allocation of the diagnostic codes. All diagnostic coding should be checked by a senior doctor.

10. Guidelines should be compiled and issued to aid understanding of the requirements of the statistical returns and to facilitate collection and collation of the data. They should include clearer definitions of component categories. The guidance should cover both the KH09 and KC60 requirements in one document.

11. There is an urgent need to establish the real workload of GUM clinics in connection with HIV/AIDS. Not only were most clinics experiencing difficulties in recording their workload through the present system of statistical returns, but most found it difficult to give accurate information on the numbers of HIV positive and AIDS patients they had ever seen, and some clinics were unable to say how many such patients were currently attending the clinic.

12. A record should be kept in each clinic of HIV tests carried out by the clinic and their results.

13. A basis is needed for a more accurate audit of the workload of the clinic as a whole, as well as the workload of the different types of staff and individual members of staff.

14. Individual clinics must be able to audit their work with reference to regional needs and national policy.

Skill mix

The research found very wide variations in staffing, work roles and responsibilities and skill mix in the clinics studied. There was particular diversity in the roles and responsibilities of medical and nursing staff on the same grade, both across clinics and within clinics. Much of this appeared to be based on custom and practice which did not necessarily reflect current needs and conditions. Training in GU medicine among nursing staff and health advisers was generally felt to be inadequate, and there was evidence of considerable demand for GUM training among both these groups of staff, as well as training in related areas. There were also concerns about the training of some medical staff and reception staff.

15. A review is needed of the skills needed in GUM clinics and the numbers and types of staff needed to fulfil these roles. There is a need for leadership in designating these skills and for assessing the required skill mix.
16. All staff employed in GUM clinics need to be clear both about their own roles and responsibilities and about those of all other staff in the clinics.
17. All staff employed in GUM clinics should have job descriptions. These should be drawn up in consultation with staff in post and with their professional managers, and regularly reviewed and revised as necessary. The job descriptions should reflect the demands and the 'culture' of the clinic and the post. They should not simply be a list of tasks.
18. Overlap and duplication of roles and responsibilities should be examined, and steps should be taken to ensure that unnecessary duplication is eliminated.
19. There is a clear need to provide proper clerical and administrative support for medical, nursing and health advising staff to avoid inappropriate use of their skills.
20. There is an urgent need to review the recruitment, retention, training and support of reception staff in some clinics.
21. The personal and professional development of all staff in GUM clinics is a high priority. Training and continuing education should be offered and maintained. There should be recognition of particular skills and aptitudes which should be developed fully. The value of interdisciplinary training courses should be acknowledged.
22. A comprehensive audit and activity analysis is required of the tasks carried out by individual members of staff. At the moment, the lack of clarity about who does what not only makes it difficult to assess the real workload of the clinic, but also inhibits the full development of individual skills.
23. A system of individual performance review should be instituted for all staff.

Management

A wide variety of management structures were found in the GUM clinics in this study, both within the clinics themselves and within the hospital, community and district. Although some clinics were experiencing changes in management structures, others were still characterised by consultant control of virtually all policy and practice. There was evidence of lack of clarity of lines of managerial and professional accountability among all types of staff, a need for more robust business and administrative management, a need for human relations management, and, not least, a need for strategic management. The design and management of the skill mix was patchy. GUM consultants have traditionally exercised greater autonomy than many other consultants within out-patients departments for a number of reasons, not least because they have no in-patient beds. However, at the time of the research few had had management training and there may well be doubts about whether consultants have either the time or the skills for the increasingly complex task of running an out-patient clinic. The following recommendations support policies which have been implemented in a number of clinics.

24. The study indicated a need for a clear management structure within each GUM clinic, however small and whatever the local conditions. The relationship between this management structure and the wider hospital or community context in which it is placed should be made explicit.
25. The research showed the need for clear lines of management and professional accountability for all types of staff in GUM clinics. Staff should be aware of the identity of the managers to whom they are both managerially and professionally accountable.
26. Professional staff should be professionally accountable to suitably qualified managers from the same professional discipline.
27. The study indicated a need for a designated clinic manager to take charge of all routine administrative and day-to-day needs of running the GUM clinic, and for a designated 'business' manager of audit, performance measurement, finance and organisational matters such as business plans.
28. The study underlined the need for a clinical director to be responsible for the clinical policy and supervision of the clinic. It is unlikely that any consultant can supervise more than two clinics adequately.
29. The development of specialty management teams within clinics, made up of the most senior staff from each discipline represented in the GUM clinic, is a priority.

Premises

In spite of increased funding for GUM over the past few years, premises and working conditions were still found to be inadequate and unsuitable in many of the clinics studied. Particular problems related to lack of soundproofing and lack of space, both for basic clinical tasks and for consultations and counselling. The reception areas of many clinics left much to be desired.

30. Adequate soundproofing of all parts of the clinic is essential to ensure confidentiality.
31. Adequate space is necessary to ensure that staff can carry out their designated responsibilities.
32. A review of the furnishing and design of reception areas is a priority.

Counselling and HIV/AIDS

With the advent of HIV/AIDS, much attention has been devoted to the need for adequate counselling and the development of counselling skills. GUM clinic staff reported that the workload of the clinic had increased mainly because of an increased demand for counselling, usually in connection with HIV/AIDS. The wide variety of interpretations of the nature and function of 'counselling' and the extent to which staff from all disciplines saw themselves as playing a role in counselling patients offered cause for concern, particularly since few staff had

had counselling training, and even among those who had, courses were usually of very short duration and not certificated. There was also evidence that counselling in connection with HIV/AIDS could take up a disproportionate amount of time of GUM clinic staff, and that the balance of work between HIV and other conditions needed to be reviewed. There was little awareness about who was counselling whom for what, and supervision and support arrangements were usually ad hoc and inadequate. There were also concerns that agencies and individuals outside the GUM clinic were also involved in counselling patients, but that there was little liaison or knowledge of the nature of this counselling. There was clearly a danger of conflicting or confusing messages being given to vulnerable people.

33. There is an urgent need for guidelines on counselling in connection with HIV and AIDS in general. These should be aimed at all agencies, professionals and individuals who may have contact with people worried about or suffering from HIV infection.

34. There is a need to review and rationalise the counselling work undertaken within GUM clinics. All staff should be made aware of the policy of the clinic on counselling in connection with different conditions, the definition of counselling and the respective functions of all staff as far as counselling is concerned. The differences between advice, information and counselling should be made clear to all staff.

35. It should be ensured that all patients requiring counselling for any reason should receive it, but that no patient should be 'over-counselled' or given conflicting or confusing messages.

36. The interaction between GUM clinics and other professionals and agencies in connection with the identification and treatment of people with HIV/AIDS should be reviewed. The question of what happens to people who are tested outside GUM clinics is a matter for investigation.

Partner notification/contact tracing

The research demonstrated wide variation in views and practice as far as partner notification/contact tracing was concerned, both in connection with HIV/AIDS and with other sexually transmitted diseases. This variation was found both within professional disciplines and across and within clinics.

37. There is need for greater discussion and sharing of experience about partner notification/contact tracing in connection with HIV/AIDS and other sexually transmitted diseases. The development of national guidelines is desirable. (Since this report was prepared, guidelines on partner notification for HIV infection have been published (Department of Health, 1992)).

Education and prevention

There was considerable interest among many GUM clinic staff, particularly nurses and health advisers, in developing their educational and preventative role, not only within the clinics but also in the community. GUM clinics have different policies about the supply of condoms to patients, often, but not always, affected by financial constraints.

38. The role of GUM clinic staff, not only in controlling the spread of infection but also in creating and maintaining 'sexual health' in the population by means of education and health promotion, both within the clinics and in the wider community, should be developed.

39. The role of GUM clinic staff in giving education in sex and personal relationships and about contraception, especially to young people, should be developed. Young people are noted for wanting 'one door to knock on' and every opportunity should be taken to give contraceptive advice and information to people who are clearly 'at risk', not only of infection but also of unwanted pregnancies.

40. Questions regarding the supply of condoms by GUM clinics should be reviewed as a matter of urgency.

Extending the boundaries

GUM clinics were still characterised by their professional and geographical isolation, which resulted in a lack of liaison with other agencies and professionals both within the hospital and in the community. There was evidence that some staff wished to extend and expand both the type of work they did and their contacts with the outside world.

41. The unique role of GUM clinics in relation to the sexual health of the nation should be recognised. The contact they have with sexually active people should be used as a basis from which to develop their services and to maximise their contribution. Encouragement should be given to GUM clinics to extend the boundaries of their work. The provision by GUM clinics of treatment and advice in areas closely related to sexual health should be encouraged, given the necessary training and expertise among staff.

42. Close and continuing links should be fostered with all professionals and agencies who may refer patients to GUM clinics and to whom GUM clinics may refer. Issues of confidentiality, which were of paramount importance to GUM clinic staff should be discussed as a matter of routine with all external agencies.

43. There is a need to conduct more research into the views and experience of patients using GUM clinics. Many of the issues examined in the study need to be looked at through the eyes of the consumer.

Appendix

A.1 Staffing establishment

Table A.1 in the Appendix shows the staffing establishment of the 20 GUM clinics in this study. It gives the details of the staffing discussed in Chapter 2.

A.2 Diagnostic codes from KC 60 forms showing details of selected conditions

The second part of the Appendix is made up of 20 graphs which show figures for diagnostic codes collated from the KC 60 forms completed by each GUM clinic for Department of Health returns. The data cover the four quarters of 1989 and the first two quarters of 1990 in all clinics apart from Clinic 6, where data were not available for the first two quarters of 1989, and Clinic 19, where data were not available for the third quarter of 1989. The figures were collated for six conditions: syphilis, gonorrhoea, chlamydia/non-specific urethritis (NSU), herpes, warts and HIV/AIDS.

The data and the graphs are discussed in Chapter 8.

Table A.1   Gum Clinic Staffing – Establishment

CLINIC CODE	1	2	3	4	5	6	7	8	9	10
Total medical	**2**	**4**	**10**	**2**	**6**	**18**	**3**	**6**	**7**	**2**
Consultants	1	1	1	1	2	6	1	2	2	1
FT	-	-	1	-	1	2	-	1	1	-
PT	1	1	-	1	1	4	1	1	1	1
Training	-	-	-	-	-	10	-	2	4	-
SReg	-	-	-	-	-	3	-	1	1	-
Reg	-	-	-	-	-	4	-	1	1	-
SHO	-	-	-	-	-	3	-	-	2	-
FT	-	-	-	-	-	10	-	1	3	-
PT	-	-	-	-	-	-	-	1	1	-
CA - no.	1	3	9	1	4	2+	2	2	1	1
- sessions	2	4	14	1	5	24	7	12	1	1
Other medical	-	-	-	-	-	-	-	-	-	-
Total nursing	**4**	**6**	**8**	**3**	**3**	**15**	**4**	**6**	**7**	**3**
Sister/CN/CNS	1	1	1	1	1	1	1	2	2	1
Staff nurse	2	3	1	1	1	10	2	2	4	1
Enrolled nurse	1	2	6	1	1	3	1	2	1	1
Auxiliary nurse	-	-	-	-	-	1	-	-	-	-
FT	1	-*	4	-	2	14	-	6	5	-
PT	3	6	4	3	1	1	4	-	2	3
Total HA	**1***	**1***	**2**	**-**	**1**	**6**	**-**	**2***	**2**	**-**
Senior HA	-	-	-	-	-	1	-	-	1	-
FT	1*	-	-	-	-	6	-	2*	2	-
PT	-	1*	2	-	1	-	-	-	-	-
Total A & C	2	2	1	1	3	14*	2	3	5	-
Receptionists	2	2	1	1	2	8	2	1	4	-
Secretary	-	-	-	-	1	4*	-	1	1	-
Supervisor	-	-	-	-	-	1	-	1	-	-
HA clerk	-	-	-	-	-	1	-	-	-	-
FT	-	-	1	-	1	13*	-	2	-	-
PT	2	2	-	1	2	1	2	1	5	-
Other profs.	**-**	**-**	**-**	**-**	**1**	**-**	**1**	**-**	**-**	**-**
HIV counsellor	-	-	-	-	1	-	-	-	-	-
MLSO/microscopist	-	-	-	-	-	-	1	-	-	-

* denotes at least one unfilled post at time of fieldwork

226

Table A.1 (continued)

CLINIC CODE	11	12	13	14	15	16	17	18	19	20
Total medical	**2**	**3**	**11**	**11**	**1**	**6**	**3**	**4**	**2**	**2**
Consultants	1	1	2	4	1	2	1	2	1	1
FT	-	-	2	-	1	1	-	2	-	-
PT	1	1	-	4	-	1	1	-	1	1
Training	-	-	-	2	-	2	-	1	-	-
SReg	-	-	-	1	-	1	-	-	-	-
Reg	-	-	-	1	-	1	-	1	-	-
SHO	-	-	-	-	-	-	-	-	-	-
FT	-	-	-	2	-	1	-	-	-	-
PT	-	-	-	-	-	1	-	1	-	-
CA - no.	1	2	8	4	-	1	2	1	1	1
- sessions	3	4	11	10	-	3	2	1	2	2
Other medical	-	-	1	1	-	1	-	-	-	-
Total nursing	**4**	**3**	**7**	**10**	**2**	**5***	**2**	**3**	**5**	**5***
Sister/CN/CNS	2	-	2	1	-	1	1	1	1	1
Staff nurse	2	-	4	4	2	2*	1	1	2	3*
Enrolled nurse	-	3	1	5	-	2	-	1	2	1
Auxiliary nurse	-	-	-	-	-	-	-	-	-	-
FT	-	-	3	8	-	5*	2	1	-	-
PT	4	3	4	2	-	-	-	2	5	5*
Total HA	**1**	**1**	**4***	**3**	**1**	**2**	**1**	**-**	**1**	**2**
Senior HA	-	-	1	1	-	-	-	-	-	-
FT	-	-	3*	3	-	2	-	-	1	-
PT	1	1	1	-	1	-	1	-	-	2
Total A & C	**2**	**4***	**9**	**8**	**2**	**3**	**1**	**3**	**1**	**3**
Receptionists	2	3*	4	5	1	2	1	2	1	2
Secretary	-	1	2	2	1	1	-	1	-	1
Supervisor	-	-	2	1	-	-	-	-	-	-
HA clerk	-	-	1	-	-	-	-	-	-	-
FT	-	-	2	4	-	-	-	-	-	-
PT	2	4*	7	4	2	3	1	3	1	3
Other profs.	**-**	**2**	**-**	**-**	**-**	**-**	**-**	**2**	**-**	**-**
HIV counsellor	-	-	-	-	-	-	-	2	-	-
MLSO/microscopist	-	2	-	-	-	-	-	2	-	-

CLINIC 1

Diagnostic codes from KC 60

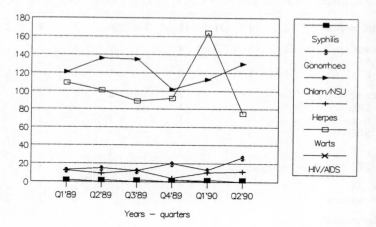

CLINIC 2

Diagnostic codes from KC 60

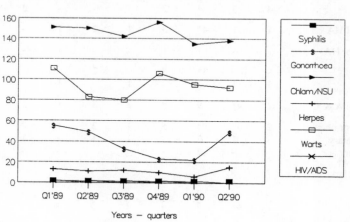

CLINIC 3

Diagnostic codes from KC 60

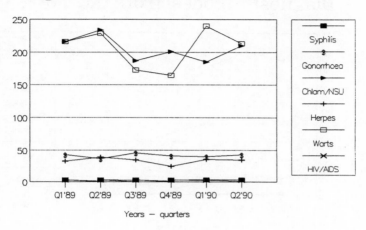

Years — quarters

CLINIC 4

Diagnostic codes from KC 60

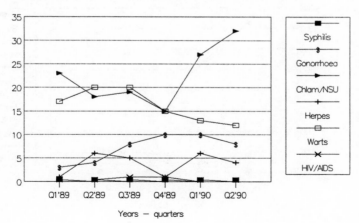

Years — quarters

CLINIC 5

Diagnostic codes from KC 60

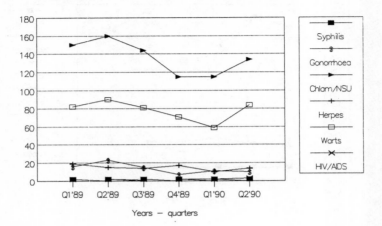

Conditions

Years — quarters

CLINIC 6

Diagnostic codes from KC 60

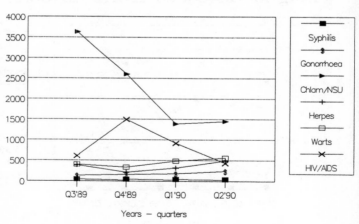

Conditions

Years — quarters

CLINIC 7

Diagnostic codes from KC 60

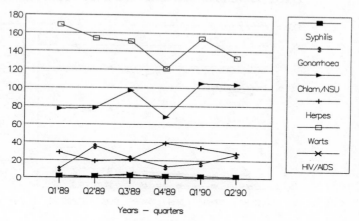

CLINIC 8

Diagnostic codes from KC 60

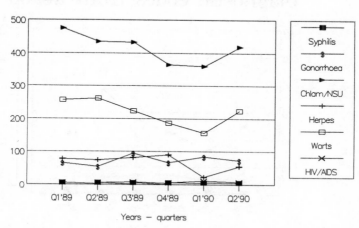

CLINIC 9

Diagnostic codes from KC 60

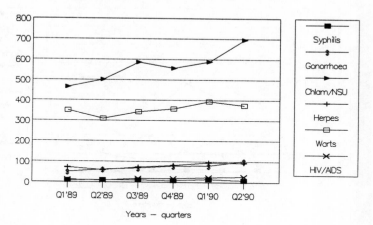

CLINIC 10

Diagnostic codes from KC 60

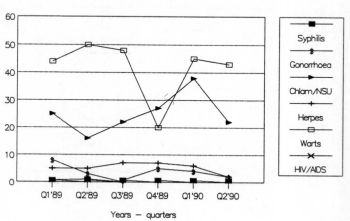

CLINIC 11

Diagnostic codes from KC 60

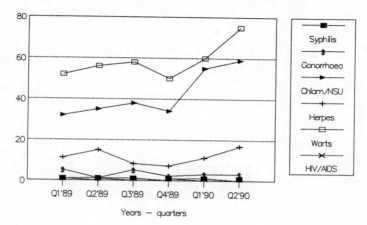

CLINIC 12

Diagnostic codes from KC 60

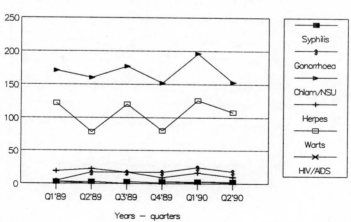

CLINIC 13

Diagnostic codes from KC 60

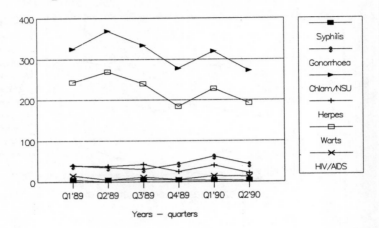

CLINIC 14

Diagnostic codes from KC 60

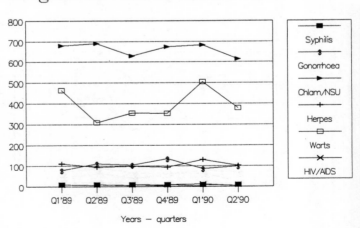

CLINIC 15

Diagnostic codes from KC 60

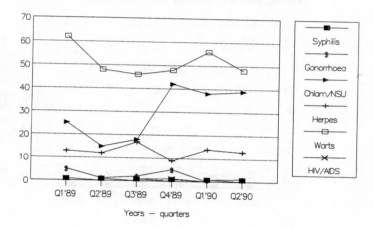

CLINIC 16

Diagnostic codes from KC 60

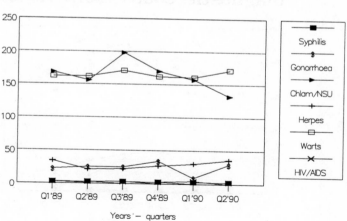

CLINIC 17

Diagnostic codes from KC 60

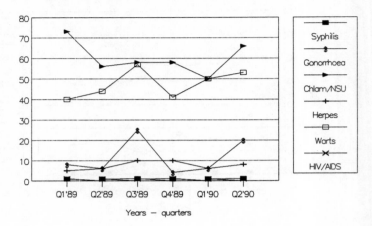

CLINIC 18

Diagnostic codes from KC 60

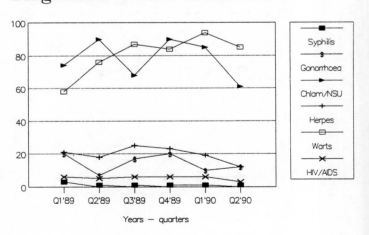

CLINIC 19

Diagnostic codes from KC 60

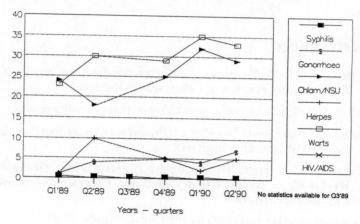

No statistics available for Q3'89

CLINIC 20

Diagnostic codes from KC 60

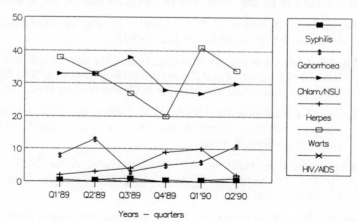

237

References

Allen, I. (1985) *Counselling Services for Sterilisation, Vasectomy and Termination of Pregnancy*. Policy Studies Institute

Allen, I. (1988) *Doctors and their Careers*. Policy Studies Institute

Allen, I. (1991) *Family Planning and Pregnancy Counselling Projects for Young People*. Policy Studies Institute

Department of Health (1988) *Report of the Working Group to Examine Workloads in Genito Urinary Medicine Clinics. (The Monks Report)*. Department of Health

Department of Health (1989) *Health Circular EL(89)P/36*.

Department of Health (1990) *Genito Urinary Medicine Clinics*. Health Building Note, 12. Supplement 1. HMSO

Department of Health (1990) (1991) (1992) *Health Circulars EL(90)P/30; EL(91)52; EL(92)18*.

Department of Health (1992) *The Health of the Nation*. Department of Health

Department of Health (1992) *Guidance on Partner Notification for HIV Infection, Professional Letter, PL/CO(92)5*.

English National Board for Nursing, Midwifery and Health Visiting (1992a) *HIV/AIDS Project. Final Report of Working group on 'The Education and Training Needs of Nurses Working in Genito-urinary Medicine'*. ENB

English National Board for Nursing, Midwifery and Health Visiting (1992b) *Caring for Persons with Genito-urinary infections and Related Problems. Course Number 276*. ENB

Keenlyside, R.A. Hawkins, A.S. Johnson, A.M. Adler, M.W. 'Attitudes to Tracing and Notifying Contacts of People with HIV Infection', *British Medical Journal* **305**, 165-8

Rogers, J.S. and Adler, M.W. (1987), 'Role and Training of Nurses Working in Departments of Genitourinary Medicine in England and Wales'. *Genitourinary Medicine* **63**, 122-32